In t

For Derek

Best wishes

Steve Lord

BA 361 LYS - LHR

30th March 2005

WALKING WITH CHARLIE

In the Footsteps of the Forty-Five

STEVE LORD

Pookus Publications

First published in Great Britain 2003
by
Pookus Publications
2 Mill Street, Eynsham, Witney
Oxon OX29 4JS

Reprinted with corrections 2004

www.pookuspublications.co.uk

enquiries@pookuspublications.co.uk

ISBN: 0-9544420-0-8

British Library Cataloguing-in-Publication Data.
A catalogue record for this book is available from the British Library.

Set in Times New Roman 11pt by
Manuscript ReSearch, Book Producers, PO Box 33, Bicester, OX26 4ZZ
Tel: 01869 323447/322552 Fax: 01869 324096

Printed by Hackman Printers Ltd., Tonypandy, Rhondda

CONTENTS

	Page
Acknowledgements	7
Foreword	9
Introduction	15
1. Two Kings: One Crown	43
2. The Standard Flies High	58
3. Over the Corrieyairack	72
4. Triumphant to Edinburgh	90
5. The March to Carlisle	123
6. To Manchester	143
7. Advancing to Retreat	158
8. Withdrawal to Scotland	173
9. Culloden	196
10. Escape to the Islands	231
11. Over the Sea to Skye	268
12. Glenmoriston Men	288
13. Cluny's Cage	314
14. Will Ye No Come Back Again?	324
Bibliography	333

ACKNOWLEDGEMENTS

My main debt of gratitude is to my wife, Momoyo, without whose understanding and support I should not have been able to complete the research, the writing and the hundreds of miles of walking. She thinks me slightly batty but that only increases my appreciation of her attitude. Many people helped in my endeavours, some with generous lifts in their cars, others with gargantuan breakfasts to fuel long hours on the hills and still more with advice and help in many ways. I am grateful to them all.

Three books deserve special mention. The first is Walter Biggar Blaikie's 'Itinerary of Prince Charles Edward Stuart'. Written in 1897 the book contains a detailed account of the Prince's journey written in the style of a diary. It was invaluable.

The second volume is a monumental work that no serious student of the '45 can do without. 'The Lyon in Mourning' is a collection of speeches, letters and articles relating to the rising. The Rev. Robert Forbes M.A., Bishop of Ross and Caithness compiled the book. Forbes was born in 1708 in Rayne, Aberdeenshire and was ordained as a priest in the Episcopalian Church in 1735. As an enthusiastic Jacobite he was determined to join the Prince and with a few friends set out to do so in early September 1745. Fate conspired against the mission and the travellers had progressed no further than Stirling when they were arrested and thrown into the castle. Robert Forbes spent the last three months of his imprisonment in Edinburgh Castle and was finally released on 29 May 1746. It is likely that he met many other Jacobite prisoners in Edinburgh and their stories encouraged him to collect information in order to build as complete a picture of the rising as possible. Forbes made 'The Lyon in Mourning' his life's work. The first of the ten manuscript volumes is dated 1747 and the bishop collected information right up to his death in 1775.

The third book is 'The Life and Adventures of Prince Charles Edward Stuart' by W. Drummond Norie. This four-volume epic is a detailed account of the rising (from a Jacobite point of view) together with Norie's description of his 1899 *'pilgrimage'* through the Highlands. The book was a pleasure to read and immensely helpful. There are places where the Prince's route is in some doubt and my opinion occasionally differs from that of Mr Norie. Where this is the case I offer my readers both itineraries from which to choose.

Lastly, I offer a word of appreciation to the memory of Bonnie Prince Charlie, the Pretender Prince who began it all.

Photography

Palazzo Muti	Roberto Piperno
Flora MacDonald's Grave	David Simmons, www.sunnyside-studio.com

FOREWORD

In 1745 the continent of Europe had been using the New Style Gregorian calendar for many years whereas Britain still used the Old Style Julian system. It was not until 1752 that the British calendar suddenly lost eleven days to bring the country in line with the rest of Europe. I have adopted the method of using New Style for the dating of events on the mainland of Europe and Old Style for those occurring in Britain.

Significant Events Leading to the Jacobite Rising of 1745

1685 James II and VII crowned King of England and Scotland.
1688 James Francis Stuart born (son of James II).
1688 James II, his wife (Mary of Modena) and son escape into exile
1689 William of Orange and wife Mary (daughter of James II and Anne Hyde) crowned as joint monarchs.
1689 James (II) arrives in Ireland in the first attempt to regain the throne.
1690 James (II) defeated by forces of William III at Battle of the Boyne.
1694 Mary dies at the age of 32 leaving no children.
1701 Act of Settlement passed stating that no Roman Catholic may become monarch.
1701 Exiled King James (II) dies.
1702 William III dies aged 53 after falling from a horse. Queen Anne (Mary's sister) ascends the throne.
1707 Act of Union passed. Great Britain comes into existence.
1708 James Francis Stuart, son of James II, unsuccessfully attempts to land in Scotland with 5,000 French troops.

1713 Treaty of Utrecht produces temporary peace between Britain and France and forbids James (III) the right to live in France.

1714 Queen Anne dies with no surviving children and George, Elector of Hanover is crowned George I.

1715 Jacobite rebellion led by the Earl of Mar captures Perth and Inverness but quickly fails through lack of French support.

1715 Louis XIV of France dies leaving Jacobites short of French support.

1717 James (III) takes up residence in Italy.

1719 Anglo-French alliance declares war on Spain

1719 Spanish financed Jacobite rebellion fails.

1719 James (III) marries Clementina Sobieska.

1720 Prince Charles Edward Stuart born in Rome.

1725 Charles' brother Henry born.

1727 George I dies, George II is crowned.

1735 Clementina Sobieska dies aged 33.

1740 Charles VI of Austria dies, precipitating the War Of Austrian Succession. Britain and France on opposing sides.

1743 French lose Battle of Dettingen. Renewed French interest in anti-British and therefore Stuart cause.

1744 Invasion troops led by Prince Charles assembled at Dunkirk. Bad weather wrecks ships and plans. Charles determined to try again.

1745 In May the French rout British forces commanded by the Duke of Cumberland at Battle of Fontenoy.

The Jacobite Rising of 1745/46

1745

5 July	Le du Teillay sails for Scotland with Charles and 'Seven Men of Moidart'
23 July	Le du Teillay arrives in Eriskay
24 July	Arrival at Loch nan Uamh

19 August	Royal Standard raised at Glenfinnan
17 September	Jacobites enter Edinburgh
21 September	Battle of Prestonpans
8 November	Charles enters England at Carlisle
10-15 November	Carlisle under siege
4 December	Jacobites enter Derby
6 December	Withdrawal to Scotland
20 December	Charles' birthday. Jacobites re-cross Scottish border
26 December	Jacobites enter Glasgow

1746

8 January	Unsuccessful siege of Stirling Castle
17 January	Battle of Falkirk
20 February	Inverness Castle surrenders
16 April	Battle of Culloden
26 April	Escape to Outer Hebrides
28 June	Over the sea to Skye
5 July	Prince Charles arrives back on mainland
5 September	In 'Cluny's Cage' in Ben Alder
20 September	Escape to France

Names of People and Places

Many people living in the Highlands during the eighteenth century shared the same surname. So many MacDonalds feature in this history that correctly identifying them is tricky. There are also numerous MacLeods, Mackinnons and Camerons to sort out one from another. To minimise the confusion Highlanders are often referred to by place of birth or domicile. Hence we refer to the Chief of Clan Cameron as Donald Cameron of Lochiel or simply 'Lochiel'. Similarly Donald Cameron of Glenpean becomes 'Glenpean' and Alexander MacDonald of Kingsburgh is 'Kingsburgh'.

Place names in the Highlands and especially the Islands of

Scotland are frequently spelled in both English and Gaelic. Good examples might be Lochboisdale (Loch Baghasdail) in South Uist (Uibhist a Deas). Other places have only a Gaelic name. Where a well-known English spelling exists I use it, with the same reasoning as I apply when referring to Rome and Florence not Roma and Firenze. In cases where I had doubts (should it be Rossinish or Rosinis?) I followed the example set by modern Ordnance Survey maps.

Many accounts were written into 'The Lyon in Mourning' from the mouths of those there at the time. Names were committed to paper using phonetic spelling. Additionally, modern ways of spelling place names are often different from those used in the eighteenth century.

Maps

The maps illustrate my personal journey and not necessarily the route of the Jacobite army. They are included to enhance the reader's perception of events and are simply sketches. The maps are not all drawn to quite the same scale and the distances recorded are inexact. No one should attempt to follow the walk using only these illustrations. The inclusion of a particular name on a map is no indication of the size of that place. Locations marked vary from large cities to single buildings.

Ordnance Survey Landranger Maps
1:50000 (2cm to 1 km or 1¼ in to 1 mile)

8 Stornoway & North Lewis
14 Tarbert & Loch Seaforth
22 Benbecula & South Uist
23 North Skye
25 Glen Carron & Glen Affric
26 Inverness & Strathglass
27 Nairn & Forres

28 Barra & South Uist
29 South Skye & Cuillin Hills
30 Loch Alsh & Glen Shiel
34 Fort Augustus & Glen Albyn
35 Kingussie & Monadhliath Mountains
36 Grantown, Aviemore & Cairngorm
40 Mallaig & Glenfinnan, Loch Shiel
41 Ben Nevis & Fort William
42 Glen Garry & Loch Rannoch
43 Braemar & Blair Atholl
52 Pitlochry to Crieff
57 Stirling & the Trossachs
58 Perth to Alloa, Auchterarder
64 Glasgow, Motherwell & Airdrie
65 Falkirk & Linlithgow, Dunfermline
66 Edinburgh, Penicuik & North Berwick
71 Lanark & Upper Nithsdale
73 Peebles, Galashiels & Selkirk
74 Kelso & Coldstream, Jedburgh & Duns
78 Nithsdale & Annandale, Sanquhar & Moffat
79 Hawick & Eskdale, Langholm
80 Cheviot Hills & Kielder Water
84 Dumfries & Castle Douglas
85 Carlisle & Solway Firth, Gretna Green
90 Penrith & Keswick, Ambleside
97 Kendal & Morecambe, Windermere & Lancaster
102 Preston, Blackpool
108 Liverpool, Southport & Wigan
109 Manchester, Bolton & Warrington
118 Stoke-on-Trent & Macclesfield
119 Buxton, Matlock & Dove Dale
128 Derby & Burton upon Trent

Guides

Guide to the Waterways (5) North West & the Pennines (Nicholson/ Ordnance Survey, 1997)
The Staffordshire Way, Official Guide (Staffordshire County Council/Countryside Commission, 1996)

INTRODUCTION

'There is no more time for deliberation; now or never is the word.'
Prince Charles Edward Stuart, September 1745

Bonnie Prince Charlie or Prince Charles Edward Stuart, to give him his more formal name, was convinced, with some good reason, that his father should be sitting on the throne of Great Britain. In July 1745 the Prince and a few companions landed on the west coast of Scotland in an ambitious and many would say foolish attempt to regain the throne for the Stuart family. Gathering support as he went, Prince Charles marched south from the Highlands with the intention of reaching London where he had the romantic notion he would be welcomed in triumph. His father would be declared James III and the reigning Hanoverian king, George II, exiled. It did not work out like that at all. True, the Bonnie Prince marched a long way south but in the end failed to reach London. His army advanced to Derby but then retreated ignominiously. At Culloden near Inverness the rebel army was badly beaten and after many adventures Prince Charlie escaped to France, his dreams of kingship shattered forever. The 1745 campaign was the last of several attempts to restore the Stuarts to the throne and is often known simply as 'The Forty-Five'.

The story of Prince Charles' exploits in Britain is famous throughout the world. Flora MacDonald, who helped him escape from the redcoat soldiers, over the sea to Skye, is almost as celebrated as the Bonnie Prince himself. The battlefield at Culloden, where Jacobite ambition was torn to pieces by British army cannon fire, is well visited and many people can sing at least the first couple of lines of 'The Skye Boat Song'. The tale is one of intrigue, high hopes, heroism, personal charisma, bravery and fortitude as well as arrogance, unreasonable expectation, butchery, fear and failure. The adventure had a poor beginning, transformed for a time by battles won and cheering crowds, into majestic success against all the odds. Yet it is a story of disillusionment, imagined betrayal, pain, death and final defeat. It is also true.

I am interested in history and I enjoy walking. It seemed like a good idea to combine the two by following the Prince's route on foot, taking into consideration the modern development of the landscape and the availability of suitable footpaths. It is crucial to my family's well-being that I work for a living and so finishing the walking in one continuous, foot-blistering slog was, fortunately, not an option. About ten days at fifteen miles a day is as much as my feet can cope with and, as I usually stay in B&Bs, the novelty of black pudding, bacon, sausage and mushroom breakfasts wears off after about a week. This journey is more than fifteen hundred miles from start to finish, many of them over rough and isolated territory. It would have taken me forever at the rate of a snatched weekend here and there. I had to reorganise my life to do it.

I have completed the first half-century of life and on the assumption that another fifty years is a bit unlikely, I decided that the wheels of corporate globalisation would have to do without me for a while. My employers have the enlightened policy of allowing their staff part time contracts. The only snag is that they only expect to pay part time salaries but I soon became used to the idea. This 'downshifting', as the fashionable jargon has it, is a good scheme if you have the finances right. I have always tried to live within my income and save a shilling or two for the future. When is the future if not when the first fifty years are completed? The mortgage is paid off and the children are almost grown up. When a fifty per cent contract was offered to me, I discussed it with Momoyo and then grabbed it with both hands. I haven't regretted it for a minute.

I began at Loch nan Uamh where Prince Charles first landed on mainland Britain. It's a wild spot just south of Arisaig on what is now 'The Road to the Isles'. The walk took me through Perth, Edinburgh, Carlisle, Manchester and finally to Derby. The Prince was determined to take London but to his enduring disappointment his commanders decided that the odds against taking and holding the capital were too great and marched the army back to Scotland. I followed the retreat to Glasgow, Inverness and the infamous battlefield

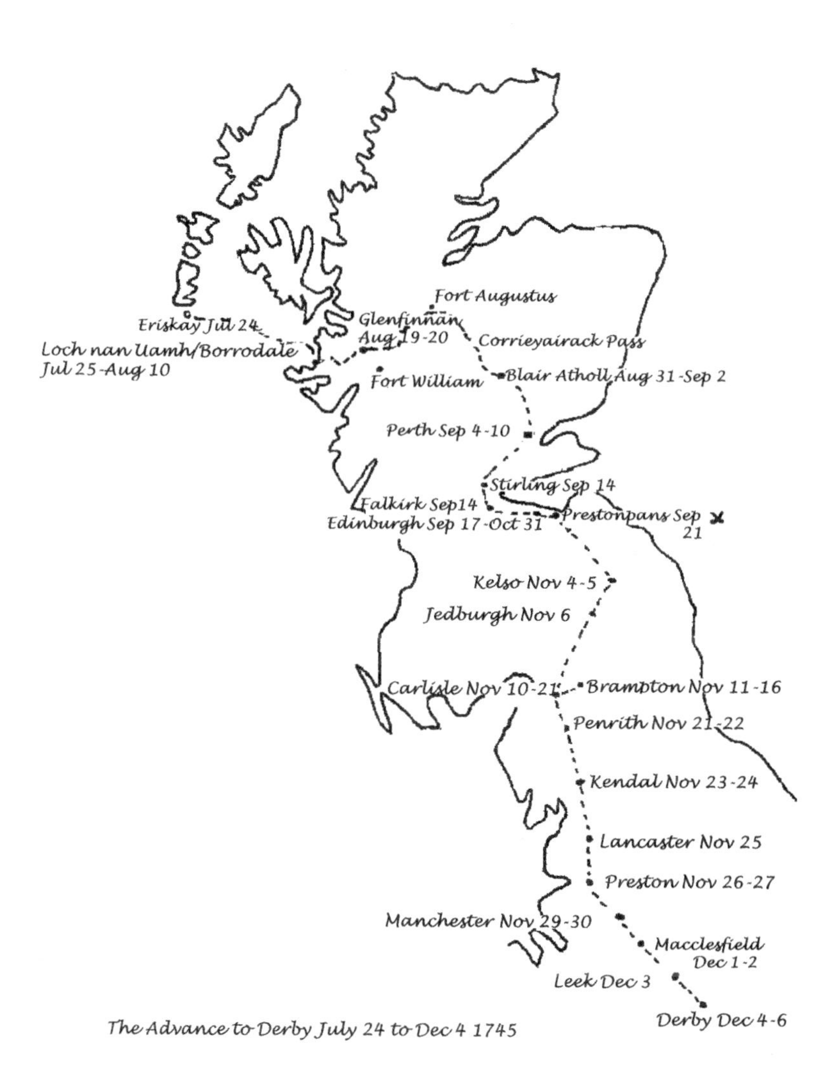

The Advance to Derby July 24 to Dec 4 1745

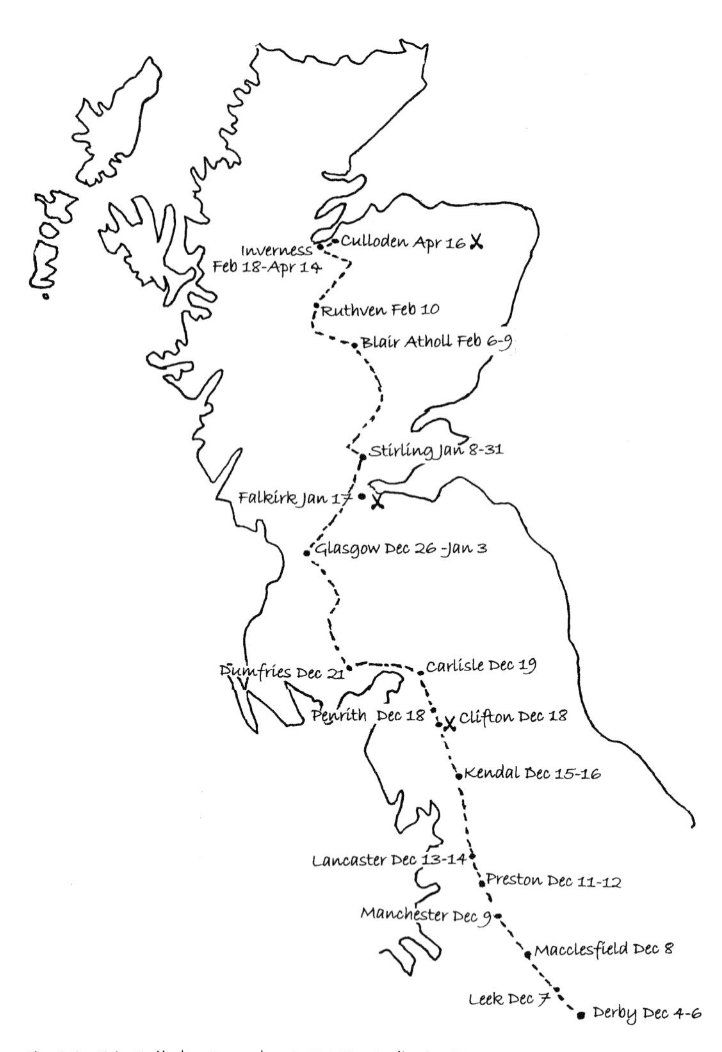

The Retreat to Culloden, December 6 1745 to April 16 1746

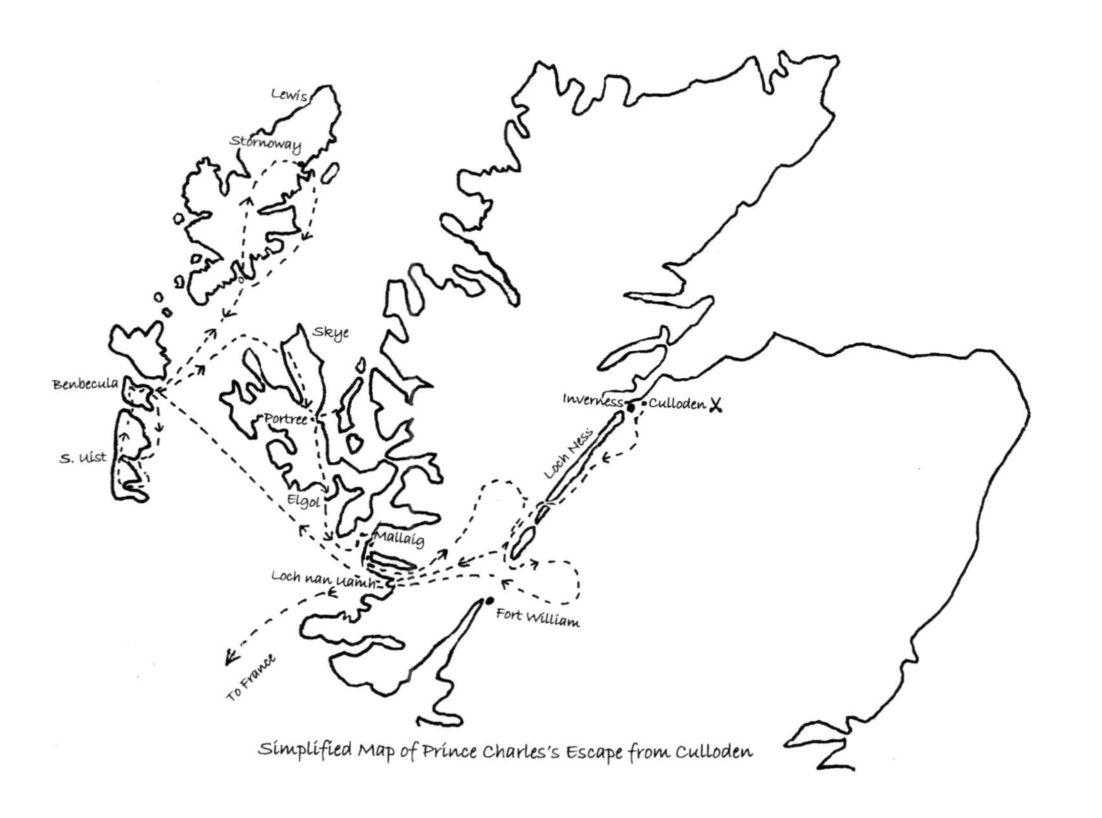

Simplified Map of Prince Charles's Escape from Culloden

at Culloden. Defeat drove Prince Charles to the Hebrides but as the noose of capture tightened he was compelled to return to the mainland and hide for weeks in the wilderness of the western Highlands. The Prince's adventure ended back at Loch nan Uamh from where he and a few companions finally escaped to France.

It is neither sensible nor practical to walk everywhere so I thought about using my car and mused over other options. Circular routes are just the job for cars. After a good day's walking you come back to the spot where you started and there is your personal transport and security blanket waiting to whisk you away to wherever your fancy takes you. Never mind that you're cold, soaking wet and have not yet found somewhere to sleep. Who cares that the last bus has just gone and there isn't another until a week on Wednesday? The car will see to it that everything is all right.

Walking on linear footpaths is different. The car that was so useful for driving to the starting place would be not a scrap of good at the end of the day unless I returned to collect it. How would I do that? Walking back was out of the question and so hitch-hiking or telephoning for a taxi might be my only option. It all looked like too much trouble. I decided to leave the car at home and rely on public transport and the occasional lift.

Many parts of Charles' route have changed out of all recognition since the eighteenth century and so I deliberately travelled some of the way by motor vehicle. I hitch-hiked frequently but warn of the possible dangers. I did a lot of it when I was an impoverished student and most people who offered me lifts were friendly and helpful. There were a couple of occasions when the male driver placed an encouraging hand on my upper thigh. I didn't much care for that and said so in a tone that made it clear that my gratitude might stretch as far as a cup of tea in a transport café but no further. There was also a notable time when a chap invited me to beat him with a springy tree branch on the slip road to the Forth Road Bridge. Well, I was with a friend, we were only eighteen and it seemed a harmless enough request to me at the time! If you do hitch, do it with a friend. At the risk of being branded a politically incorrect sexist, females would be mad to hitch alone. Be careful!

The requirements of family and work meant that I completed the walk in stages over six years. I researched the Prince's route before setting out on each part of my journey and chose the exact path to take on a daily basis. I used O.S. Landranger maps and walked on existing footpaths, disused railway lines, canal towpaths and minor roads. If you complete any part of this walk you will have an achievement on which to congratulate yourself. I wish you much enjoyment.

The journey took me through glens and over mountains, across some of the wildest country in the land as well as over gentler terrain and into towns and villages. I am not a rock climber and so the walk offers none of the dangers associated with that activity. Much of the journey is through easy walking territory. Provided you are physically fit you could try it yourself and the qualities you will find essential are fortitude and no aversion to rain. Nonetheless some of the route is through the most remote region of Britain and took me considerable distances from roads and settlements. The Highlands of Scotland are thinly populated. Those who have never been there before will be amazed at the scarcity of towns or villages with any sizeable number of people. It is possible to walk all day in the more remote areas and not see anyone. A twisted ankle or worse would be serious problem for a lone walker and it could be a long time, perhaps even days, before anyone came along. The mobile phone, a sometimes-useful device in adverse circumstances, will probably not provide an operational line at the vital time.

The weather anywhere in Britain, but particularly in the west of Scotland, is capable of rapid change. A beautiful day at nine in the morning might deteriorate into a howling gale by four in the afternoon. Appropriate clothing is essential and should include good, comfortable walking boots, waterproofs and something warm. The boots are important. Feet are going to ache after a while no matter what, but chafing boots that produce blisters are the last things anyone needs.

I'm a great believer in wearing a hat but then I am somewhat 'follically challenged'. A hat keeps off the sun and helps deter buzzing insects. A wide brim gives a split second's warning of tree branches or other potentially painful objects. Yes, get a hat but not a baseball cap, and especially not one worn back to front. Buy a proper hat, one with a bit of style. You won't regret it. Sun tan cream and insect repellent are useful and a plastic survival bag or similar protection might save your life if you're stranded in a remote area. Carry a compass (know how to use it!) and a whistle and never walk without a suitable map. Acquire a decent walking stick. There are all sorts available, from expensive high tech affairs that look like ski poles to ones fashioned from bits of dead branch. A stick is useful for providing balance when crossing streams or difficult terrain. It provides additional leverage for uphill climbs or a little braking for downhill ones. Lastly, a stick offers some comfort when confronted with the barking dogs you are likely to encounter along the way.

Try not to do too much in each day, particularly if you find you're not quite as fit as you think you are. There is a commonly held view that a human being can walk at about four miles an hour, and for short distances, over smooth, flat ground this may be true. However experience tells me that I am hard pushed to do more than two miles an hour over the whole day and less than that in the more arduous areas of the Highlands. I admit right here, right now that there were occasions where I failed to follow in the Prince's footsteps as closely as I should have liked. Some of the journey was hard and my plan was to enjoy the experience, not wear myself out. Occasionally, time constraints, weather, personal motivation, fitness and perhaps even age conspired together to leave my achievements short of the ideal. However the reader may be assured that if I say I walked a particular route then I did so and if I did not then I say that too.

I have tried to make my route clear without becoming bogged down in too much detail. However, my endeavours should not be regarded as the only way of completing the journey. There are often alternative paths. I prepared each day's walk but still occasionally took the wrong path and had to backtrack a little. The secret here, I discovered, was to be vigilant with both map and compass. I checked my position frequently, especially when the slightest suspicion that I might be moving in the wrong direction crept into my mind. I decided not to book accommodation in advance, as I preferred the flexibility of taking pot-luck. Finding somewhere to sleep in the Highlands was occasionally difficult and so I left plenty of time each day to locate a place to stay. I considered camping, but not for long. I'm a bed and breakfast man. I do camp sometimes but only in good weather and in places where I can return to the site easily. I'm far too long in the tooth for carrying a heavy pack and never much liked it when I was younger. Camping is tremendous fun, cheap and you meet some super people but at the end of a hard day's walk there is nothing like a hot bath and a comfortable bed.

I mentioned earlier that the story is true; but is it? Certainly if the broad thrust of my version of the tale is examined in terms of dates, battles and principal characters then it is as true as the next writer's. But the truth we perceive and hope to understand depends on how events are portrayed. We need to learn not simply the bare facts but the underlying motivation behind the action. We ought to see what happened from more than one point of view. These truths are more difficult to define. How did the ordinary soldier in the Jacobite army feel? What of the motivation of the various commanders or the attitude of the French? What were the reasons for the decision to retreat from Derby? Could the Jacobite army have regrouped successfully after Culloden? Who supported the Prince and why? There are endless questions and even more answers. Although I have tried to throw a little light onto events it is not within the scope of this book to delve deeply into these subjective matters. There are dozens of books on the Forty-Five for those who wish to further their knowledge and come to their own conclusions about the rebellion.

Several factors may influence our perception of these events 250 years ago. The tourist industry long ago concluded that there is a lot of money to be made from the 'Highlandisation' of Scotland. Tartans, claymores, kilts, bagpipes and the like are on everything from whisky bottles to tea towels. These images are not only found north of the Highland line but throughout the country. The Royal

Mile in Edinburgh has never been a centre of Highland culture or support but its shops are full of the stuff. The image of a masculine Highlander with rippling muscles, struggling against the odds to maintain his traditional way of life is an integral part of the hard sell. The portrayal of the Jacobite risings as plucky but unequal struggles against the English fits neatly into the mythology.

The marketing people have a field day with the names Bonnie Prince Charlie and Flora MacDonald. If the kilted Highlander is thrown into the melting pot and we view the rebellion of 1745-46 through rose tinted spectacles, as we are encouraged to do, the resulting image becomes endowed with a mysticism that sells huge quantities of shortbread! Do we see the Bonnie Prince as a ruthless, vain, despotic prince who believes in the divine right of kings and is willing to sacrifice any number of people to achieve his ends? No we do not. We see a young, handsome, almost angelic prince who, very nearly single-handed, has come from afar to deliver his faithful Highlanders from poverty and oppression and avenge the wrongful exile of his grandfather king. In Flora, do we see a frightened young woman terrified of government troops but compelled by the authority of her visitors and a misguided sense of Highland hospitality to undertake her dangerous mission? Again we do not. We are encouraged to see Flora as a romantic heroine, perhaps a little in love with her handsome Highland prince. She is willing to risk her life to protect him from the wicked English in the furtherance of a desperate cause dear to her heart. The whole Flora MacDonald episode is overblown in the popular 'faction' version of the '45. True, the woman played a useful role but she was only with the Prince for twelve days. Her prominence is attributable to the perceived romantic involvement and because she is one of only a few women to play active and significant parts. Collectively these images play upon our thinking and may convince us, without any good foundation, of the right of the Jacobite cause and perhaps persuade us that the Prince's supporters were all Highlanders.

It was in the British government's interest to initially play down the importance of the Forty-Five and later transmogrify the image of the Highlander from a rebellious savage into that of patriotic British soldier fighting valiantly for freedom throughout the world. The belittling and denigration of the rising facilitated an atmosphere that precluded further unrest on behalf of the Stuart dynasty and was deemed essential for decades. The Prince's army was portrayed as a hastily thrown together band of desperate men with little training and no hope of success. Highland dress was forbidden and the Highland way of life was depicted as flawed and dying in response to challenges of the Britain so recently born out of the Act of Union. Thomas Pennant, who was no Jacobite, made these comments during a tour of Scotland twenty-three years after the rising.

> *The houses of the common people in these parts are shocking to humanity, formed of loose stones, and covered with clods, which they call devish, or with heath, broom or branches of fir: they look at a distance like so many black molehills. The inhabitants live very poorly, on oatmeal, barley-cakes and potatoes; their drink whisky sweetened with honey. The men are thin, but strong; idle and lazy, except employed in the chase, or anything that looks like amusement; are content with their hard fare, and will not exert themselves farther than to get what they deem necessaries.*

When the threat of renewed Jacobite activity was deemed to be over, the gradual rehabilitation of the Highlander into mainstream Scottish and British life took place. Sir Walter Scott's Jacobite novel, 'Waverley' was published in 1814 and that was followed by 'Rob Roy' and other romantic Highland works. Caroline Oliphant who was the daughter of a prominent supporter of Prince Charles Edward wrote popular songs sentimentalising the Highlands in general and the Prince in particular. 'Charlie is my Darling' uncompromisingly illustrates the interest in romantic Jacobitism.

Wi' Hieland bonnets on their heads,
And claymores bright and clear,
They came to fight for Scotland's right,
And the young Chevalier.

Oh, Charlie is my darling,
My darling, my darling;
Oh, Charlie is my darling,
The young Chevalier.

They've left their bonnie Hieland hills,
Their wives and bairnies dear,
To draw the sword for Scotland's lord,
The young Chevalier.

Queen Victoria continued the process and gave the tartan a new respect and validity. The Forty-Five was coated with a syrupy veneer and portrayed as a wild, impulsive, almost teenage escapade. After all it was a long time ago, the Jacobites lost and the monarchy and country were safe and prosperous. The establishment could afford to be generous to a distant rebellion that no longer produced a moment's disquiet in the drawing rooms of England.

The '45 is frequently described as either a rebellion against the legitimate British government of the day or a rising by supporters of a wrongly dispossessed royal dynasty to recover its rightful position on the throne of Great Britain. Sometimes the rising is portrayed as an 'England v. Scotland' contest as though it were a football match. Clearly this is a simplistic and inaccurate representation of the conflict. Although it cannot be denied that government support was mostly English and Welsh while Jacobite support was mostly Scottish, neither side drew their assistance exclusively from these sources. The custom of referring to Prince Charles' forces as the Highland army is understandable but erroneous. Highlanders were the biggest single group in the Prince's army at all times and as the high points of the campaign might be seen as the Battle of Prestonpans and the advance to Derby where the majority of the marching army were Highlanders the popular description may be excused. Prince Charles is partly to blame as he adopted Highland dress as the standard uniform for his army, even providing the Manchester Regiment with white cockades and tartan sashes. However, there were English, French and Irish in the army and not a small number of Lowland Scots. Gordon of Glenbucket and Lord Pitsligo each recruited several hundred men from the Aberdeen and Banff regions where Episcopalianism, with its concept of the indefeasibility of kings, was strong. Lord Ogilvy produced 600 or so from Angus and John Roy Stewart led the Edinburgh Regiment. The second line of the Prince's army at Culloden contained more Lowlanders than Highlanders. Rivalry between the Highland regiments in the front line was intense and clansmen would take orders from their own chief but not from any other. To resolve these difficulties overall command of clan regiments fell to The Duke of Perth and Lord George Murray.

It is similarly incorrect to believe that all, or even most, Highlanders supported the Prince, let alone did any fighting for him. The memory of how previous Jacobite risings had ended and the arrival of Prince Charles with almost no support did nothing to convince clan chiefs that enthusiastically rallying to the Jacobite Standard was a great idea. The chiefs of the MacDonalds and MacLeods of Skye ignored the pleas for help, as did Lord Seaforth, leader of the Mackenzies, despite the fact that his clan had been 'out' for the Jacobites in 1715. Indeed it can be argued that few of the western clans came out en masse to support the Prince and it was not until the Jacobite army entered Perth that its numbers matched those of the '15.

The popular image of the rising does not encourage the casual observer to believe that the government attracted much Highland support other than that raised by The Duke of Argyll and his cousin General John Campbell of Mamore. However, Duncan Forbes who was the most senior government officer in Scotland spent much time and energy raising twenty independent companies of Highland militia composed of MacDonalds of Sleat, MacLeods, Grants, Munros,

Rosses and Gordons.

Finally, it is sometimes said that more Scots fought on the 'English' side at Culloden than for *'Scotland and Prince Charlie.'* This is also untrue. Of the 9,000 men who fought in the government lines at Culloden about 2,400 were Scots. These were predominantly in three regiments: The Royal Scots (1st), Campbell's Royal Scots Fusiliers (21st) and Sempill's King's Own Scottish Borderers (25th). In addition there were the Argyll Militia and Lord Louden's men. Of approximately 5,000 men fighting in the Prince's lines most were Scots with the notable exceptions of the Irish Piquets, the Manchester regiment and the Régiment Écossais Royaux.

Prince's Cairn, Loch nan Uamh

Head of Loch Shiel

Corrieyairack Pass

St. George's Bridge, Garvamore

Dalkeith Palace

Carlisle Castle

Bonnie Prince Charlie, Derby

Swarkestone Bridge, Derbyshire

Battle of Falkirk
Monument

Bantaskine Windows

St. Ninian's Tower, Stirling

Culloden Memorial

Lochan Leum an t-Sagairt

Swampy Green Lochan

J. J. MacDonald, Prince's Cave, Corradale

Colin and Author (left) on a Fishing Trip

Cloud Over Monkstadt, Skye

Flora MacDonald's
Grave

Flora's Cottage, Flodigarry

Gardens at Armadale

'Western Isles' at Inverie, Knoydart

Over the Top from Kinloch Hourn

Glenmoriston Men's Cave

Sourlies Bothy

White Falls

Cluny's Cage? Ben Alder

ONE

TWO KINGS: ONE CROWN

'I have been, above six months ago, invited by our friends to go to Scotland.'
Letter from Prince Charles to his father, 12 June 1745

Before I begin to describe the Prince's campaign and my own efforts to follow the route, it might be a good idea to have a brief look at the history of events leading to the '45. It perhaps all began when Elizabeth I of England died childless in 1603 and the crown passed from the Tudors to the Stuarts. James VI of Scotland was crowned James I of England, his entitlement stemming from Henry VIII's sister Margaret, who had married King James IV of Scotland.

Charles I came next but the Civil War led to his execution in 1649 and Oliver Cromwell replaced royalty. The monarchy was restored in 1660 and Charles II reigned until he died on 6 February 1685. Charles II had no legitimate children and so despite the passing of the Test Acts specifically designed to prevent Catholics holding public office, Charles' brother was crowned James II.

James had converted to Roman Catholicism in the 1660s and had married an Italian, Mary Beatrice, Princess d'Este, in 1673 when he was Duke of York. Despite disapproval from many quarters and a period of banishment James never really understood the antipathy felt in both England and Scotland towards the Catholic Church. After his accession King James instituted a programme of reversing the existing anti-Catholic laws and encouraged the holding of Mass. The size of the army was increased without reference to Parliament and an ambassador was sent to Rome expressing obedience to the Pope. These acts were thought by some to be a precursor to the forceful restoration of England to full Catholicism. Many were of the opinion that the King was full of religious fanaticism.

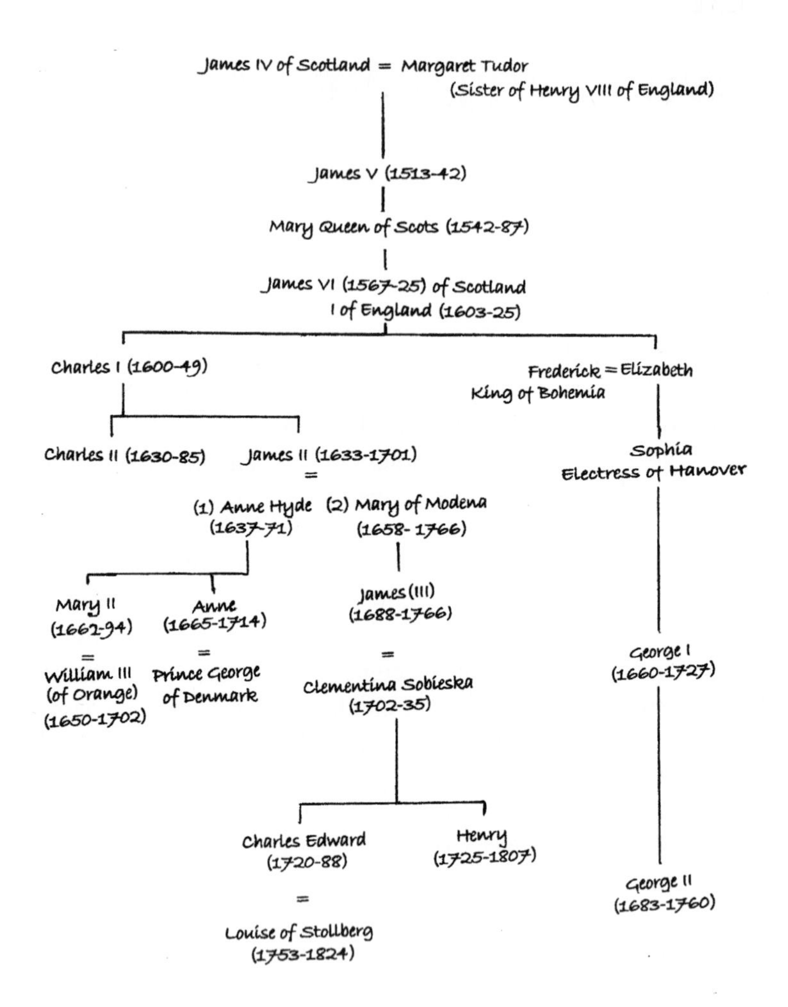

James IV of Scotland = Margaret Tudor
(Sister of Henry VIII of England)
James V (1513-42)
Mary Queen of Scots (1542-87)
James VI (1567-25) of Scotland
I of England (1603-25)
Charles I (1600-49)
Frederick = Elizabeth
King of Bohemia
Charles II (1630-85)
James II (1633-1701)
=
(1) Anne Hyde
(1637-71)
(2) Mary of Modena
(1658-1766)
Sophia
Electress of Hanover
Mary II
(1662-94)
=
William III
(of Orange)
(1650-1702)
Anne
(1665-1714)
=
Prince George
of Denmark
James (III)
(1688-1766)
=
Clementina Sobieska
(1702-35)
George I
(1660-1727)
Charles Edward
(1720-88)
=
Louise of Stollberg
(1753-1824)
Henry
(1725-1807)
George II
(1683-1760)

To complicate matters Mary Beatrice or Mary of Modena as she is often known was James' second wife. The King had previously been married to Anne Hyde who had given him two daughters: Mary born in 1662 and Anne in 1665. Both princesses were brought up as Protestants by their uncle, Charles II, after the death of their mother in 1671. Mary was not quite sixteen when, on 4 November 1677, she married her Protestant cousin, William of Orange, the son of James' sister.

King James II was fifty-one years old when he ascended the throne and no Stuart had lived beyond the age of sixty. Queen Mary Beatrice had been pregnant eight times but suffered four miscarriages and of the four children born all died before the age of five. The political thought of the day was that the reversion towards Catholicism would end with the King's death and that the throne would pass without trouble to his Protestant daughter, Mary.

In December 1687 Mary of Modena surprised everyone by announcing she was pregnant again and James Francis Edward Stuart was born on 10 June 1688. Princess Mary was no longer heir to the throne and William of Orange, decided to come to England to investigate the circumstances of this unexpected and controversial birth. A rumour spread that the boy was not Mary's child but had been smuggled into the bedchamber in a warming pan. This seems improbable, as there were almost seventy people in the room to witness the birth!

William landed at Torbay in Devon and marched on London, gathering support as he went. Despite desperate attempts to reverse some of the recent measures favouring Catholics James could elicit little sympathy or support and had to face the reality that neither he nor his newborn heir were wanted in the country. Remembering the fate of his father, Charles I, James fled the country on Christmas Eve 1688, and was reunited with his wife and son who had arrived in France two weeks earlier. The exiled family was welcomed by King Louis XIV who provided James with a sumptuous residence twelve miles west of Paris at St Germain-en-Laye where he could set up his court in exile. King James neither abdicated nor renounced his claim to the throne. Despite any legal justification the crown was offered to Mary who was only prepared to become Queen if her husband was appointed King. Parliament was anxious for a swift and painless transfer of power and so agreed to this unprecedented request.

William and Mary were crowned as joint monarchs in Westminster Abbey in April 1689. A joint monarchy had never previously ruled England or Scotland and the orb created for Mary's coronation has not been used since. In accepting the crown in what has become known as 'The Glorious Revolution' William and Mary agreed to the terms of the Bill of Rights Act of 1689. The Act ended the concept of divine right of kings and made the monarch subject to laws passed by Parliament. From James's point of view one clause is particularly relevant. '*It hath been found by experience that it is inconsistent with the safety and welfare of this Protestant kingdom to be governed by a popish prince.*'

Although political union between England and Scotland had been considered, a continuing desire amongst Scots to control their own affairs had so far prevented this happening and many Scots refused to swear allegiance to the new monarchs. Feelings were strongest in the Highlands, where many clan chiefs had no desire for centralised government from London. Those who held King James to be their legitimate monarch were dubbed Jacobites from Jacobus, the Latin word for James. Amongst the most passionate of the Jacobites was John Graham of Claverhouse, Viscount of Dundee who rallied the clans loyal to King James. On 27 July 1689 'Bonnie Dundee' confronted an army of government troops in a narrow gorge close to Killiecrankie in Perthshire. The Highlanders routed their enemy but Dundee was killed. Without their charismatic leader the Highlanders lost direction and were badly beaten at the subsequent battle of Dunkeld.

The French King, Louis XIV, was persuaded to finance an expedition to restore the Stuart monarchy through Roman Catholic Ireland as it had no great taste for the rule of William and Mary and was fiercely Jacobite. King James landed supplied with French arms, men and money. Things went well at first; city after city declared for James and his army swelled to 30,000 men who initially encountered little opposition. However when King William arrived in June 1690 with a well-trained army of 36,000, the tide turned and James was thoroughly beaten on 1 July at the Battle of the Boyne.

The English government decided to clamp down on the Jacobite clans and issued an edict requiring the chiefs to swear an oath of allegiance to King William by New Year's Day 1692. The chiefs felt themselves to be in an impossible position and appealed to exiled King James for special dispensation to take the oath. Unfortunately James did not grant this authorisation until almost the end of 1691. Unwillingness to co-operate, bad weather and a belief that the oath should be sworn at Fort William conspired to make MacIan, chief of the Glencoe MacDonalds, miss the deadline and by the time he swore allegiance it was 6 January. The government decided to punish the clan in a way that would encourage others to abide by their new loyalties and forget Jacobitism. Captain Robert Campbell of Glenlyon was sent to Glencoe where he and his men were hospitably received after making up a story that there was no accommodation available at Fort William. They stayed for two weeks before orders arrived to massacre every Glencoe MacDonald under the age of seventy. In the early hours of 13 February they fell upon their hosts. MacIan was murdered in his bed and his wife forced out into the snow where she was left to die. Forty were killed but despite the ruthless brutality of Campbell and his men many MacDonalds escaped into the relative safety of the snowy night.

William and Mary, who had no children, were joint monarchs until Mary died of smallpox in 1694, leaving William to rule alone. Mary's sister Anne, who was next in line to the throne had at least seventeen pregnancies, most of which ended in miscarriage or stillbirth. Of the children born alive all died in infancy except the Duke of Gloucester who was frail and diseased and expired at the age of eleven in 1700. The Duke and his siblings are all interred in Westminster Abbey's Lady Chapel. This inability of the sisters to produce a child who could inherit produced speculation and conversation with 'King' James suggesting that the throne might be offered to his son James Francis if only he could be brought up in the Protestant faith. James was furious and of course refused.

In 1701, despite doubts regarding the succession, the English Parliament passed the Act of Settlement that cemented the law that no future monarch could be of the Catholic faith. James I's daughter, Elizabeth had married Frederick V of Bohemia and their Protestant daughter Sophia married the Elector of Hanover. In England it was decreed that after the death of Anne, Sophia or her descendants would inherit the throne. Three months after the Act was passed, exiled King James died.

I began my visit to St Germain-en-Laye with a short train journey from Etoile station at the Arc de Triomphe. The chateau that provided ex-King James with sanctuary for the last thirteen years of his life dominates the town and was immediately visible as I emerged from the station into Place Charles de Gaulle. Unfortunately almost no evidence remains of the chateau's Jacobite history as the interior was gutted in the nineteenth century. The elegant exterior now houses the Musée des Antiquités Nationales. L'Eglise St Germain is opposite the chateau on the other side of the road. The church was consecrated in 1827 and is the third to be built on the site. At the back on the right hand side is a marble monument to the memory of James II/VII. The Latin inscription reads,

FERALE QUISQUIS HOC MONUMENTUM SUSPICIS
RERUM HUMANARUM VICES MEDITARE.
MAGNUS IN PROSPERIS, IN ADVERSIS MAJOR.
JACOBUS II ANGLORUM REX
INSIGNES ÆRUMNAS DOLENDA QUI NIMIUM FATA
PIO, PLACIDI QUE OBITU EXSOLVIT
IN HÂC URBE
DIE XVI SEPTEMBRIS ANNI 1701,
ET NOBILIORES QUÆDAM CORPORIS EJUS PARTES
HIC RECONDITÆ ASSERVANTUR

L'Eglise Saint Germain

Whoever you are who are looking up at this funeral monument, consider the changes of fortune in human affairs. Great in times of prosperity, greater in times of adversity. James II, King of England. As a result of misfortunes which are to be grieved over because of his well-known hardships, he died with a Holy and calm death in this city on September 16 1701, and the more distinguished parts of his body are declared to lie here.

A plaque attached to an exterior wall of the church reads,

In this church is the shrine to the memory of James II The last Stuart King of England who died in exile at the castle of St Germain-en-Laye on September 16th 1701. The monument was erected by her Majesty, Queen Victoria.

As the Latin inscription points out King James II is not buried in his entirety in this church. Various bits of his body; heart, entrails etc were buried at four churches but the main part of his body was taken to the chapel of the English Benedictines in Paris where it lay unburied, encased in both wooden and lead coffins, for almost a hundred years. It seems that the coffins were broken open during the French Revolution and the lead melted down to make ammunition. Where the body of King James now lies is not known.

In February 1702 King William fell from his horse after it caught a hoof on a molehill. William broke his collarbone and the fall weakened him to the point where he contracted pleurisy and died on 8 March. Jacobites celebrated and drank toasts to 'the little gentleman in black velvet' that was the cause of the King's demise. Anne became Queen. During her reign the unification of England and Scotland finally came about with the passing of The Act of Union in 1707. This coupling of the ancient kingdom of Scotland with England angered a large number Scots and many became willing to support the Jacobite cause.

In 1708 Louis XIV financed titular King James III, 'The King over the Water', to go to Scotland with 6,000 soldiers in an attempt to rally support for the restoration of the former Stuart line. The expedition began badly as James contracted measles soon after he arrived in Dunkirk. The ships sailed but were confronted at the mouth of the Firth of Forth by twenty-eight British warships. The French fleet turned tail and fled back to France losing vesels and men in the terrible gales that struck them during the voyage.

In the years immediately preceding Queen Anne's death in 1714 there was a good opportunity for the difficulties regarding succession to be reconsidered. The Act of Settlement was not popular with everyone and the House of Commons contained many pro-Jacobite Tories. Queen Anne was not adamantly against the throne being inherited by James Francis if she could not produce a successor who would outlive her. There was a real possibility that the throne would be passed to Sophia's son George, the Elector of Hanover. That would be the end of the Stuarts and Anne was not enthusiastic about being succeeded by an obscure German princeling. James had the considerable advantages of the Stuart name and of being the Queen's half-brother. As before the sticking point was religion. James believed that God had ordained his right to the British throne. He would not renounce his Roman Catholic faith and so when Anne died the Elector was crowned George I.

The year 1715 brought the most ambitious scheme so far to place James on the throne of Britain. Three risings were to take place simultaneously: in the south-west and north of England and in Scotland. The main effort depended upon the seizure of Bristol and Plymouth through which ports continental help could flow. The government discovered the plot and struck pre-emptive blows arresting many prominent Jacobites and causing the rising in the south to be over before it had started. In Scotland a rebellion led by John Erskine, Earl of Mar and 10,000 clansmen was planned. The Earl's men raised the Royal Standard at Braemar on 6 September and soon controlled most of Scotland from Perth to Inverness. A bungled attempt to take Edinburgh Castle left Mar and his badly equipped men inactively garrisoned in Perth and facing the Duke of Argyll who was quartered in Stirling doing not much more than biding his time in expectation of Mar marching south. The rising here was a stalemate. The north of England saw Jacobites marching about Northumberland, ineffectively threatening Newcastle and proclaiming James to be King. They were joined by a number of Scots and some men from the failed rebellion in the south. The northern Jacobites initially encountered little opposition but then discovered that General George Carpenter and 900 cavalry were on their way to confront them. Hoping to gather more recruits in the north-west of England the Jacobites moved west and then south. Carpenter caught up with them at Preston and after a couple of days skirmishing the Jacobites surrendered. Back in Scotland Mar fought an inconclusive battle at Sheriffmuir on 13 November but was forced to abandon Inverness and many Highlanders returned home for the winter. By the time 'King' James arrived on 22 December the rising was all but over. What remained of the Jacobite army fled north pursuing a scorched earth policy as it did so. This action caused untold hardship on the people and slowed their pursers not a bit. The cause was lost and on 4 February 1716 James and a few of his followers sailed back to France.

The death of Louis XIV was a significant setback to the Pretender's hopes. The French King had been his main supporter and to make matters worse England was at peace with France. The Treaty of Utrecht contained a clause that bound the French government to refuse James residence in France. When James returned from the '15, the Duke of Orleans informed him that he must leave French territory. He reluctantly did so and moved his household to Italy. By mid January 1719 a Franco/British alliance declared war on Spain, eliminating the chance of collusion between James and the French government.

In 1719 an attempt was made to invade both England and Scotland simultaneously. It is sometimes known as 'The Spanish Plot', as King Philip V of Spain financed the venture. The plan involved a large force under the command of the Duke of Ormonde landing in England, and a smaller one commanded by the 10th Earl of Marischal, destined for Scotland. Ormonde's force met with a violent storm and returned to port but Marischal's force of 307 Spaniards landed at Stornoway on the Isle of Lewis where they learned of the failure of the other group. The Jacobites found no welcome in Lewis, so sailed south and made their headquarters on the mainland at Eilean Donan Castle at the head of Loch Alsh. Before long the Royal Navy sent a squadron of ships into the sea loch and the Spanish garrison was overwhelmed. Weapons and stores were captured and the castle destroyed. With no means of withdrawal Marischal was forced to retreat inland where Major General Wightman defeated the Jacobite army at the Battle of Glenshiel on James Francis' thirty-first birthday 10 June. The rising of 1719 emulated its 1715 predecessor by ending in failure.

It was imperative that the 'King over the Water' should marry and produce a son and heir. British disapproval of the continuation of the Stuart line meant that finding a bride was proving difficult. An Irishman, Charles Wogan, was commissioned to search the courts of Europe for James' potential queen and after several disappointments eventually found the Polish Sobieski family willing to provide a suitable young woman. James Sobieski's father had been King John III of Poland but the throne was not hereditary and James had not been elected. This left him in a similar position to James Stuart as both men felt they had a right to the thrones of their respective countries but had little chance of seeing their ambitions fulfilled. Sobieski had a daughter named Clementina and the family accepted James Stuart's proposal of marriage. As the Pretender was in Spain involved with the rising of 1719, the wedding ceremony on 9 May took place by proxy. James was thirty-one years old, Clementina seventeen. Their first son Prince Charles Edward Louis John Casimir Silvester Severino Maria Stuart was born in the Palazzo Muti, in Rome, on 31 December 1720 (New Style). In Scotland the birth was recorded as 20 December (Old Style).

There was fresh hope for the Jacobites when George I died in 1727. James returned uninvited to France to judge the measure of support for his cause. He was to be sorely disappointed. The French were furious at the visit and considered it a threat to peace with

Palazzo Muti, Rome

Britain. James was unable to drum up much assistance and returned to Italy. Despite the absence of French aid, the efforts to restore the Stuart line to the British throne had not been abandoned. Numerous Jacobite sympathisers visited the Stuarts in Rome and James and his sons were reasonably well supplied with money. James' marriage was not thriving although another child, Henry, arrived in March 1725. Disillusioned with marriage Clementina became reclusive and devoted herself to religion. Just a few months after Prince Henry's birth Clementina took herself off to find refuge in a convent for a couple of years. In January 1735, at the age of thirty-three, she died, probably from tuberculosis brought on by constant fasting and malnutrition. The funeral was magnificent and Clementina is buried in St Peter's, where today a monument stands opposite the one dedicated to her husband and sons. She requested that her heart be interred in the Basilica of the Twelve Apostles where she worshipped every day. The church is in the Piazza Santi Apostoli, a few yards from the Palazzo Muti. About half way into the basilica and just to the right is a pillar bearing a Latin inscription. The translation reads, *'Here rests the outer part of the heart of Clementina, for heavenly love did not allow the heart itself to survive. To Maria Clementina, Queen of Great Britain etc., the convent of the Franciscans reverently placed this.'*

The Palazzo Muti (now called the Palazzo Ballestra) is at the top of the Via dei Santa Apostoli just off the Via del Corso. Inside the passageway leading to the internal courtyard is a plaque high on the wall.

ABITÓ QUESTO PALAZZO
ENRICO DUCA POI CARDINALE DI YORK
CHE FIGLIO SUPERSTITE DI GIACOMO III
D'INGHILTERRA
PRESE IL NOME D'ENRICO IX
IN LUI NELL' ANNO MDCCCVII
S'ESTINSE LA DINASTIA DE' STUARDI

In this building lived Henry, Duke later Cardinal of York, who, surviving son of James III of England, took the name of Henry IX. In him in the year 1807 the Stuart dynasty became extinct.

By 1740 events in Europe were moving in a direction favourable to the Stuarts. Charles VI of Austria died, leaving the throne to his daughter Maria Theresa. The event brought long-standing difficulties regarding the Austrian succession into focus and several claims to the new Empress's territory were made. Most of Europe was involved in the dispute and Britain and France soon took opposite sides. In 1743, despite no declaration of war, George II's troops beat the French at the Battle of Dettingen. King George's son, The Duke of Cumberland was wounded in the fighting.

Exchanges recommenced between the French government and various Jacobite interests and relations with James improved. In 1743 new plans were laid for an assault on Britain, the force to be led by twenty-three year old Prince Charles. Thirty-eight ships and 12,000 men were made ready in Dunkirk, while an additional 3,000 soldiers were to be sent to Scotland under Earl Marischal. The enterprise was abandoned when once again storms wrecked the chance of invasion and many transports were lost with all hands. The English demanded that Charles be forced from French territory. Louis XV was furious and although the War of Austrian Succession had already been rumbling along for four years France formally declared war on both Maria Theresa and Britain on 20 March 1744.

By April the French had about-turned and were making conciliatory gestures to the British. Although they allowed Charles to stay in the country the French were again losing interest in the Jacobite cause. Despite having no guaranteed French support, Charles, encouraged from Rome by his father, raised sufficient money to commission two ships, buy 1500 muskets, 1800 broadswords, some small pieces of artillery and quantities of ammunition. Most of these arms and about 700 men were loaded aboard one of the ships,

L'Elisabeth. By the middle of 1745 all was ready for the last and most determined attempt to restore the Stuart dynasty to the British throne.

TWO

THE STANDARD FLIES HIGH

'On the 23d they arrived at the island of Erisca, belonging to Clanranald, which lies betwixt the isles of Barra and South Uist.'
From an account by Aeneas MacDonald ~ The Lyon in Mourning

On 22 June 1745 Prince Charles Edward Stuart, the Young Pretender, boarded Le du Teillay anchored off St Nazaire in the mouth of the Loire. The owner of the ship was Antoine Walsh, a Franco-Irish merchant, adventurer and slave trader. The party sailed to Belle Isle and awaited the appearance of L'Elisabeth. On 4 July Old Style (15 July New Style) L'Elisabeth arrived and the next day the ships set sail, bound for Scotland.

The French ships were spotted and HMS Lyon brought L'Elisabeth to battle stations in the late afternoon of 9 July. The Lyon had fifty-eight guns and L'Elisabeth sixty-four. A ferocious exchange of fire ensued and the two ships fought until nightfall with heavy losses on both sides. At least forty-five men died on the Lyon and fifty-seven, possibly including the Captain, on L'Elisabeth. Many more were seriously injured. L'Elisabeth was so badly damaged she had to limp back to Brest taking most of the Prince's ability to fight with her. Le du Teillay continued on her way with Prince Charles and a tiny band of revolutionaries some of whom are known as 'The Seven Men of Moidart'. These seven are mentioned in every history of the period although a number of them had little bearing on the campaign. Perhaps they have retained their position in the histories because at this point in the rising there are few others to write about.

The seven included William, Duke of Atholl who was fifty-six years old and in poor health. He had supported the Jacobites in both the '15 and the '19 and was deprived of his estates at Blair Atholl, in favour of his younger brother James, for his trouble. The only other of Scottish birth was Aeneas MacDonald, a banker and brother of Donald MacDonald of Kinlochmoidart who was among the first to join the Prince. Sir Thomas Sheridan, the Prince's Irish tutor who was over seventy years of age was in the group as was Colonel Francis Strickland, the only Englishman. Strickland's father had supported James II (and VII) and followed him into exile in France where Francis was born. Parson George Kelly and Sir John MacDonald, a cavalry officer in the French forces, are included in the seven. MacDonald was appointed 'Instructor of Cavalry' in the Jacobite forces. There was never much cavalry to instruct and Sir John's post seems to have been somewhat nominal. He kept a journal throughout the campaign and so it is fortunate for historians that he was there. The main man turned out to be Irishman John William O'Sullivan, whose opinions the Prince came to greatly and, some would say, foolishly value. O'Sullivan was born in County Kerry in about 1700. His parents sent him to Paris and Rome with a view to him entering the priesthood. After spending some time as a tutor in a French military household he abandoned his intended life in the church and took up soldiering. Quite when O'Sullivan met Prince Charles is not clear but they became friends. The Irishman was to play a prominent part in the Forty-Five.

Le Du Teillay sailed close to Barra in the Outer Hebrides. Duncan Cameron who was a native of the island went ashore to find a pilot to guide them through the hazardous waters. The ship at last made safe harbour on the west coast of the island of Eriskay, between Barra and South Uist. Eriskay belonged to the clan chief MacDonald of Clanranald and was held for him by his half brother Alexander MacDonald of Boisdale. Late in the evening of 23 July, at a place still known as 'Coilleag a' Phrionnsa' or 'The Prince's Shore', Charles Edward Stuart first set foot on British soil.

Boisdale was shocked that the Prince had arrived with so little support and left him in no doubt as to his opinion, which was that he should return home. Prince Charles replied, '*I am come home, sir, and I will entertain no notion at all of returning to that place from whence I came; for I am persuaded that my faithful*

Highlanders will stand by me.' In addition Prince Charles expressed his confidence that Alexander MacDonald of Sleat and Norman MacLeod of MacLeod, the two influential chiefs from Skye, would rally to his Standard, as they had been fiercely Jacobite in the past. Boisdale was astonished and *'Begged leave to tell him that he had pitched upon the wrong persons; for from his own certain knowledge he could assure him that these gentlemen would not adhere to his interest; on the contrary they might chance to act an opposite part.'* He added *'That if Sir Alexander MacDonald and the Laird of MacLeod declared for him then it was his opinion then he might land on the continent* (mainland). *But if they should happen to refuse their assistance, then their example would prove of bad consequence, and would tend only to make others backward and to keep at home.'* This news came as a huge shock to Prince Charles and O'Sullivan comments, *'Every body was strock as with a thunder boult to hear yt sentence.'*

MacLeod and Sleat had decided that the preservation of peace was better than the risk of failure involved in supporting another Jacobite rising; especially one which had got off to such an inauspicious start. However, there was another reason why these two men failed to 'come out' for the Prince. In 1739 both MacLeod and Sleat were connected with a plan to ship a number of their tenants to North America to be sold as indentured servants if not quite slaves. These people were not criminals and the motivation for their 'export' seems to have been simply mercenary. The plan was discovered and it was only after MacLeod appealed to Duncan Forbes, Lord President of Scotland that the perpetrators escaped prosecution. Forbes was the senior law officer of the Crown in Scotland and was a patriotic Scot who disliked Jacobitism. He had made strenuous efforts to produce reform in the Highlands and bring some prosperity by the introduction of justice and industry. *'Honest, learned and kind, he was an excellent golfer, and the most hospitable of hosts.'* Forbes believed that Scotland's future lay in strengthening the Union and he travelled widely attempting to keep unsettled clans loyal. His efforts in keeping Sleat and MacLeod out of trouble bore rewards, for as soon as MacLeod heard of the Young Pretender's arrival in Scotland he informed the government. Despite the Lord President's intervention and the urgings of MacLeod, had the Prince arrived with a fighting force of men and arms then it is possible that the Skye MacDonalds would have joined the rising. Indeed, after the disaster of Culloden when Sir Alexander went to pay his respects to the victorious Duke of Cumberland he was heard to remark, '*Is it not very hard that I should be obliged to come and bow to that puppy and to kiss his fingers, whom not long ago I thought to have given a kick in the breech? Had I ever imagined that my country would have been so served I should have shewn them another thing of it, for had I raised my men MacLeod durst not have stayed home.*' The day after Le du Teillay arrived she sailed away from Eriskay and dropped anchor in Loch nan Uamh, a rocky inlet of sea between Morar and Arisaig. Prince Charles Edward Stuart had reached the British mainland. The rising was about to begin.

The Prince spent his first two weeks in Britain on board ship or at Borrodale, a house owned by Angus MacDonald. The time was used to gather support and the campaign was boosted enormously when the Chief of Clan Cameron, Donald Cameron of Lochiel, pledged the 800 fighting men under his command. Lochiel was by no means certain of the Prince's success but had a great sense of loyalty to the Jacobite cause. He also had much influence in the Highlands not least because each of his twelve sisters had married into other clans. Being determined to go forward in his mission no matter what the end might be, Charles knighted Antoine Walsh and sent Le du Teillay back to France.

Once Lochiel was committed, other local clan chiefs including MacDonald of Keppoch and Stewart of Ardshiel, the leader of the Stewarts of Appin, promised support. MacDonald of Clanranald was dubious but hedged his bets by sending his son, Young Clanranald, to lead his men to the Prince's Standard. Notable by his vacillation was Simon Fraser, Lord Lovat and Chief of Clan Fraser. Fraser sent a message to Prince Charles by way of Lochiel wishing the cause well but complaining of illness and age. At the same time he wrote to the commander of the garrison in Edinburgh warning of the uprising about to begin.

The Prince sailed around the Ardnish point and into Loch Moidart where John Murray of Broughton, King James' Secretary of State for Scottish Affairs, joined the campaign. The next week was spent at Kinlochmoidart House collecting supplies and planning future moves. The first actions of the campaign took place while Charles was at Kinlochmoidart. Captain Swetenham of Guise's regiment was captured and clansmen led by MacDonald of Tiendrish attacked a party of Royal Scots at Highbridge.

Charles, his close companions and fifty of Clanranald's men marched from Kinlochmoidart to Loch Shiel on 18 August and rowed up the loch to Glenaladale. The next morning the party continued to Glenfinnan where the clans had been instructed to gather. The Prince hoped to disembark to the cheers of a great crowd of supporters. He was to be disappointed. The shore was silent. At mid-day there was still no one there. At last 150 MacDonalds led by MacDonald of Morar arrived but it was not until about four o'clock that first the sound and then the especially welcome sight of Lochiel's Camerons put a smile on the Young Pretender's face. MacDonald of Keppoch arrived next and by late afternoon on 19 August more than 1200 loyal clansmen were assembled at the head of the loch. With the support of two men at his side the ailing Duke William of Atholl unfurled the Royal Standard to the sound of the pipes and roars of approval from the clansmen. A commission from King James appointing Charles as Prince Regent was read aloud and then the assembly heard a manifesto amounting to a declaration of war on King George II.

Landranger Map
40 Mallaig & Glenfinnan

Prince's Cairn	**NM720844**
Polloch Pier	**NM780694**
Borrodale	**NM693849**
Glenfinnan	**NM900808**
Kinlochmoidart	**NM707728**

I considered travelling to Eriskay to begin at the beginning but as Prince Charles did not stay long before continuing to the mainland I concluded that my visit could wait until later. I would take my first steps from Loch nan Uamh and so began my adventure by flying to Inverness. The bus to Fort William leaves every couple of hours or so and the trip was worth the fare simply for the views of Loch Ness.

When the Bonnie Prince landed in northern Scotland, he did us all a favour by choosing Loch nan Uamh as the place. Railway lines are rare in the western Highlands but luckily the Fort William to Mallaig line goes right past the spot where H.R.H. disembarked and the nearest station is Beasdale. Life is rarely perfect and there is probably a very good reason why the bus that I took from Inverness arrived in Fort William at 1205 and the train to Beasdale left at 1154. The next train was several hours away and so I walked out of town to the junction with the 'Road to the Isles' and stuck out a tentative thumb at the passing traffic. Without exception it roared past as though I did not exist.

Eventually a kindly old gentleman picked me up. Mr Cameron was in his eighties and spent much of our journey telling me about his exploits fighting his way through North Africa and Italy during the Second World War. This old soldier knew quite a bit about the '45 and was none too keen on the Campbells who fought in the government lines at Culloden. We travelled through Glenfinnan and then Mr Cameron took me out of his way and dropped me on the lochside near the cairn (picture p29) that commemorates the Prince. It is unlikely that Prince Charles stepped off Le du Teillay at exactly this spot but it is a good place to stand and contemplate on how he

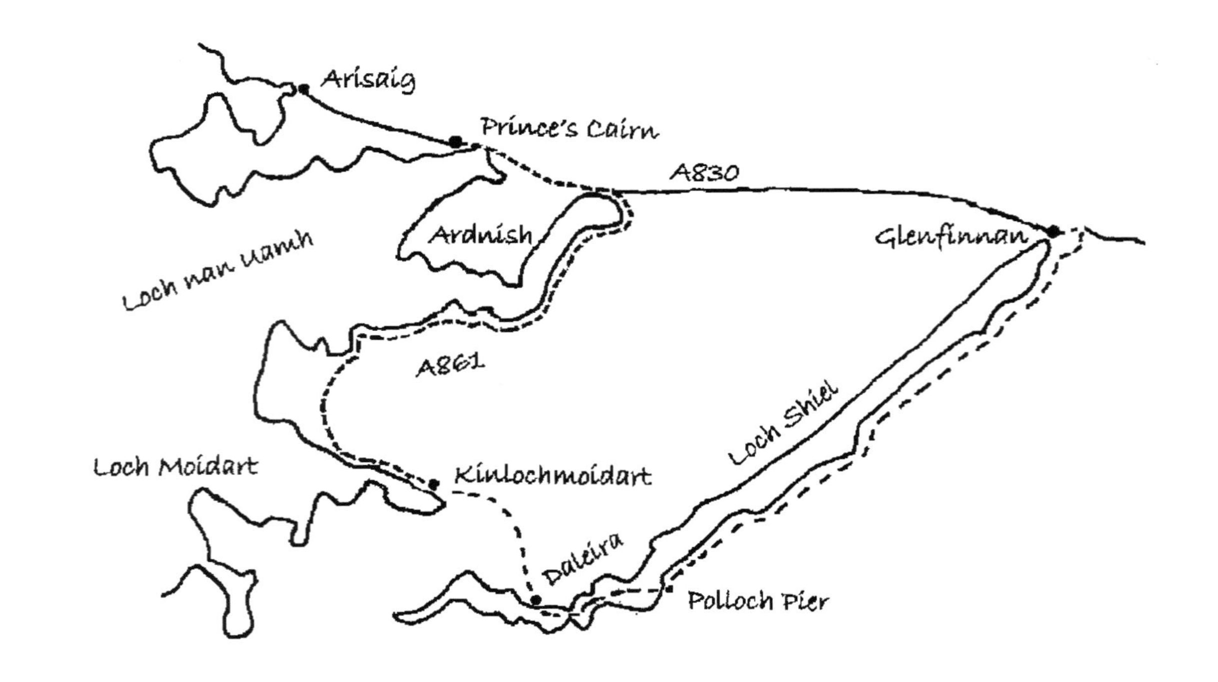

Prince's Cairn to Kinlochmoidart and Glenfinnan (34 Miles)

must have felt at the beginning of his campaign. In front of him was the huge task of restoring the monarchy to his family. The Prince believed it to be both his birthright and his destiny.

I spent a few minutes at the cairn and gazing at the spectacular view over the loch. The weather was fabulous, the sun was shining and the day warm. I was tremendously pleased with myself for having at last arrived at the start of the Prince's journey. My next task was to travel to Kinlochmoidart and so, for the first but certainly not last time, I had to deviate from Prince Charles' travel arrangements. The Prince sailed to Kinlochmoidart but I had no boat and so once again took to the road making heavy weather of the small pack I was carrying. A few minutes later a young couple with whom I had exchanged a few words of conversation back at the cairn, stopped their car and offered me a lift to the junction of the A861. There were few cars on the road but fortunately the less traffic there is, the more likely it is to stop for a hitch-hiker because two quick lifts later I was in Kinlochmoidart. Many Jacobite houses were razed to the ground after the Battle of Culloden and the one at Kinlochmoidart was no exception. The present day Kinlochmoidart House dates only from 1884. Seven beech trees and a commemorative cairn stand on the side of the loch in memory of the 'Seven Men of Moidart' and the beginning of the Forty-Five.

The daylight was fading, I needed somewhere to stay and Kinlochmoidart is not exactly a metropolis. I could see nowhere offering accommodation. Fortunately I had not yet left the sanctuary of the car and, seeing my spirits start to sag, the driver offered to take me to a nearby hotel he had noticed earlier in the day. Ten minutes later I was safely installed in the Clanranald Hotel, at Acharacle. The room was agreeable enough and there was a private bathroom with no bath but a shower. If I am offered a choice I'll take a bath rather than a shower any time. Showers have their uses but what I need after a hard day's walking, especially if the weather has not been too clever, is a long soak in a hot bath. I used the shower, put on some clean clothes and two pints of beer and a salmon steak dinner later I was ready for a little light television and a good night's sleep.

The next morning dawned fine and a young lady brought some excellent smoked haddock and poached eggs to my breakfast table. Not many guests were staying in the hotel but I fell into conversation over the tea and toast with a fellow who was selling space on the Internet. He was quite pleased with himself as he had successfully signed up the Clanranald and was about drive to another remote hotel and offer it the chance to be part of the global economy. More to the point of this journal he offered me a lift back to Kinlochmoidart. I jumped at it.

I began by walking along the road to Glenmoidart, following the path the Jacobites took to Dalelia on the shore of Loch Shiel. At Brunery I crossed the river and found the track leading uphill to Ty Coat. Fortunately the owner of this interestingly named wooden house was bumping towards me in his car and stopped to provide confirmation that this was the right route. 'In the steps of the Prince,' were his very words and you can't get clearer than that. Three miles later I arrived at Dalelia to discover that although there are trails along the northern side of the loch they peter out quickly. To reach Glenfinnan I had either to travel by boat as the Prince did, or somehow find my way to Polloch pier on the far side of the loch, from where there is a forest road to Glenfinnan. Polloch is only about three miles in a straight line from Dalelia but about twenty-five by road. I quickly determined that the thing to do was to take a boat. The only trouble was, I didn't have one.

I visited the big house in Dalelia to ask if anyone would be prepared to take me over the water. It seemed that someone working on the fish farm might, but quite when was impossible to say. There was nothing for it but to potter about and hope for a boat to tie up at the pier. Half an hour later one did and the offer of a twenty-pound note saw me scudding across the loch to Polloch. I wanted to travel the whole length of the Loch Shiel to Glenfinnan but my ship's captain had neither time nor inclination for that. My tiny craft cut its engine and the twenty pounds fare stretched far enough to have the pilot pull the boat into the shallows so that I could avoid getting my boots soaked. I said goodbye and leapt out onto the wide forest road to Glenfinnan.

Forty minutes walking took me past Gorstanvorran, an isolated house marked on the map for want of anything else to note. The sun was shining and I was entertained by the splendid views of the loch and its tiny islands. Eventually the welcome sight of the massive Glenfinnan railway viaduct came into view and a few moments later I caught my first glimpse of the Jacobite monument (picture p29) at the head of Loch Shiel. Four hours walking from Polloch brought me opposite the monument, but the bridge over the river was another foot-aching mile down the track. The last two miles along the main road were something of a downhearted struggle but eventually I trailed thankfully into the village.

Since my visit a boat service has started to offer trips between Acharacle and Glenfinnan and one day I must return and make the trip in a similar way to Prince Charles. The company offering the service uses a 52ft ex-admiralty launch and a one-way trip takes two and a half hours.

Why did Prince Charles choose this part of Britain for the commencement of his campaign? Why was there more support for the Jacobites in the Highlands of Scotland than anywhere else in Britain? The answers, as you might imagine, are not simple. The seeds of Highland Jacobite support were in both politics and religion. They were able to grow into full-scale rebellion against the British government by the nature of Highland society and the clan structure. Before the Act of Union in 1707, Scotland was an independent country with its own monarch and parliament. Many Scots saw unification with their larger, more prosperous southern neighbour as a betrayal of a long and proud tradition. This was particularly true in the feudally based Highlands with its autonomous clans that brooked no interference from outside their borders. For generations the clan chiefs had been beholden to no one and felt they owed little allegiance to kings and their parliaments. However, if homage had to be paid to any king, better he be a Stuart king of Scotland than a Hanoverian king of England.

Loyalty and honour based on supposed and actual blood relationships expressed through the sharing of the same surname formed the basis of clan society. At the apex was the chief who was an all-powerful if often patriarchal figure. Although clan land was theoretically held in common, in reality it belonged to the chief who leased it to tenants known as tacksmen. The chief dispensed the law and was the ultimate source of authority holding the right of life and death over his people. His power was balanced by a sense of responsibility for his people's welfare and most chiefs took this part of their duties seriously.

The ground was hard and difficult to farm. The meagre diet consisted mainly of oatmeal, milk, butter and cheese. Domestic animals provided a little meat and there was venison occasionally. Those near the coast supplemented their food with shellfish. Sadly farming methods were not sufficiently advanced to support the population adequately. There are tales of Highlanders becoming so desperate that they were reduced to bleeding their animals and mixing the blood with oatmeal to avoid starvation. The housing was poor. The low one-roomed huts were made of stones and sods of earth, thatched with heather. A smoky fire provided heat, light and the ability to cook but life was tough for everyone. Most Highlanders were roving herdsmen, tending black cattle, goats and a few sheep and the clan measured its wealth by the stock it owned. Cattle stealing raids were frequent and became such a matter of clan honour that the herdsmen became warriors. Every male old enough to carry a broadsword was enlisted in the clan regiment and the prestige of the chief depended on the number of fighting men he could put into the field. Those reluctant to take up arms were likely to have the roofs burned from their houses by the tacksmen and so 'persuaded' into military service.

Each clan was a unique, separate unit with loyalties to its members and those others to whom the chief might from time to time offer allegiance. Clans identified themselves by name, by pipe tunes and battle cries. A distinctive sprig of vegetation was often tied to a man's bonnet. Tartans did not so closely identify clans in the eighteenth century as modern day tourist offices would have you believe. Most clan members were too poor to be concerned with such niceties of style. The notions of family honour, hierarchical authority and the rights of dynastic succession were engraved deeply into Highland society. These ideas were not far removed from Stuart views on kingship and an attempt by an exiled king's son to recapture the throne he regarded as his by right, struck a resonant chord. The ability of clan chiefs to raise bodies of armed men had been attractive to Jacobites in 1715 and 1719 and was once again in 1745.

The clans were by no means united in support for the Prince. They were rarely united about anything. In 1745 approximately 32,000 Highlanders bore arms and yet the Young Pretender could never command more than 6,000 of them at any one time. Many chiefs did not 'come out' for the Stuarts at all and others did so reluctantly, from a sense of personal duty to the Prince. Clansmen were equally unsure of their obligations to this stranger who had come over the sea with neither troops nor arms. The chief could force men into military service by threats of house burning or worse but throughout the campaign desertion was common.

The failure of the Forty-Five and subsequent government determination after Culloden meant that the clan system as it had existed for centuries was doomed. Even without the rebellion it is certain that big changes in Highland society would have come about within a few decades. The Lowland areas of Scotland had already succumbed to economic and political influence from England and the Highlands could not long remain insulated from these pressures. Communications with the south had been greatly improved by the construction of military roads that took no account of clan boundaries.

The monument at Glenfinnan was erected in 1815 and is now in the care of the National Trust. A narrow internal staircase leads to the statue at the summit. Circling the top is a low safety barrier. I do not recommend the climb to the top if it is crowded. If you're not as young as you used to be or if you are not too keen on heights, stay at the bottom and pretend you don't want to go up anyway.

The exact spot where the Standard was raised is unclear and

the place where the monument stands was chosen for its beautiful and dramatic position at the head of Loch Shiel. The statue is not that of the Prince but is of a typical Highlander, representing the body of support that rallied to the Prince at Glenfinnan. Surrounding the monument is an enclosed garden and the plants are symbolic of the clans that met here. Attached to the garden wall are large plaques, which in English, Latin and Gaelic bear the words:

> *On the spot where Prince Charles Edward first raised his standard on the nineteenth day of August 1745, when he made the daring and romantic attempt to recover the throne lost by the imprudence of his ancestors, this column was erected by Alexander MacDonald Esquire of Glenaladale.*

Glenfinnan is marked on all the road maps and as it has a railway station you might be forgiven for thinking it is a sizeable place. It is not. However the village does have a Visitor Centre, a couple of hotels and a few houses offering bed and breakfast. I stayed at the appropriately named Prince's House Hotel and my room provided me with a with a telephone, a selection of books and tea and coffee making facilities. Breakfast was good. I went for the kippers and ate them in 'Flora's Restaurant'. They don't miss a trick in Glenfinnan you know!

Twenty minutes later I paid the bill and strolled out into another lovely day. As I walked down the hill towards the monument my thoughts were drawn not only to Flora MacDonald but also to other women involved in the Forty-Five. A few were committed Jacobites and rallied to the Prince's cause independently of male influence. These became the butt of Hanoverian propaganda and were frequently portrayed as being wild, undisciplined women of dubious moral standards. Among the first was Jenny Cameron of Glen Dessarry who is better known for her alleged sexual escapades with Prince Charles than for her efforts in raising clansmen for his army. According to the rumours she became the Prince's mistress at Glenfinnan and accompanied him throughout the campaign. There is not a shred of evidence to substantiate the tale but the mud stuck firmly and the rumours were difficult to dispel. Aneas MacDonald did his best in his account of the event. *'She was so far from accompanying the Prince's army that she went off with the rest of the spectators as soon as the army marched. Neither did she ever follow camp, nor was ever with the Prince, but in public when he had his Court at Edinburgh.'*

Other women supported their Jacobite husbands and these included Margaret, wife of John Murray of Broughton, and another Margaret, the twenty-year-old Lady Ogilvy both of whom accompanied the army for much of the campaign. Many writers consider that Anne, the wife of Lord Kilmarnock, persuaded her husband to follow the Prince's star although letters from the Duke to his wife indicate that it might have been him who was persuading her of the desirability of joining the Jacobites. No matter, unfortunately for the Duke the decision was a bad one. Kilmarnock ended his days on the scaffold. Anne Mackintosh came out for Charles despite the fact that her husband was fighting on the Hanoverian side. Many others including Lady Margaret MacDonald of Sleat, MacDonald of Boisdale's wife and the famous Flora herself were sympathetic to the cause or offered help out of a sense of duty or perhaps simple kindness to a person in need.

THREE

OVER THE CORRIEYAIRACK

'On Friday August 23d, the Prince lodged in Fassafern, three miles down Loch Eil, and about five miles from Fort William.'
Duncan Cameron, pilot who guided Le du Teillay to Eriskay.
The Lyon in Mourning

Charles remained at Glenfinnan until 22 August and by then had perhaps three thousand men under arms. The army marched to Kinlochiel from where the Prince wrote letters asking for men, money and weapons. The government had placed a reward of £30,000 on his head and the forces of King George II, under the command of General Sir John Cope, were marching north through Dalnacardoch towards Fort Augustus. However, when Cope heard reports of Highlander strength and that the Prince intended to attack his troops as they crossed the Corrieyairack pass, he changed his plans and withdrew to Inverness.

At Fassfern Prince Charles stayed the night at John Cameron's house. Despite being Lochiel's brother, Cameron refused to join the campaign as he was of the opinion that the whole expedition was foolish and probably doomed. The following day the Highlanders trudged over the hills to Moy on the north side of the River Lochy, staying well out of range of the guns at Fort William.

The Prince moved on to Highbridge and took General Wade's road north, along the south side of Loch Lochy, through Letterfinlay to Laggan where Donald MacDonell of Lochgarry added 400 men to the army. At Invergarry hundreds more joined the cause. Stewart of Ardshiel with 260 Appin men was there to greet Prince Charles. There were men from Knoydart and Morar, Arisaig and Moidart, under the command of Coll MacDonald of Barrisdale and Donald MacDonald of Scotus. The jubilant warriors marched on to

Aberchalder where more Glengarry men, a few Grants from Glenmoriston and some MacDonalds of Glencoe marched into camp. Believing that General Cope was preparing to cross the Corrieyairack pass from the south the Jacobites decided to seize it and block his advance. Once the pass had been occupied the Highlanders came upon redcoat deserters who informed them that their army had withdrawn. Having secured the way south without needing to fight and, perhaps in order to placate those who were anxious for some action, Prince Charles gave permission for a couple of raids.

The first was an attack on the government garrison at Ruthven, which was commanded by Sergeant Terrence Mulloy. A hundred men, jointly led by Archibald Cameron and John O'Sullivan, attacked the barracks. The venture failed and the Highlanders were driven off with one killed and several wounded. The second raid captured Ewan Macpherson of Cluny who was an officer in the government army. The event may have been arranged beforehand as Cluny does not seem to have been too upset by his capture. He was introduced to Prince Charles and quickly promised to raise his clan in support. Some discussion took place as to whether to pursue General Cope but as the Lowlands were now unprotected the decision was made to march south.

After crossing the Corrieyairack pass Prince Charles slept the night of 29 August in the heather at Dalwhinnie and then marched to Dalnacardoch Lodge, an inn on Wade's road. The following day, 31 August, the army received an enthusiastic welcome at Blair Atholl to where it had marched at the suggestion of Duke William who was anxious to oust his Hanoverian brother, James.

LANDRANGER MAPS

40 Mallaig & Glenfinnan
35 Kingussie
41 Ben Nevis, Fort William
42 Glen Garry
34 Fort Augustus & Glen Albyn
43 Braemar & Blair Atholl

Blair Atholl Castle

Fassfern (41)	**NN021788**
Invergarry (34)	**NH305011**
Achnanellan (41)	**NN091849**
Melgarve (34)	**NN464959**
Clunes (34)	**NN202886**
Laggan Bridge (35)	**NN615943**
Gairlochy (34)	**NN176841**
Blair Atholl (43)	**NN871653**

I began the nine-mile walk from Glenfinnan to Fassfern by retracing my steps past the exit from the Polloch forest road. It seemed a shorter distance now than it had at the end of a long day's walk the previous evening. There is no footpath along the shore of Loch Eil and so I continued along the road. It was an uncomfortable walk on a narrow grass verge with cars buzzing past too frequently for comfort. I was thinking I might hitch-hike when luck came to my rescue and a car stopped a few yards down the road. It was the owner of Ty Coat. He opened his car door and I leapt in with a word of thanks. A few minutes later I was back on my feet at the junction for Fassfern. The imposing house has been considerably altered over the years and is no longer in the hands of the Cameron family. As the Jacobite army progressed from Fassfern they needed to stay away from the garrison at Fort William and so *'on sight of a warship which lay opposite to the garrison, the Prince crossed a hill and went to Moy.'* I followed their tracks north, through the wild, spectacular scenery of Gleann Suileag to the bothy bearing the same name.

Shortly after leaving the bothy and despite being marked on the map the track that had been passable by motor vehicles disappeared. Fortunately the general direction through the wide valley was easy to see. I met no one and the only sounds were the gurgling of the burns and the strange grunting sounds of deer, high in the hills. The going was damp to very wet and the principal burn has dozens of tributaries. Most are no more than a few inches wide but about a foot deep and covered with vegetation. I could hear them all around

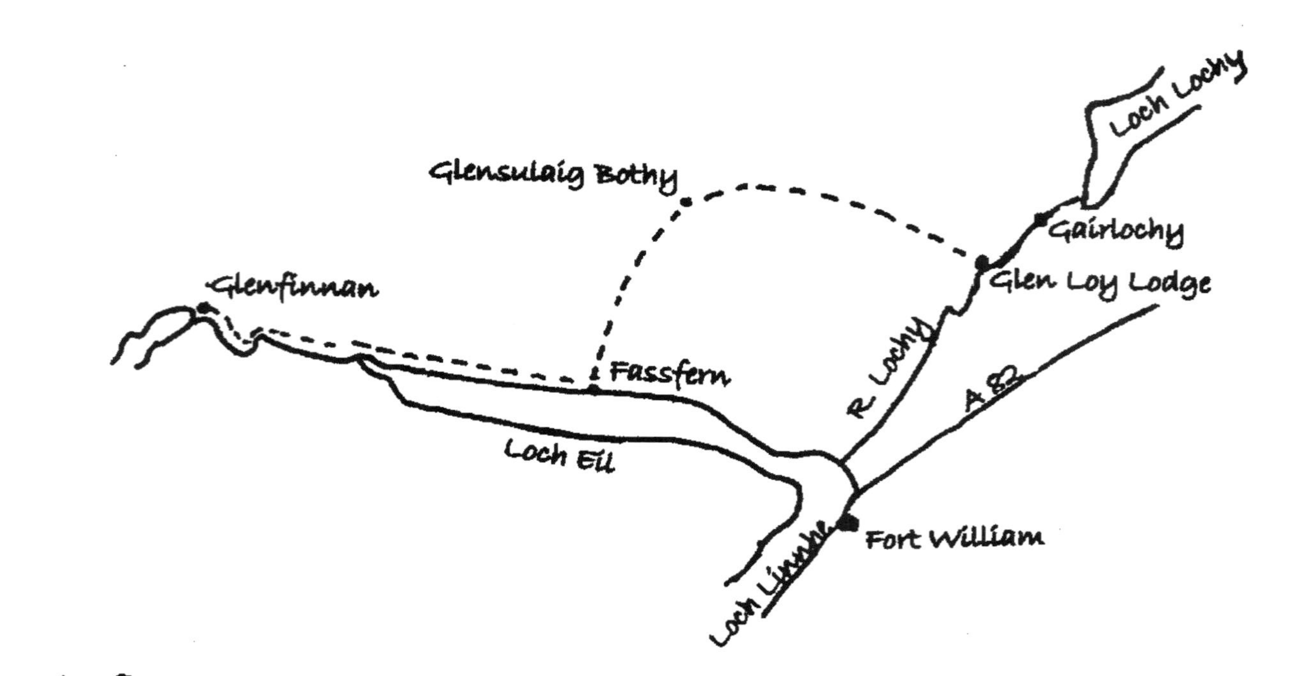
Loch Lochy
Glensulaig Bothy
Gairlochy
Glen Loy Lodge
Glenfinnan
Fassfern
R Lochy
A 82
Loch Eil
Fort William
Loch Linnhe
Glenfinnan to Gairlochy (22½ Miles)

but they were difficult to see and a constant source of danger. A twisted ankle was the last thing I needed. Eventually the footpath re-emerged as a white scar cut into the hillside and I came to Achnanellan where a road winds gently down Glen Loy to the B8004. I was ambling down the road thinking that there were miles to go before I slept, when a car drew up and offered me a lift. Could I resist climbing in? I could not. I can walk all day on footpaths but on roads I find it difficult to stop my mind calculating how quickly I could cover the ground in a car. Anyway, part of the pleasure of walking is not having to do it for a while. During the speedy ride to the road junction my feet were given a rest and the conversation lifted my spirits. We parted company and I walked to the farmhouse at Moy from where a footpath between the River Lochy and the Caledonian Canal runs to Gairlochy.

I only saw one bed and breakfast establishment in Gairlochy and that was closed for the winter. There may be others but I wouldn't bank on it. The village has a few houses, a telephone box and some lock gates across the Caledonian Canal. That's about it. The nearest place with plenty of accommodation is Spean Bridge, three and a half miles away, so that is where I went. The following morning I made the short journey to Highbridge where one of the first encounters of the rising took place. Constructed in 1736 Highbridge was *'a fine bridge of three arches flung over the torrent Spean, founded on rocks; two of the arches are 95ft high.'* In 1819 Thomas Telford built a new bridge over the river and so relegated Highbridge to obscurity and eventual collapse. However, the skirmish is not forgotten and a memorial cairn tells the story.

ACTION AT HIGH BRIDGE

Near this spot on August 16 1745, the first action of the "Forty-Five" took place. Donald MacDonell of Tirnadris, with eleven men and a piper from Keppoch's clan, by making use of the now demolished High Bridge Inn and surrounding trees to conceal the smallness of their number, succeeding in

Clan Cameron Museum, Achnacarry

preventing two companies of the 1st Royal Regiment of Foot (later the Royal Scots) from crossing the High Bridge over the River Spean. This force consisting of about eighty-five men had been sent from Fort Augustus to reinforce the garrison at Fort William.

I returned to Gairlochy but before continuing my journey I crossed the canal and walked up the hill towards the seat of the Camerons of Lochiel at Achnacarry. The Clan Cameron museum on the estate offers much to see relating to Cameron involvement with the Jacobite rebellion, including a waistcoat worn by Prince Charles and letters written by Charles and his brother Henry. Bonnie Prince Charlie's men wore white cockades in their headgear and the story goes that the first were made from roses at Fassfern. The 'Jacobite White' rose bushes growing by the front wall of the museum were planted from Fassfern cuttings.

Donald Cameron of Lochiel, 19th Chief of Clan Cameron, ran the estate at Achnacarry in 1745 in the place of his father who had been exiled to France after the '15. Born in 1695, 'The Gentle Lochiel', as he is often known was an ardent Jacobite but his first thoughts were that as Prince Charles had landed with no troops, few weapons and little money then success was unlikely. The Prince summoned Lochiel who was persuaded by the strength of Charles' character to offer his wholehearted support. It is likely that the assertion that should Lochiel decline to join he, *'may stay at home and learn from the newspapers the fate of his Prince'* had a bearing on his decision. Another telling argument may have been that as the French had trounced the Duke of Cumberland at the Battle of Fontenoy in May, the Great Glen garrisons at Fort William and elsewhere would be reduced to provide reinforcements for the British army.

Lochiel's brother, Archibald Cameron, finds a place in this excellent little museum. Dr Archie studied medicine at Edinburgh, was made Aide de Camp to Prince Charles and fell wounded at the Battle of Falkirk. After the rising was over Dr Archie escaped to

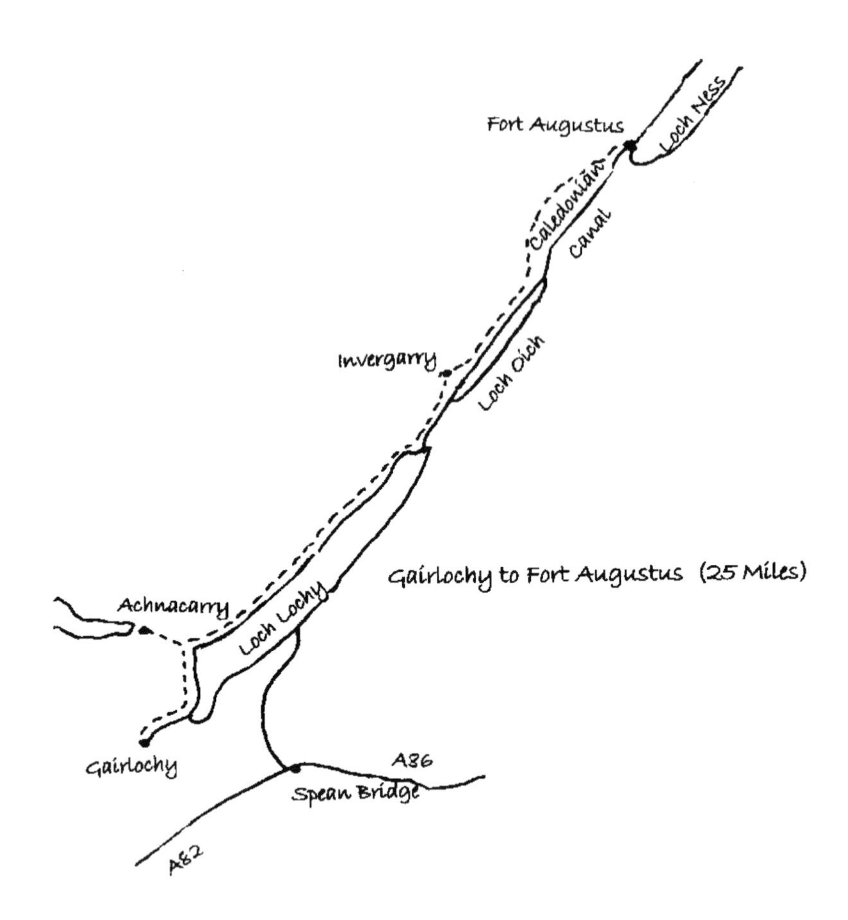

Gairlochy to Fort Augustus (25 Miles)

France with Lochiel and the Prince but later returned to Scotland in an attempt to rekindle Jacobite sympathies. He was arrested after the failure of a crazy scheme to assassinate the Royal family and executed in the summer of 1753. Dr Cameron's body was buried in the Savoy Chapel in The Strand, London where a plaque remembers the event. Another brother, Alexander, who was chaplain to Prince Charles fought throughout the campaign and was captured after Culloden. He was put on board the sloop HMS Furnace and kept there with other Jacobites before being transferred to a prison hulk in the Thames at Gravesend. He died in appalling conditions, while waiting to be transported to the West Indies. The Crown confiscated Cameron lands after Culloden and visited much hardship on the people by government edicts and brutal behaviour. However in 1784 the 'General Act of Indemnity' was passed and Donald Cameron, the 22nd Clan Chief, was able to buy back the estate for £3,433 9/1d. The estate remains in Cameron ownership to this day and the present house was built in 1802.

I left the splendours of Achnacarry and walked to Clunes and the Great Glen Cycle Route that runs along the northern side of Loch Lochy. Wade's road through Letterfinlay on the other side of the loch, is now the busy A82 and not so good for walkers. The cycle route provides magnificent views as it runs through the South Laggan forest to Invergarry and Aberchalder. Two and a half hours walking from Clunes brought me to the other end of Loch Lochy. I crossed the Kilfinnan burn and continued for about half a mile until the road divided into two. The cycle route takes the left hand fork uphill to meet the A82 at the southern end of Loch Oich. The right hand fork passes through Kilfinnan Holiday Park to Laggan Locks and the start of another section of the canal. I went to look at the locks and afterwards was tempted to turn left along the canal towpath. The path began well enough but soon became overgrown and difficult, with sections that had fallen away completely. It became impassable after perhaps half a mile, forcing me to scramble uphill to the A82 about a mile south of Laggan swing bridge. The busy main road provides only a narrow grass verge upon which to walk. I do not recommend it.

After visiting the locks I should have retraced my steps and followed the cycle route to Loch Oich. The track climbs steeply and offers spectacular views of the loch before it drops onto the minor road just east of the quaintly named Easter Mandally. Invergarry is on the far side of the River Garry and one way to approach the village is to follow the cycle route over the road bridge. I chose an alternative path and turned left across the cattle grid. My feet were aching and I had lost a little concentration so it took me some time to spot the iron gate in a wooden fence twenty yards along the road. The footpath heads to a footbridge over the river and into Invergarry.

I was tired and as I couldn't find the cycle track from Invergarry to the Bridge of Oich I wrongly presumed it did not exist. The day was ending and rain falling so I began to seek out somewhere to stay. There are not many bed and breakfast enterprises in Invergarry and most of the ones I saw were closed. There is the Invergarry Hotel but that was a bit pricey for me and in any event they had no rooms free. Having found no accommodation I decided to travel the eight miles to Fort Augustus by bus. I waited in the rain and hoped one would arrive soon as it was becoming chilly. Hedging my bets against the non-arrival of public transport I did a bit of hitch-hiking as well. A dispiriting dark and wet hour later no bus had come and no cars had stopped. It was seven in the evening, I was tired, wet and had nowhere to sleep. There was a filling station about a hundred yards from the bus stop. I walked into it and waited for the next car to stop for petrol and waved a modest five-pound note in front of the young driver's eyes. Fifteen minutes later we said goodbye in Fort Augustus. There's a lot to be said for capitalism don't you think?

Fort Augustus is an engaging little town and still possesses the stone fort built by General Wade in 1729. The passing years have greatly changed the building and it was until recently an abbey and has also been a boys' school. The monks have left now and there is some doubt as to what will happen to the buildings. The town was once called Kilcumin but was re-named after H.R.H. William

Augustus, the Duke of Cumberland, second son of George II. There are a few shops and plenty of places to stay. The Caledonian Canal with its attractive flight of locks comes straight through the middle of town.

The following day I travelled back to Invergarry and this time, being perfectly fit and refreshed, easily found the continuation of the cycle route next to the Invergarry Hotel. The path climbs steeply but the views of Glen Garry from the summit are fabulous and make the effort required worthwhile. The track exits onto the road at the Bridge of Oich near Aberchalder. The Jacobites took the military road from Aberchalder towards Fort Augustus and the start of the road (picture p30) over the Corrieyairack pass. I could have followed them along the A82 but the route along the canal is much more pleasing. The towpath is on a causeway between the canal and the River Oich and took me past the huge gates of Cullochy and Kytra locks and into Fort Augustus.

The Caledonian Canal is a sizeable piece of civil engineering even by today's standards and quite remarkable for the time when it was constructed. It is 61 miles long and links the Atlantic and the North Sea across the breadth of Scotland. Only a 23-mile stretch is artificial, the rest being composed of Lochs Lochy, Oich, and Ness. Thomas Telford built the canal (presumably with a bit of help) between 1803 and 1823.

To find the military road from Fort Augustus over the Corrieyairack I tramped uphill towards Fort William. About a mile out of town the route to the pass tracks uphill to the left of the Kilchuiman Burial Ground and past a house called Lower Culachy. At the junction with the driveway to Culachy House I turned right and a few minutes later stood at the boulder-strewn entrance to Wade's military road to Laggan.

General George Wade was an Englishman who was assigned the task of improving road communications in the Highlands after the Jacobite rebellion of 1715 so that troops could be moved about quickly. Between 1725 and 1740 about 250 miles of new or greatly improved road were completed. Sixty miles were in the Great Glen linking Fort William with Inverness and a further two roads linked Inverness with Perth and Stirling. Yet another was built in 1731 and led from Fort Augustus to Dalwhinnie climbing to 2,500 ft over the Corrieyairack pass. Ironically the only time this road played a decisive role in a military campaign was to help Prince Charles' army in its initial military success. The road provided work for more than 500 soldiers, cost £70 per mile to build and was originally fifteen feet wide. Modern road builders have often followed the line of Wade's roads but the one from Fort Augustus to Laggan Bridge has not been further improved and is now a track sometimes no more than five feet wide.

The notice board outside the Tourist Information Office in Fort Augustus describes the walk over the Corrieyairack as 'not for the fainthearted' and with that sentiment I readily agree. Once begun there are only the possibilities of going on or returning to the start. The road is just about suitable for four-wheel drive vehicles, but at the time of writing these have been banned while thought is given to their effect on this wilderness landscape. It is clear to me that except for essential maintenance or agriculture, vehicles should be permanently excluded. The road crosses no others and there are no houses. Walkers and mountain bikers might be able to help someone in difficulty but this is a long and isolated walk. It is not to be undertaken except by those who are properly equipped and physically fit. From Fort Augustus to the start of the road is one and a half miles. Then follow eleven miles over the pass to Melgarve, the first place to which ordinary cars can drive. From Melgarve to Laggan Bridge is a similar distance along a narrow, very quiet road. Do not expect to be able to catch a bus!

Wade's road climbs past Culachy House and continues uphill in a series of zigzags. It loops around so frequently that attempting short cuts through the heather across the hairpin bends is irresistibly tempting but non-productive as I quickly discovered. Walking through deep heather is exhausting and I soon gave up and kept to the road. As I puffed my way up I was thankful that I did not have to carry a

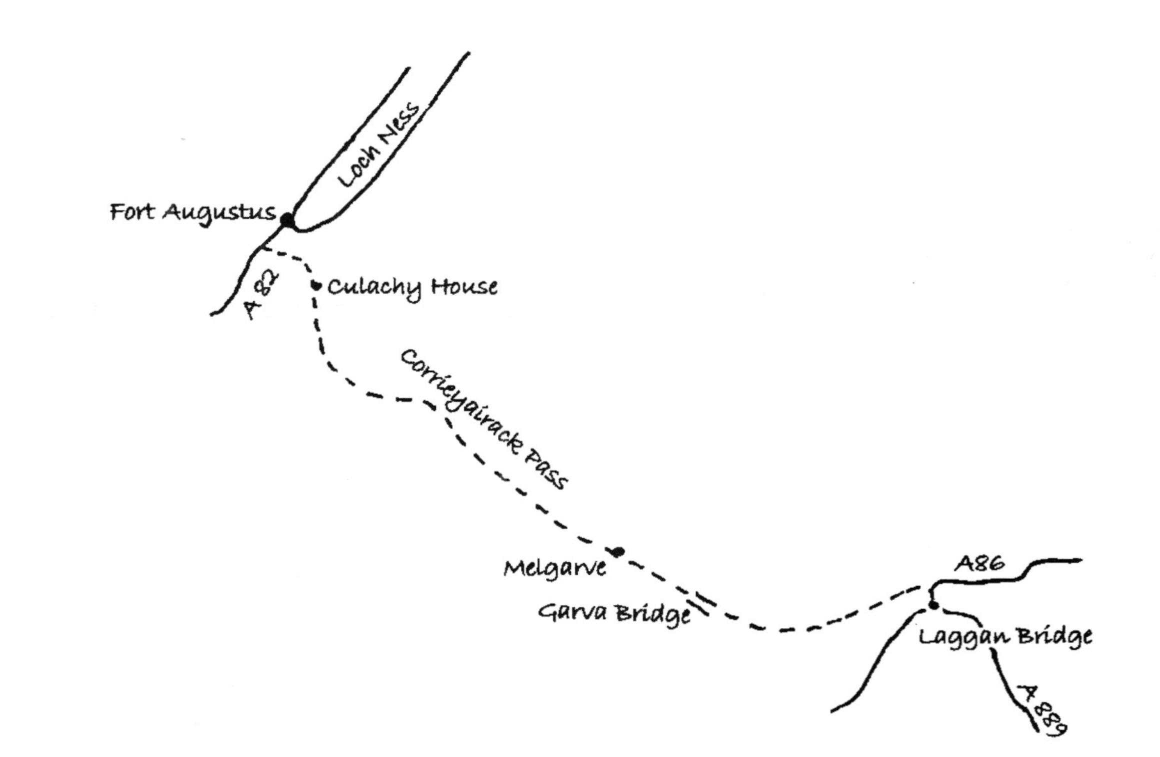

Fort Augustus to Laggan Bridge (23½ Miles)

heavy load of weapons and supplies over the pass as the clansmen did.

If the weather is good the path provides excellent views of Fort Augustus at the end of Loch Ness amid the wonderful surrounding countryside. There is little evidence of man's influence on the landscape other than the road itself and the electricity pylons that somewhat mar the view. General Wade constructed several bridges as part of the road but most of them are now in a state of poor repair, although renovation work has been carried out in places.

It took me about three and a half hours to reach the top of the pass and begin winding down to the huge hole in the ground, which is the Corrie Yairack. Another two hours' steady plodding brought me to Melgarve, about half way to Laggan Bridge. Although the walking is easier from here I began to think that I should have organised a car to meet me. There was no traffic for a long time when suddenly out of the distance came the delightful sound of the internal combustion engine. The driver stopped and offered me a lift to Laggan. I took it gratefully and we were off down the road to St. George's Bridge near Garvamore. (picture p30) The bridge, built in 1732, is a fine example of General Wade's work and is still good enough to be used by motor vehicles. In Laggan Bridge I was lucky enough to find the lovely Monadhliath Hotel on the southern side of the river and it fortunately had a room available for me. The hotel was once a manse for the ruined church that stands in its grounds.

The railway line and the A9 already take the only suitable way through the Drumochter Pass and so I opted to travel by car from Laggan Bridge to Dalnacardoch Lodge. The A9 continues to thunder south from Dalnacardoch but at least there is now the possibility of sensible walking. The construction of the main road left behind the earlier road alongside. This minor thoroughfare still serves several farms and houses and in the absence of a proper footpath provides an enjoyable route along the bank of the rushing River Garry. At Calvine I crossed the Garry and picked up a footpath to Old Struan. This is an agreeable stroll along the riverbank to Struan kirk and then over Errochty Water.

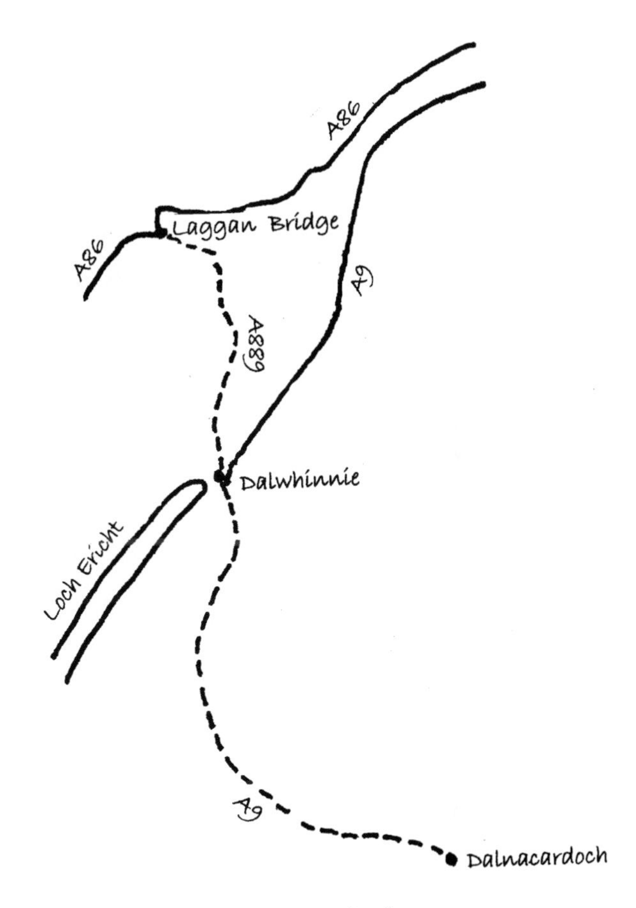

Laggan Bridge to Dalnacardoch (20½ Miles)

Dalnacardoch to Blair Atholl (13 Miles)

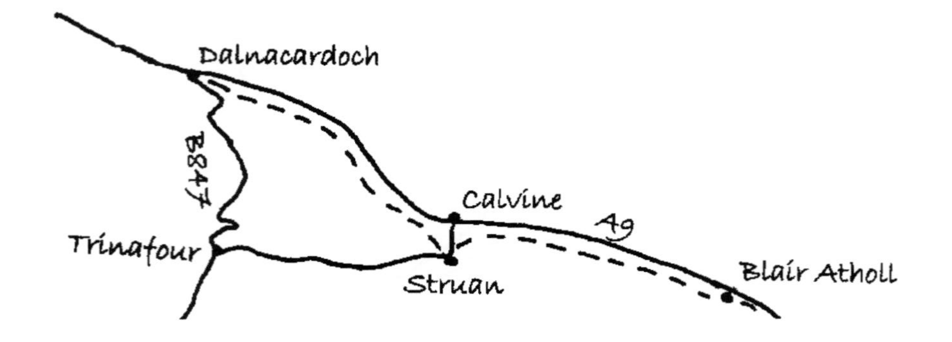

A left turn took me along a road running parallel to the river. Across the valley to my left was the roar of the traffic on the A9, in marked contrast with my tranquil little byway. The road passes under the A9 and emerges as a footpath on the other side. The path forces its way along a corridor between the river and the main road for another mile and eventually I crossed a suspension bridge to enter the Blair Atholl estate through the impressive gates of a lodge house with fairytale turrets. Blair Castle contains huge displays of furniture, arms, china and other treasures. A small section in the Treasure Room is given over to Jacobite relics, including Prince Charles Edward's pipe and a pair of eyeglasses and case belonging to Lord George Murray, one of the Prince's greatest commanders. Lord George's White Cockade is on display as is a piece of plaid reputedly worn by the Prince and a lock of HRH's hair.

FOUR

TRIUMPHANT TO EDINBURGH

'This morning I have gained a most signal victory with little or no loss.'
Letter from Prince Charles to his father after the Battle of Prestonpans ~ The Lyon in Mourning

The Prince rested at Blair Castle until 3 September and then marched through Killiecrankie and Dunkeld towards Perth. While Prince Charles was at Blair, Lochiel went ahead with 400 men and took possession of Perth in anticipation of the Prince's arrival the following day. Wearing tartan trimmed with gold lace and riding at the head of his army, Prince Charles made a triumphal entrance to the city on the evening of 4 September. He set up his headquarters in an inn that is now the Salutation Hotel, and possibly also stayed at Lord Stormont's house in the High Street. Despite the impressive display, the Jacobite army was short of supplies and money as all that had been brought from France had now gone. Charles spent his week in Perth raising both 'taxes' and troops. Lord Strathallan and Oliphant of Gask joined the rising as did Lord Ogilvy, the twenty-year old son of the Earl of Airlie. James Drummond, Duke of Perth was an important recruit but the most important of all was Lord George Murray.

George Murray was fifty years old and a younger brother of William, Duke of Atholl. He had acquired some military experience and was exiled after taking part in the Jacobite risings of 1715 and 1719. When pardoned in 1725 he returned to live on his estates at Tullibardine. In 1739, perhaps despairing of success for the Jacobite cause and in order to take part in political life he took oaths of allegiance to King George and for a time seemed to be sharing the views of his Hanoverian brother James. The Lord President of Scotland even went so far as to appoint Lord George as a Sheriff Deputy, responsible for supplying government troops with their requirements in the Highlands. However, Murray maintained his Jacobite sympathies and on 3 September wrote to his brother declaring his support for the Stuarts. *'My life, my fortune, my expectations, the happiness of my wife and children are all at stake (and the chances are against me), and yet a principle of (what seems to me) honour, and my duty to King and Country, outweighs everything.'* This decision to actively support the Prince must have been very hard especially as his pregnant wife Amelia disapproved.

Charles recognised Murray's value immediately and granted him the rank of Lieutenant-General and Deputy Commander of the Jacobite forces. However, because of his previous involvement with the government, the relationship between Lord George and the Prince was never an easy one. Murray's arrogant manner and quick temper were not well liked by others in the Prince's inner circle. Some resented the sudden rise to power of this newcomer and placed doubts in the Prince's mind as to Lord George's loyalty. Colonel John William O'Sullivan bitterly resented Murray's influence in matters he considered to be within his own jurisdiction. Both he and Sir John MacDonald refer to Lord George in derogatory terms. O'Sullivan remarks that, *'His carracter was not of the best, & yt his own friends and relations were a feard of it, & yt some of them spook openly, especially a Lady, who told the Prince yt he cou'd not be trusted to, & yt he wou'd soon or leat ruine the Kings case.'*

MacDonald is harsher still, and wrote, *'The woman told me she had come on purpose to warn H.R.H that Lord George was one of his greatest enemies. I asked her what proof she had of this and she told me that she had known him for many years for a scoundrel.'* A further complication in the leadership struggle was that Charles also awarded the rank of Lieutenant-General to the thirty-two year old, enthusiastic but inexperienced Duke of Perth.

During Charles' stay in Perth his troop numbers rose to 2,400.

Balhaldie House, Dunblane

The Jacobites received news that General Cope and his army were marching to Aberdeen, from where they intended to sail to ports near Edinburgh and help defend the city. Charles immediately decided to march in the hope of reaching Edinburgh before Cope and 11 September saw the army moving south on the Stirling road. It seems an ambitious itinerary but Donald Cameron reports in 'The Lyon in Mourning' that on the day Prince Charles left Perth he visited Scone Palace in the manner of a tourist. On the same day Charles had breakfast with Laurence Oliphant at Gask House and dined with Lord George Murray at Tullibardine before heading off for Dunblane where he probably stayed at Balhaldie House.

Prince Charles and his army continued the march towards Edinburgh on 12 September. They encountered no opposition. The next day, after crossing the River Forth at the Fords of Frew, the Prince dropped in at Leckie House for refreshments and meanwhile much of his army made camp at Touch House, five miles to the east. While Charles was at Leckie he dashed off a letter to the Provost of Glasgow demanding £15,000 and all the weapons the city could lay its hands on. When the Provost discovered that Prince Charles was marching away from his city towards Stirling he declined to comply. The Jacobites did not attempt to take Stirling Castle and it did no more than fire a few cannon balls at the approaching army. The army halted briefly on the field of the Battle of Bannockburn and then took Falkirk without difficulty. In Falkirk Charles stayed with Lord Kilmarnock at Callendar House. James Livingston had forfeited the house to the government after the Jacobite defeat in 1715 and the York Buildings Company snapped it up in 1720. The company could not find a suitable tenant and so in the end leased it to Livingston's daughter, Anne, who married the Earl of Kilmarnock in 1724. The Earl was in serious financial difficulties and so, possibly feeling he had little to lose and perhaps much to gain, offered Prince Charles his support. Kilmarnock brought his personal servants into the army but had difficulty in persuading others to enlist. Robert Chambers notes, *'His lordship assembled them in the town-hall, and tried them first with entreaties and then with threats; but not one man would consent to join his standard.'*

Charles' army arrived at Corstorphine, three miles from Edinburgh, on 16 September and made camp a little to the south at Slateford, where the Prince used Gray's Mill as his headquarters. It was here that David, Lord Elcho, the son of Lord Wemyss, a faithful Jacobite, became a welcome addition to the cause. Elcho was born on 21 August 1721 and so was almost the same age as the Prince. The two had met in Rome some years earlier and found that they enjoyed each other's company. Elcho was appointed aide-de-camp and raised a company of cavalry, soon to become the Prince's lifeguards. Further evidence of the Prince's mistrust of those he had not known before his arrival in Scotland emerged from a conversation between Elcho and Charles on the day they renewed their friendship. Elcho reports that Charles Edward offered an opinion that perhaps Lord George Murray had joined the campaign in order to sabotage it and that he (Elcho) must be on his guard in his dealings with the man. Lord Elcho came to value Lord George's military skill and attributes the Prince's suspicions to the influence of Secretary Murray of Broughton who possibly saw Lord George as a rival for the Prince's attention. In a further conversation Prince Charles confided that he was rather short of money and Elcho came immediately to the rescue by providing fifteen hundred guineas from his own pocket.

The story of the Jacobite capture of Edinburgh is one of incompetence on the part of those responsible for its defence. The town council had intended to strengthen the city walls and to raise additional men, but little had yet been done. The castle was impregnable, but its cannon were obsolete. Indeed nobody was sure whether the guns could be fired at all, or what the results might be if they were. The Governor of the castle was eighty-five years old, and the garrison quite inadequate for the protection of the city. In short, nothing was done to prevent the progress of the Jacobite army and hope was rested upon the anticipated imminent arrival of Cope's men from Aberdeen. Such troops as were available to defend Edinburgh were camped at Coltbridge, just west of the town centre. They chose to fall back to Leith and join up with Cope's army when it arrived. However when they heard that shots had been fired at their rearguard in Corstorphine and that the Jacobites were advancing they panicked and fled in disarray in what has become known as the 'Canter of Coltbrigg'.

The Prince sent a letter to the Provost of Edinburgh demanding that the city surrender to him. Its terms are quite clear.

> *Being now in a condition to make our way into the capital of his Majesty's ancient kingdom of Scotland, we hereby summon you to receive us, as you are in duty bound to do so, and in order to it we hereby require upon receipt of this to summon the Town Council and take proper measures in it for securing the peace and quiet of the city, which we are very desirous to protect. But if you suffer any of the Usurper's troops to enter the town, or any of the cannon, arms or ammunition now in it, whether belonging to the publick or to private persons, to be carried off, we shall take it as a breach of your duty and a heinous offence against the king and us, and shall resent it accordingly. We promise to preserve all the rights and liberties of the city, and the particular property of every one of his Majesty's subjects. But if any opposition be made to us we cannot answer for the consequences, being firmly resolved at any rate to enter the city, and in that case, if any of the inhabitants are found in arms against us, they must not be expected to be treated as prisoners of war.*
>
> *(Signed) Charles Prince Regent*
>
> *From Our Camp, 16th September 1745*

The town council began to prevaricate, hoping for news of the arrival of Cope's army. This provoked another letter setting a deadline of two o'clock in the morning for a *'positive answer'* in the absence of which *'he will think himself obliged to take measure conform.'*

At about three o' clock in the morning of 17 September Prince

Charles began to lose patience and sent Lochiel and a force of 1,000 men to occupy the town. To begin with the Highlanders were unsuccessful in their attempts to have the city gates opened but a little good luck came their way when the deputation sent by the council to negotiate with the Jacobites returned. Netherbow Port was opened to admit them and the Highlanders rushed through to take possession of the city. Although Charles marched unopposed into Edinburgh, the castle was still in government hands and remained so throughout the period of occupation. The Prince took up residence in the Palace of Holyroodhouse and later that day at the Mercat Cross in the High Street the City Herald proclaimed his father King of Scotland, England, France and Ireland. Having his father declared King of France might be considered an unusual step considering Charles expected help from the French, but it was a traditional proclamation for newly crowned kings.

Meanwhile, Sir John Cope's men were being disembarked twenty miles away at Dunbar. When Charles heard of this he demanded that Edinburgh provide him with arms and this brought in 1,200 muskets, a supply of ammunition and some clothing. On 19 September the Prince moved camp to Duddingston where a Council of War resolved to attack government forces as soon as possible.

Cope marched towards Edinburgh and camped at Haddington, fifteen miles from the Jacobites. The following day the Prince crossed the Esk at Musselburgh and took up a position on high ground at Birsley Brae between Preston and Tranent. In response Cope placed his army to the north of the Jacobites a little to the east of Preston. There was a deep ditch and a large area of marshland between the two forces and O'Sullivan was not happy with the Jacobite position. *'This was not a proper Scituation for highlanders for they must have nothing before them that can hinder them to run upon the enemy.'* Lord George was equally worried. An incident occurred when Prince Charles ordered O'Sullivan to use the Athollmen to guard the Musselburgh road, so preventing any attempt by Cope to march towards Edinburgh. Neither man had thought to inform Lord George who furiously *'threw his gun on the Ground in a great passion and Swore God he'd never draw his sword for the cause if the Bregade was not brought back.'* Lord George, also without any consultation, concluded that the sensible course was to move the army east, to the other side of Tranent, and then around the boggy ground in an attempt to find a sound position from which to attack. Sir John MacDonald notes that O'Sullivan was *'in great distress because Lord George would do nothing that he advised.'* Since Bannockburn the MacDonalds had fought proudly on the right flank in every battle. While in Perth the Prince had decided that the clans should draw lots for position in the front line. At Prestonpans (called Gladsmuir at the time) the Camerons drew the right hand side, infuriating the MacDonalds. Lochiel diffused the anger by generously allowing the MacDonalds their traditional place. These actions and discussions were perhaps intended to resolve problems but are indicative of serious disagreement between the commanders and perhaps show a lack of overall control.

As the army rested for the night a local man, Robert Anderson, came forward with the information that he knew of a way through the swamp, so enabling the Jacobites to attack with the advantage of surprise. Anderson was brought to Lord George who adopted the idea immediately. In the early hours of 21 September the Highlanders moved quietly over the marsh. The MacDonalds were at the front led by Clanranald's men. Next came Glengarry and Keppoch together with the MacDonalds of Glencoe. The Duke of Perth followed and then the MacGregors with the Appin Stewarts and Lochiel's Camerons in the rear. The second line was made up of a number of clans including Menzies, Athollmen, Robertsons and Maclaclans. The cavalry remained at the back as a silent approach was essential. The men were not quite all safely through the morass when their enemy at last noticed them and an alarm gun was fired. Despite failing to take their enemy completely unawares the Jacobite army *'advanced with such rapidity that General Cope had hardly time to form his troops in order of battle, before the Highlanders rushed on them sword in hand.'*

An armed Highlander would expect to be equipped with a

claymore, a dirk and a targe (or 'target'). The claymore was originally a huge double-handed sword but this weapon had largely been superseded by the lighter basket-hilted version by 1745. The dirk was a knife about eighteen inches long and the targe a round wooden shield covered in animal skin and embossed with metal studs. Some targes were embellished with a metal spike protruding from the centre. Clan chiefs and the 'gentlemen' of the clan carried a pair of pistols and all clansmen hoped to have a musket which, after being fired once, would probably be thrown to the ground during the headlong charge that characterised Highlander attacks. Some men carried the fearsome Lochaber axe. This was a hatchet-shaped blade fixed to a long pole at the end of which was a hook designed to pull a man to the ground should the blade not have completed its work.

Facing the Jacobites were Murray's, Guise's, Lascelles' and Lee's regiments. Squadrons of both Hamilton's and Gardiner's dragoons were deployed and in total General Cope had some 2,400 men under his command, a similar number to that mustered by Prince Charles. The Hanoverian forces possessed six 1½ pound guns and a few mortars manned by gunners borrowed from the Navy. Highland battle plans, if such they can be called, did not accord with the usual military thinking of the time and the fearsome charge at dawn succeeded more by causing panic in the enemy lines than by any military superiority.

> *They advanced with the utmost rapidity towards the enemy, gave fire when within a musket-length of the object, and then throwing down their pieces, drew their swords, and holding a dirk in their left hand along with the target, darted with fury on the enemy through the smoke and fire. When within reach of the enemy's bayonets, bending their left knee, they contrived to receive the thrust of that weapon on their targets; then raising their arm, and with it the enemy's point, they rushed in upon the soldier, now defenceless, killed him at one blow.*

One tactic was to strike at the noses of government horses causing them to rear and wheel in terror and pain, throwing the enemy front line into confusion. Lacking sufficient muskets the MacGregors had found scythes and tied them to long poles and with these crude but efficient weapons *'cut the legs of the horses in two, and their riders through the middle of their bodies.'*

Unfortunately for General Cope, his gunners deserted before the action began and, in the face of the Highland charge, so had their replacements. The guns had to be manned by a Marine Lieutenant-Colonel and the elderly Master-Gunner of Edinburgh Castle. They managed to fire the weapons and this gave the Jacobites a bit of a shock but produced few casualties. The Highland charge was unstoppable, causing Cope's badly disciplined men to turn and flee, despite desperate attempts to rally them. Perhaps the mood of the battle can best be illustrated by Cope's statement at the government inquiry that his men were seized by *'a sudden Pannick'* and by Prince Charles' comment in a letter to his father where he noted that the redcoats *'eskaped like rabets.'*

King George's army was soundly beaten although it is difficult to be sure of casualty figures. The Chevalier de Johnstone's figure of 1300 Hanoverian dead is certainly a huge exaggeration. Murray of Broughton reported no more than 300 government soldiers killed, with between 400 and 500 wounded. Jacobite casualties were at most thirty killed and eighty injured. Amongst the Hanoverian casualties was Colonel James Gardiner. He was a religious man who had predicted his death shortly before the 'Canter of Coltbrigg'. He fell not a mile from his house and lies buried in Tranent churchyard. The battle lasted for no more than fifteen minutes, after which Cope left his infantry to their fate and escaped south to Berwick with two regiments of dragoons.

The Prince stayed the night at Pinkie House in Musselburgh and the day after the battle returned in triumph to Edinburgh and Holyroodhouse, accompanied by the sounds of pipes and drums. The victory gave the Jacobite army an immense psychological boost and provided them with much booty, including large quantities of arms,

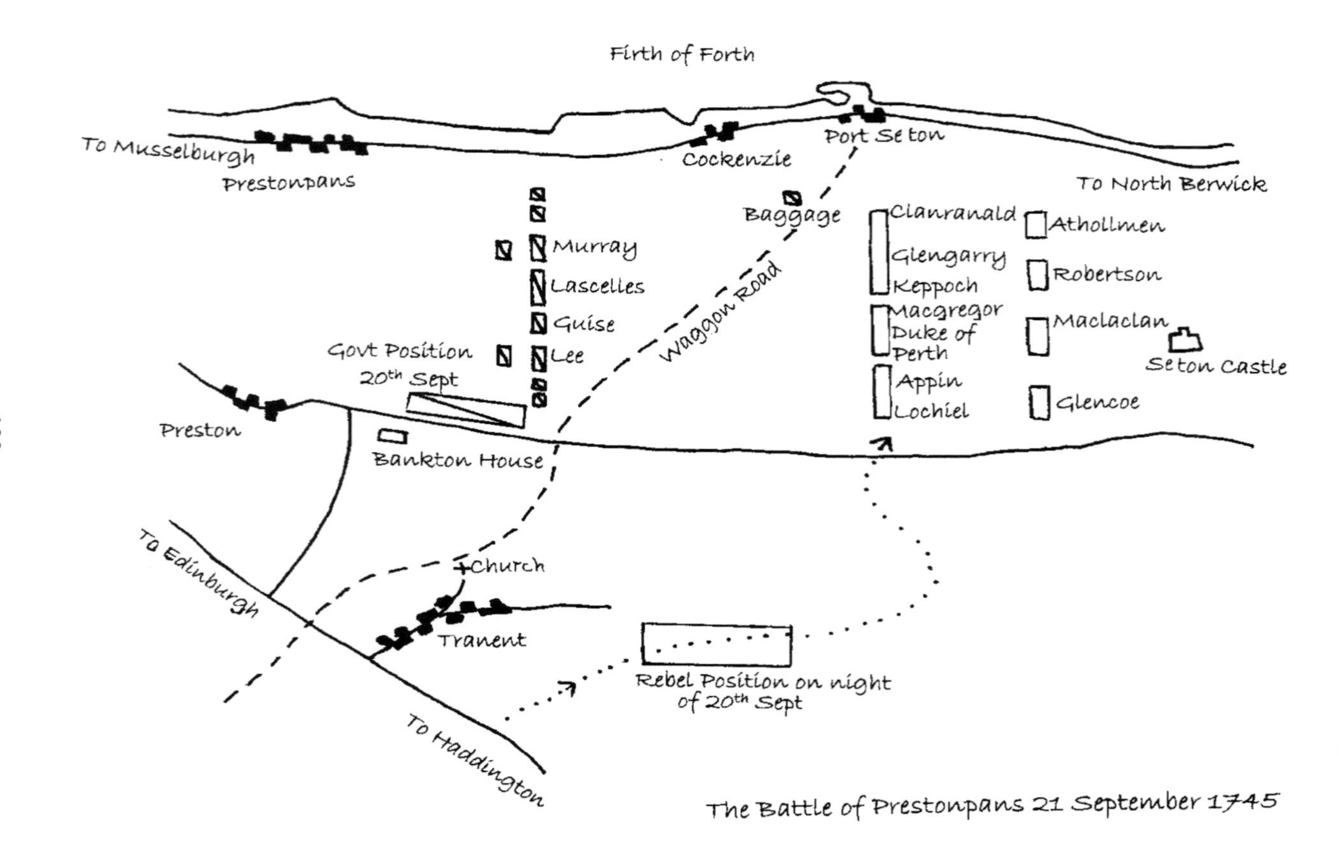
Firth of Forth
To Musselburgh
Prestonpans
Cockenzie
Port Seton
To North Berwick
Baggage
Clanranald
Glengarry
Keppoch
Macgregor
Duke of Perth
Appin
Lochiel
Athollmen
Robertson
Maclaclan
Glencoe
Seton Castle
Murray
Lascelles
Guise
Lee
Waggon Road
Govt Position 20th Sept
Preston
Bankton House
Church
Tranent
To Edinburgh
To Haddington
Rebel Position on night of 20th Sept
The Battle of Prestonpans 21 September 1745

ammunition and clothing from the battlefield. As the Jacobite army was short of just about everything these spoils of war were extremely useful. One simple soul found himself a watch but after it had wound down, sold it the following day remarking that he was glad to be rid of it, *'for it had died last night.'*

Jacobite morale was high. The castles at Edinburgh and Stirling and a few garrisons in the north were still in government hands but the victory gave Prince Charles effective command of Scotland. The Jacobites attempted to cut off supplies to Edinburgh Castle and this prompted the elderly commanders, Generals Guest and Preston, to fire cannon into the city. The blockade began on 29 September but the cannonade caused several casualties and so much civilian unrest that on 5 October the siege was lifted.

The Young Pretender was at Holyrood for several weeks and during that time he was undisputed 'king' of Scotland although he behaved quietly with no great shows of ostentation. His morale was boosted by the arrival from France of the Marquis d'Eguilles who was granted the title of French Ambassador. The Prince dressed elegantly at a number of balls in his honour but according to O'Sullivan he could not bring himself to dance saying, *'I like danceing, & am very glad to the Lady's and yu divert yr selfs, but I have now another Air to dance, until that be finished I'l dance no other.'*

John Home who joined the Hanoverian army in Edinburgh, describes the Prince in his 'History of the Rebellion':

> *He was in the prime of youth, tall and handsome, of a fair complexion; he had a light coloured periwig with his own hair combed over the front: he wore the Highland dress, that is a tartan short coat without the plaid, a blue bonnet on his head, and on his breast the star of St. Andrew. Charles stood some time in the park to shew himself to the people; and then, though he was very near the palace, mounted his horse, either to render himself more conspicuous, or because he rode well, and looked graceful on horseback. The Jacobites were charmed with his appearance: they compared*

him to Robert the Bruce, whom he resembled (they said) in his figure as in his fortune. The Whigs looked upon him with other eyes. They acknowledged that he was a goodly person; but they observed, that even in that triumphant hour, when he was about to enter the palace of his fathers, the air of his countenance was languid and melancholy: that he looked like a gentleman of fashion, but not like a hero or a conqueror.

Throughout the campaign Prince Charles was dilatory in his communications with English and Welsh Jacobites despite his hope of support from them. However, the day following Prestonpans a messenger was despatched to, *'my friends and particularly those in the north and north-west'* with the news that, *'it is my full intention, in a few days, to move towards them; and that they will be inexcusable before God and man, if they do not do all in their power to assist and support me.'* On 10 October Charles released a statement declaring his father's intention to *'reinstate all his subjects in the full enjoyment of their religion, laws and liberties'* and railing self-righteously against the injustices suffered by his family over the preceding decades. *'Is not my royal father represented as a blood thirsty tyrant, breathing out nothing but destruction to all who will not immediately embrace an odious religion? ~ I with my own money, hired a small vessel, ill supplied with money, arms or friends. ~ That our family has suffered exile during these fifty-seven years, everybody knows. Has the nation, during that period of time, been the more happy and flourishing for it?'*

A number of Jacobite soldiers deserted after Prestonpans and it is likely that the Prince's strength was down to about 1,500. Emissaries were dispatched on recruiting missions to both Highland and Lowland areas. Arthur Elphingstone, soon to become Lord Balmerino, joined the Prince in Edinburgh, as did Gordon of Glenbucket and Lord Pitsligo who each brought a few hundred men. Mackinnon of Mackinnon from Skye added about 200; Lord Ogilvy turned up with 500 from Angus and John Roy Stewart, who had joined the Prince at Blair Atholl, took command of the 400 strong Edinburgh regiment. Macpherson of Cluny was marching to the Jacobite banner and by the end of October the army mustered some 5,500 men of which 500 were mounted.

Alexander MacLeod took news of the recent victory to MacDonald of Sleat and MacLeod of MacLeod in Skye. The Prince assured them *'that we cannot impute their not joining us hitherto to any failure of loyalty or zeal for His Majesty's cause'* and informed them *'of the complete victory which, by the assistance of God, we have gained over the forces of the usurper.'* The chiefs were to be acquainted, *'that we have most undoubted assurances of assistance from France and Spain.'* To begin with the message seemed to produce the desired result. Sleat immediately called a meeting of local leaders to discuss how they should react. *'Sir Alexander said that this was certainly a most remarkable and surprizing victory the Prince had obtained; that he doubted not now of the Prince's succeeding in the attempt.'* Turning to the Laird of Raasay he said, *'Raaza, tis true you cannot raise many men; but the men you have are good. You can easily raise an hundred, and I resolve to raise nine hundred, which will make out a thousand good stout fellows betwixt us.'*

The very next morning Sir Alexander received letters from Lord President Duncan Forbes and MacLeod of MacLeod. The precise content of the letters is not certain but they had a remarkable effect on the reader. *'Immediately he left his former chearfulness and frank way, and was quite upon the grave and thoughtful. He spoke not another word of the matter. To the importunities of the President and MacLeod had Sir Alexander in an instant yielded himself up entirely, and dropt the declared resolution of his own mind.'*

News of Prestonpans was relayed to Lord Lovat who was pleased with the victory but frightened of total commitment to the cause. In an attempt to be on the winning side no matter how the venture turned out he encouraged Fraser of Gorthleck to muster 500 of the clan and called home his eighteen-year old son from St Andrews to lead the march to the Prince's Standard. Simultaneously Fraser wrote to his neighbour, Duncan Forbes, declaring his loyalty to King George and adding, *'I do solemnly declare to your lordship that nothing ever vexed my soul so much as the resolution of my son to go and join the Prince.'*

Defeat at Prestonpans shocked London and Parliament was recalled. Troops returned from Flanders and the Dutch government sent 6,000 men to bolster the British army. Three groups were formed. The first, consisting of approximately 14,000 men under the command of General Wade marched to Newcastle where they arrived on 29 October. Sir John Ligonier marched the second towards Lancashire and the third was deployed along the south-east coast in case of French invasion.

A new verse of the National Anthem was written to engender patriotism.

God grant that Marshal Wade
May by thy mighty aid
Victory bring.
May he sedition hush
And like a torrent rush
Rebellious Scots to crush
God save the King.

LANDRANGER MAPS

43 Braemar & Blair Atholl
57 Stirling & the Trossachs
52 Pitlochry to Crieff
65 Falkirk & Linlithgow
58 Perth to Alloa
66 Edinburgh

Milton of Dalcapon (52)	**NN979549**
Sheriffmuir (57)	**NN829028**
Bungalow Countlich (52)	**NO005498**
Old Leckie (57)	**NS689947**
Moneydie (52)	**NO066296**
Callendar House (65)	**NS898793**
Kinkell Bridge (58)	**NN932166**
Ratho (65)	**NT139709**
Buttergask (58)	**NN877086**
Prestonpans (66)	**NT404744**
Fords of Frew (57)	**NS668960**

I left Blair Atholl Castle grounds by the main gate and walked down to the Atholl Arms Hotel in the centre of town. A nearby footpath leads down Ford Road to a bridge over the river and then a left turn took me to a minuscule road running alongside the A9 to the junction with the Killiecrankie road. The Killiecrankie Visitor Centre provides details of the battle fought on 27 July 1689 when a Jacobite force led by 'Bonnie Dundee' routed government forces. The Killiecrankie Walk took me along the River Garry and then the shore of Loch Faskally into the centre of Pitlochry. The walk passes the Soldier's Leap, where Donald MacBean, a government trooper, is supposed to have made a leap of eighteen feet across the river to escape his pursuers. When Queen Victoria visited she declared the leap 'impossible' and I agree with her.

I couldn't find suitable footpaths for the fifteen-mile walk from Pitlochry to Dunkeld and so I began by walking down the main street past the Blair Atholl distillery to the junction for Croftinloan. I climbed the hill to Balchandy and Milton of Dalcapon and gazed back at the fantastic view of the river valley and Pitlochry. The weather was fine and the road quiet. Only one car passed me in the first hour of walking. There is a T-junction a couple of miles after Dalcapon and I took the road through Tulliemet and Kilmorich. A few yards before the Bungalow Countlich a left turn took me most of the way to the Dunkeld Highland Lodges and Resort Hotel along a woodland road.

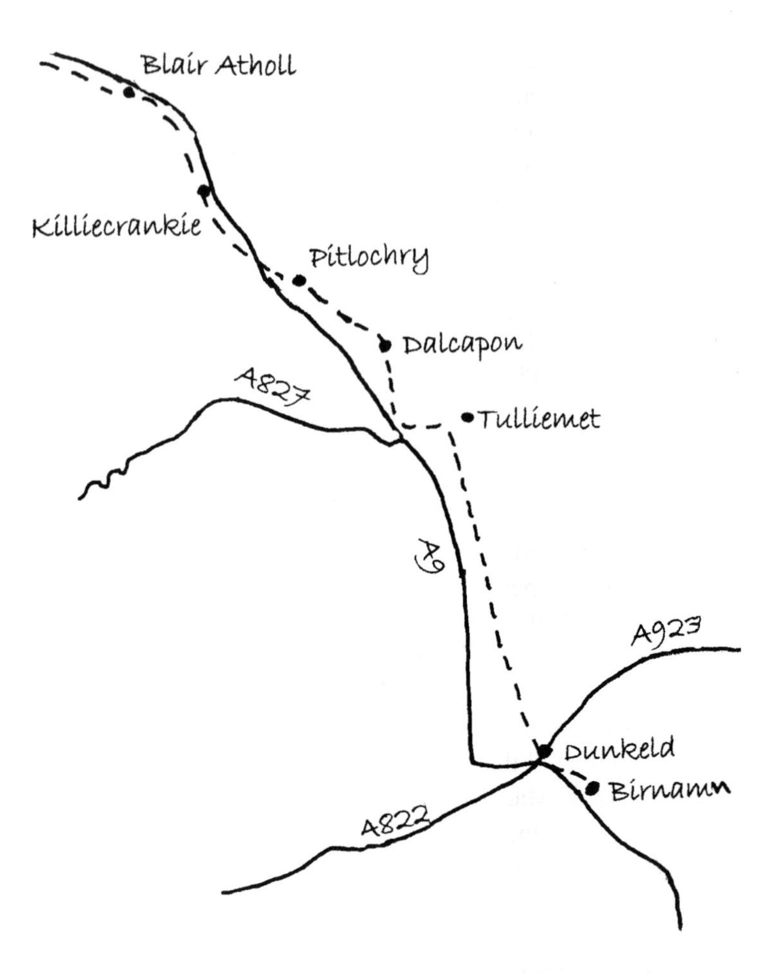

Blair Atholl to Birnam (20 Miles)

Dunkeld House, where Prince Charles stayed, was demolished in 1830 and the hotel now stands in the grounds. The path through the gardens leads to the river and town centre. The partly ruined cathedral in Dunkeld contains an exhibition mentioning the Battle of Killiecrankie and Bonnie Prince Charlie's visit to Dunkeld.

In the cathedral square I noticed the Ell House. An ell is a measure, initially taken from the length of a weaver's arm and later standardised in Scotland at 37 inches. There is a standard ell fastened to the side of the house, against which others could be measured. The length gave rise to the expression, *'Give him an inch and he'll take an ell.'* Ells being now redundant the much longer mile has become the distance likely to be taken. A reflection of our more selfish times I wonder? I walked out of the square to Atholl Street, crossed the River Tay to the Birnam side and found a place to stay.

The following day I strolled along the riverbank Birnam Walk. I wanted to see the Birnam Oak. The tree is several hundred years old and its limbs are supported by half a dozen strong crutches. It is reputed to be the last remaining tree from the Birnam Wood mentioned in Shakespeare's 'Macbeth'. The play has it (Act IV, Scene I) that Macbeth need not fear for his position or life until, *'Great Birnam Wood to high Dunsinane hill shall come against him.'* Macbeth, not surprisingly, thought this unlikely to happen. However soldiers under the command of Malcolm, son of King Duncan, camouflaged themselves with branches cut from Birnam Wood and defeated Macbeth's army in battle at Dunsinane.

In due course the walk turns back upon itself and finds the A9. The traffic hammered past and I was pleased when I had scurried across the highway to the quieter B867. Just after Bee Cottage I turned left, towards Kingswood and the curiously named Byres of Murthly. From Kingswood House I climbed past Kingswood Cottages along a green road leading to Bankfoot. A short stretch of the B867 brought me to Hunter's Lodge Hotel and the turn to Moneydie and Almondbank. Again I could find no footpath but was spared some of the long walk by extending my thumb into the path of an oncoming van. The driver dropped me in Kinvaid and I walked on to

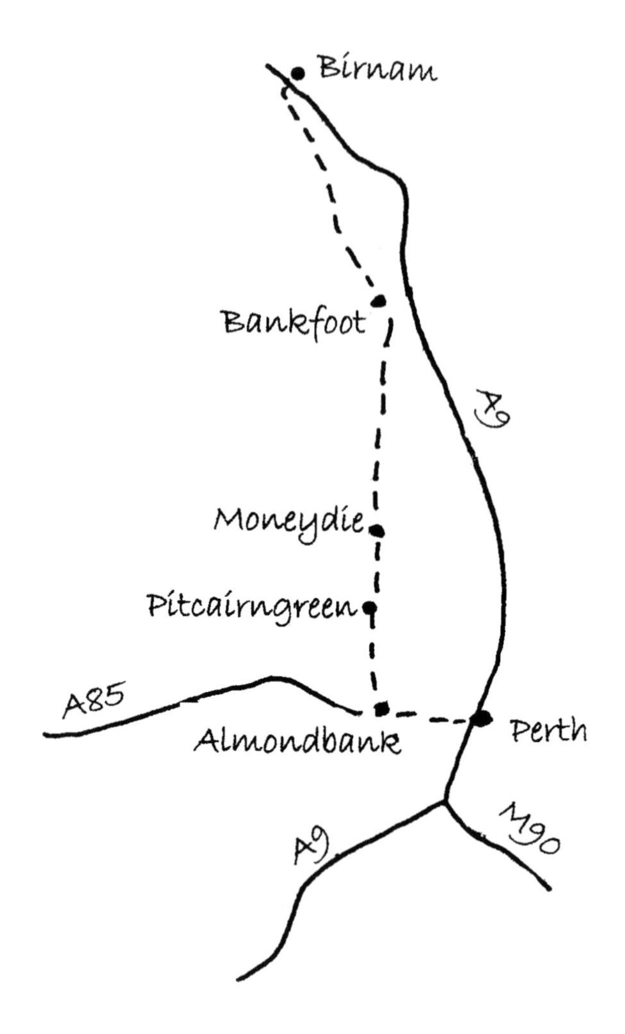

Birnam to Perth (15 Miles)

Pitcairngreen. Almondbank is not as pretty a place as Pitcairngreen but it has the advantage of a bus service to Perth. In the absence of any reasonable walking route to the city, I caught one.

I made for South Street to have a look at the Salutation Hotel which claims to be the oldest established hotel in Scotland. The room Prince Charles is thought to have slept in is now called the Stuart Room, and the management was kind enough to let me see it. It is used as a conference room at present and has nothing remarkable about it with the exception of a fireplace with the date 1699 carved on its stone surround. Lord Stormont's House, where Prince Charles also possibly stayed, and the King's Arms, in which councils of war were held, have long since been demolished.

I wanted to avoid the A9 completely on my way to Auchterarder but there is a dearth of suitable footpaths. There is plenty public transport that could have whisked me all the way, but that would have been cheating. I left Perth by York Place and the Glasgow Road, heading towards Cherrybank Gardens, where I compromised and took a bus along the A9 to Crossgates and the junction to Kinkell Bridge. This is a quiet old Roman road and is fine for walking. At Kinkell Bridge I crossed the River Earn to join the B8062 and then turned off to visit Tullibardine's ancient chapel, founded in 1446. From Tullibardine I chose the road through Backburn and Castleton to Auchterarder.

I boarded another bus in Auchterarder for the few miles through Blackford to Buttergask where I jumped off and took to my feet again. The footpath, through Topfauld Farm, joins the remote and narrow Sheriffmuir road at East Biggs Farm. I was hopeful that a passing car might take pity on me a give me a ride through this wild landscape of heather moor. No such luck I'm afraid. I persevered with the gentle slog to the top where I came within sight of the Sheriffmuir Inn. The inn is all alone on the moor and it looked not just the perfect place to rest and enjoy a pint of its best draught beer, but also the only place for miles around. I strode towards it with a spring in my step, only to be crushed with disappointment when I pushed at the door and found it locked.

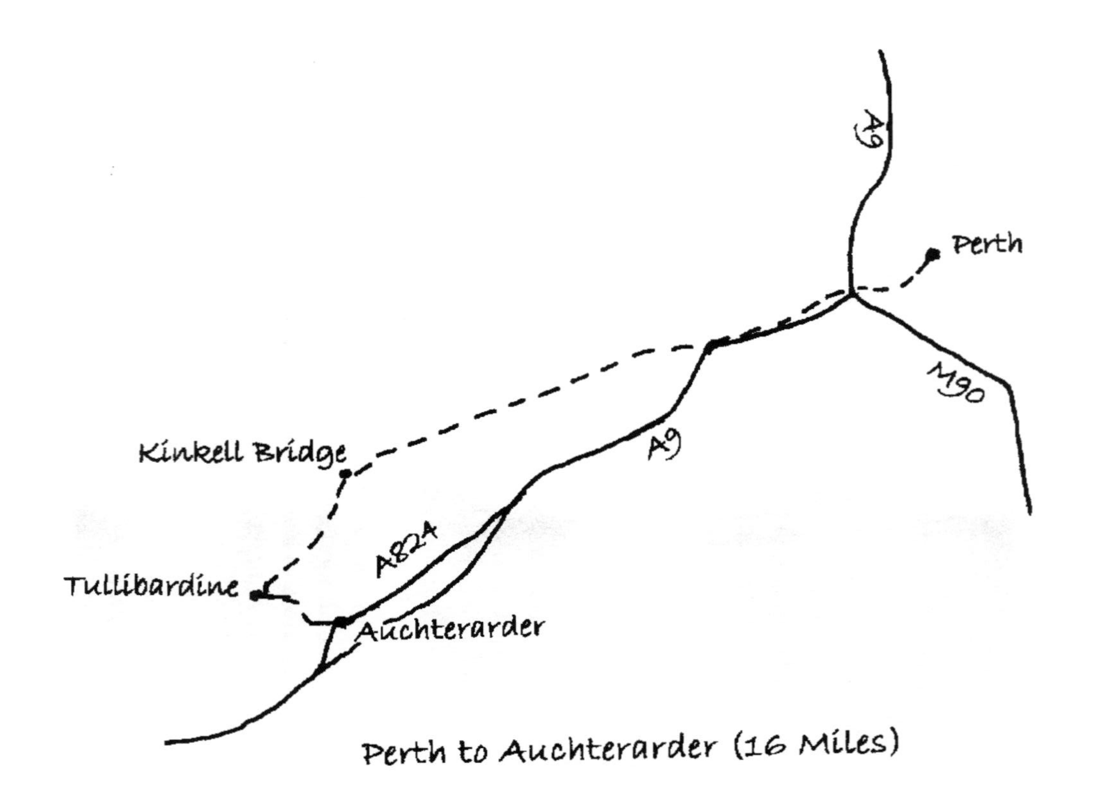

Perth to Auchterarder (16 Miles)

Salutation Hotel, Perth

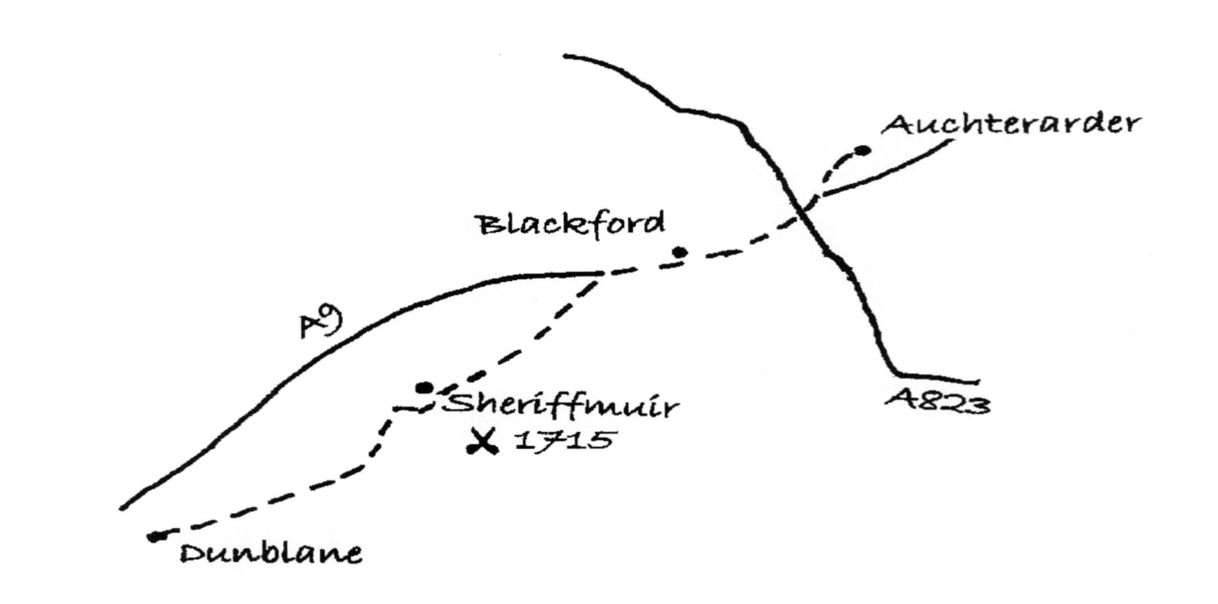

Auchterarder to Dunblane (13½ Miles)

Just past the inn the road splits into two, one branch going to Bridge of Allan and the other to Dunblane. Luckily I was not the only one who was put out by the fact that the pub was closed. I had not gone far along the Dunblane road when two people, who had driven up to the inn for lunch and were now disappointedly returning home, generously picked me up. I was grateful but if they had come along five minutes later I would have been able to take a closer look at the monument commemorating the Battle of Sheriffmuir, fought here on 13 November 1715.

Balhaldie House where Prince Charles probably spent the night 11 September is next to the public library on Dunblane High Street close to the junction with Smithy Loan. The rooms used by the Pretender still exist and are in everyday use. A plaque on the gable end wall informs us that this is '*The Townhouse of Alexander Drummond or MacGregor of Balhaldie, a notable Jacobite supporter. Prince Charles Edward Stuart stayed here on night of 11th September 1745.*'

From the railway station in Dunblane I walked down Old Doune Road past Dunblane High School. A footbridge provided a safe route over the busy A9 and then the footpath led me past Greenyards and Glenhead cottages and eventually joined the main road into Doune. Half a mile south of the River Teith I picked up an under-used footpath leading south-west to the A873 at the junction with the B8031 Coldoch Road. From here it was road all the way past Craighead and South Mid Frew to the Fords of Frew used by the Jacobite army. I crossed the modern road bridge and straight away found an ancient bridge that carries a footpath over Boquhan Burn south to the A811 and the Boqhuan Estate. Leckie House or Old Leckie as it is now called is midway between Kippen and Gargunnock and although in 1745 it was on the highway to Stirling, today that road is no more than a farm track. At the time of the Prince Charles' visit the house was owned by George Moir who was not privileged to greet his guest in person, having been arrested the previous evening by a troop of government dragoons.

Touch House is five miles to the east of Leckie and while it is

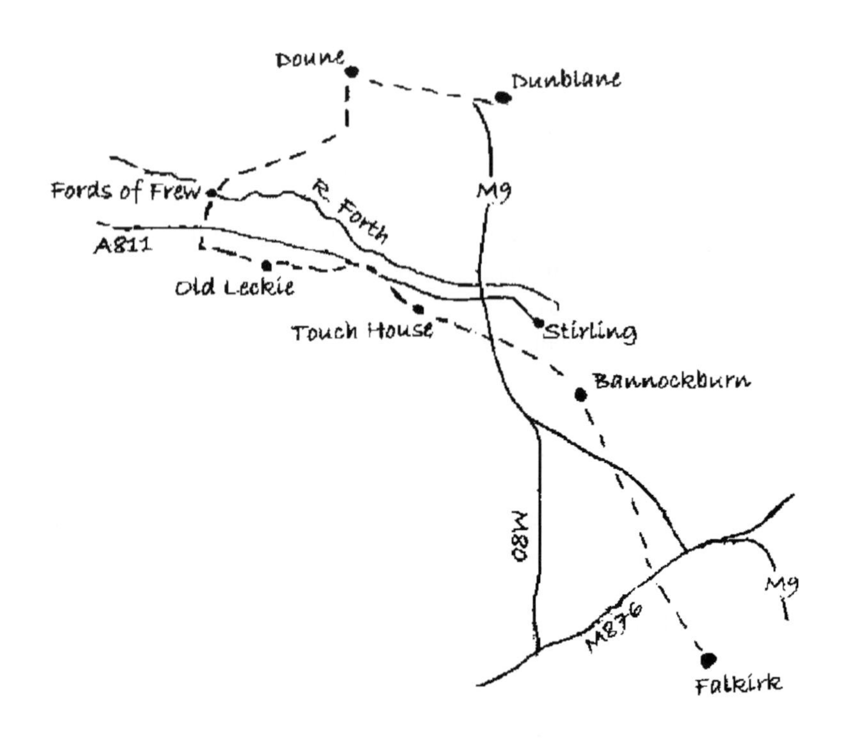

Dunblane to Falkirk (24 Miles)

probable that Prince Charles visited both houses it is possible that he spent the night at neither, although he needed a bed somewhere on the evening of 13 September before arriving at Callendar House in Falkirk the following day. Drummond Norie asserts that The Young Pretender spent the night at Touch although his host Hugh Seton had taken the precaution of making himself absent in order to avoid the fate of his neighbour at Leckie. Today Touch House stands elegant as ever in grounds of 4,500 acres and although continuing its agricultural work is also developing an office and conference centre. Hugh Seton commenced building the magnificent south front of the house in 1757 and, despite the man's Jacobite sympathies; this addition to the house can best be described as 'Georgian!'

From Touch I walked into Stirling and then took the weight off my feet and travelled through the urban landscape to Falkirk by bus. On arrival I made my way to Callendar Park and House. The Prince chose his accommodation well. A visit to this handsome house is worth the entrance fee if only to see the kitchen that is just as it would have been in 1825. I was lucky enough to visit on a day when a huge coal fire was blazing away in preparation for the spit roasting of an ox.

Reluctantly I left Callendar Park and walked up to the Union Canal. I could find no more excuses about being unable to find a suitable walking route as the towpath stretches all the way to Edinburgh. The waterway was constructed between 1818 and 1822 and is almost thirty-two miles long. Together with the Forth and Clyde Canal the Union carried coal and other goods from Edinburgh to Glasgow. It closed to through navigation in 1965 and then gradually fell into disrepair. In March 1999 work began to revitalise the two canals and re-establish continuous navigation between the capital and Scotland's biggest city. The centrepiece of the £78m project is the 115ft high Falkirk Wheel, an ingenious device designed to lift or lower boats from one canal to the other and so once again connect the two waterways.

The Palace of Linlithgow where Mary Queen of Scots was born is nine miles east of Falkirk. There has been a royal house on

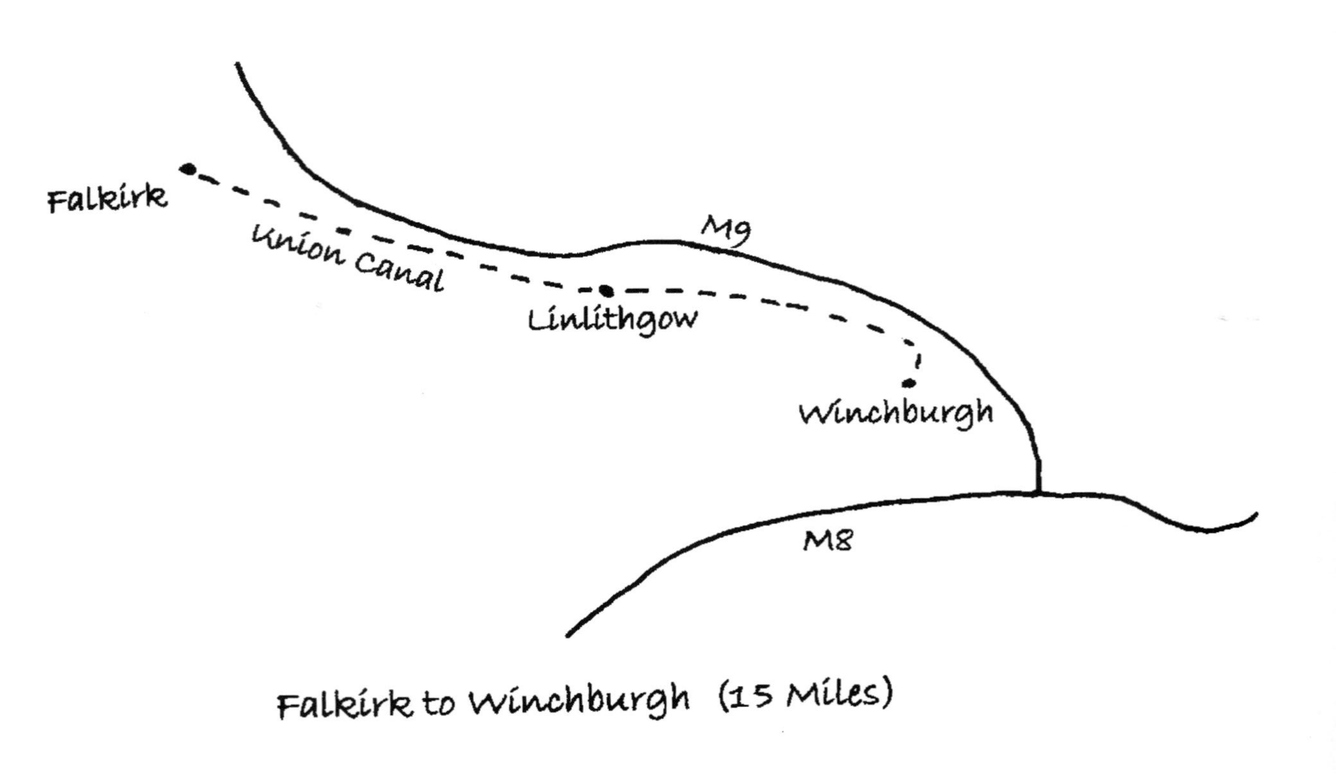

Falkirk to Winchburgh (15 Miles)

the site since the time of King David I in 1124. King Edward I of England used the manor house in 1301 and fire destroyed it in 1424. Construction of the present palace began soon after the fire and the building continued developing for the next two centuries. Prince Charles Edward was made welcome on his journey south and the Duke of Cumberland's army stayed at Linlithgow on 31 January 1746. During their stay, either on purpose or by accident, Cumberland's troops set the palace on fire, reducing it to the ruin it is today.

An aqueduct takes the canal over the River Almond and from here to Ratho the canal is frequently in woodland. The sunshine filtering through the trees and glinting on the water produced a restful scene that helped me forget my aching feet. Canal boats and the Bridge Inn at Ratho kept me amused for a while before I made the final assault on Edinburgh. As I left Ratho I could see the impregnable castle thrusting into the horizon sky.

Gray's Mill, where the Prince first halted on approaching Edinburgh has been destroyed. It stood on the Water of Leith and originally milled flour but was a paper mill at the beginning of the twentieth century. The site is now occupied by Bookers Cash and Carry warehouse and a B&Q DIY store on Inglis Green Road. Happily the name has survived. There is a street in the area called Gray's Loan, a modern and unattractive pub on Slateford Road called Gray's Mill and Graysmill School, about half a mile south of Slateford station. At the point where Slateford Road becomes Lanark Road an aqueduct, built in 1937, carries the Union Canal over the road. A dingy plaque, high on the underside of the bridge, is rarely noticed by passing motorists or pedestrians. *'Prince Charlie Bridge ~ Near this spot at Gray's Mill Prince Charlie's army halted in 1745 prior to the occupation of Edinburgh.'*

At the time of my visit the canal ended quietly in the middle of a housing estate on the outskirts of the city. I had to return home and I could see aeroplanes taking off not far away. Unfortunately there seemed to be no way of arriving at the airport without going into Edinburgh and then out again on public transport. I tried the 'Fort Augustus Fiver' method on a chap who was tinkering with his car on the street. He was unable to help but called his daughter and without hesitation she agreed to give me a lift. Such faith in a complete stranger is rare. I even had some difficulty in persuading her to accept the modest amount of money I offered. Fifteen minutes later I was checking in at the British Airways desk, away from the eighteenth century rural canal towpath and back in the ways of the modern world.

A few months later I was back in Edinburgh and champing at the bit to visit the Palace of Holyroodhouse and the battle site at Prestonpans. I managed to restrain my enthusiasm long enough to drop into The National Portrait Gallery in Queen Street where several paintings connected with the '45 are displayed. One of them is a portrait of Prince Charles painted in Paris by Maurice Quentin de la Tour shortly after the Battle of Culloden. There are pictures of Prince Charles and his brother Henry, painted by Antonio David in 1732 and a 1747 portrait of Flora MacDonald by Richard Wilson.

Next I made a short detour to Constitution Street in Leith where Robert Forbes, the compiler of 'The Lyon in Mourning' is buried in South Leith Church. There has been a church on the site since 1483 but most of the present building is Victorian. A framed seating plan of the church before its reconstruction in the 1840s hangs on the wall and this shows the pews allocated to the representatives of a variety of organisations and tradesmen including bakers, hammermen, tailors and maltmen. Forbes' tomb is unmarked but according to the church's guide to memorials and burial sites he is buried along with his wife in one of the maltmen's aisles.

From the Palace I set off through Holyrood Park. Edinburgh crowds in on all sides but the Park's hilly terrain has managed to resist the encroaching city and so it resembles a little piece of the Highlands in the capital. As I walked I began to think of John Roy Stewart, the commander of the Edinburgh Regiment. He was a remarkable man, a poet as well as a soldier. Stewart was born round about 1700 and enlisted in the Scots Greys in his twenties. After being refused a commission in the Black Watch he joined the French army and helped defeat the Duke of Cumberland's army at Fontenoy

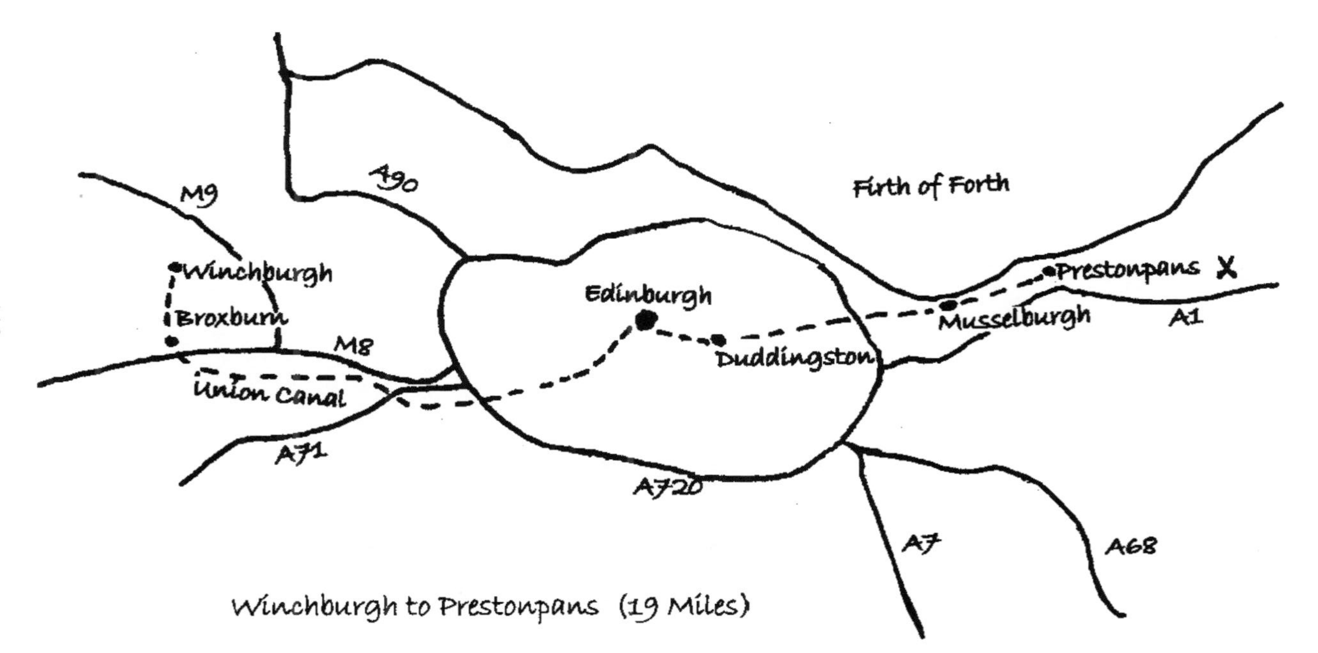

Winchburgh to Prestonpans (19 Miles)

in May 1745. While in France Stewart became active in the Jacobite cause and often acted as a liaison officer between Jacobites in France and those in Scotland. At the outbreak of the Forty-Five John Roy was in Ghent with the French army but joined Prince Charles as quickly as he could. Stewart gained a reputation as a wit, raconteur and poet but sadly much of his poetry has been lost. The best known and most entertaining of that remaining is a parody of the 23rd Psalm.

The Lord's my targe, I will be stout
With dirk and trusty blade,
Though Campbells come in flocks about
I will not be afraid.

The Lord's the same as heretofore,
He's always good to me.
Though redcoats come a thousand more,
Afraid I will not be.

I arrived in Duddingston and made my way to a street named The Causeway. No 8 has a stone above the door commemorating the Prince's visit. *'In this house on 19 September 1745 Prince Charles held his Council of War before the Battle of Prestonpans.'* The battlefield is three miles further east and there are no suitable footpaths from Duddingston. It was pouring with rain so I decided to take the bus. Unfortunately, but perhaps inevitably, the site has greatly changed over the years. The railway, the A1 and industrial development have all imposed themselves on this historic location. A modest cairn with the simple inscription, '1745' has been on the roadside for many years but recently an impressive, pyramid shaped memorial overlooking the battlefield has been built at Meadowmill. A small enclosure at the top holds a general description of the background and development of the battle. As I gazed around I wondered why such a huge pyramid of earth had been expensively constructed to house at the top such a modest memorial. I later discovered that the pyramid was not built for the battlefield at all, but as an artificial ski slope; part of the Meadowmill sports complex. The slope was never used for its original purpose and the memorial was simply an afterthought.

A path from the Meadowmill memorial leads towards Bankton House, where Colonel James Gardiner lived. After being derelict for years the house has been restored and converted into private flats. Nearby is a monument to Gardiner erected by public subscription in 1853. It bears several inscriptions including, *'To Colonel Gardiner who fell in the battle of Prestonpans, 21 September 1745.'* There is some remarkable poetry on the obelisk. I include it here not least because it introduced me to a word I had not met before. The word 'meed' means 'reward' (for those of you who do not already know). I have no idea who wrote the lines that follow but I think he must have put up a sizeable chunk of the subscription money.

His valour, his high scorn of death, to fame's proud meed no impulse owed.
His was a pure unsullied zeal for Britain and for God.
He fell, he died; the exulting foe trod careless o'er his noble clay.
Yet not in vain our champion fought in that disastrous fray.

Unfortunately Tranent churchyard has no stone marking the grave of James Gardiner. The present minister believes that Gardiner was laid to rest close to the church wall. When the building was enlarged the remains were probably moved so that they remained outside the wall. Somehow the headstone disappeared and now the place is lost. The churchyard contains a wonderful example of where some local sympathy lay. On the middle of the wall to the left is a large commemorative stone celebrating the life and death of the Vallance family. One of the people mentioned is William Cumberland Vallance who was born in 1746, the year of Culloden. It is unlikely that the family were Jacobites! I walked from the church to Cockenzie House where the Jacobite army captured General Cope's papers and military chest containing about £2,500. The house is close to the sea front and is now a residential nursing home. Pinkie House, where the Prince stayed after the battle is almost in the centre of Musselburgh. It is currently being used as a private school and is not open to the public.

FIVE

THE MARCH TO CARLISLE

'The chiefs represented to the Prince that nothing could be more ridiculous than to attempt an invasion of England with such a handful of men.'
Chevalier de Johnstone ~ A Memoir of the Forty-Five

News that the rising was under way had arrived in France before Edinburgh was taken and Antoine Walsh urged the King to give assistance to Prince Charles. Several small privateers were commissioned and landed men and armaments at Montrose and Stonehaven in early October. The news of Jacobite victory at Prestonpans delighted Louis XV and on 24 October a treaty was signed at Fontainebleau promising greater French support. However, not everyone at the French Court was bursting with enthusiasm. The Comte de Maurepas, Minister of the Navy, on hearing of the success at Prestonpans was cautious and wrote, *'This news causes a great sensation in Paris, but it does not seem to be doing so to the British nation. Those who are favourably inclined to him, if indeed he has a party in which he can rely, seem to want still greater success before they show themselves.'* Despite this gloomy assessment the Régiment Écossais Royaux and 300 soldiers from the Irish regiments in French service all under the command of Lord John Drummond, the brother of the Duke of Perth, were embarked from Dunkirk in the middle of November. Once again the weather turned against the French and only La Renommée managed to land her men and munitions at Montrose. The other ships were either captured or driven back to France. While in the Montrose channel La Renommée's guns helped local Jacobites capture the government sloop Hazard which was renamed Le Prince Charles.

The Prince formed a Council that met every morning. The

Duke of Perth, Lord George Murray, Lord Elcho, Lochiel, Keppoch, Clanranald, Colonel O'Sullivan, Secretary Murray, Sir Thomas Sheridan and other important commanders and advisors attended. Lord Elcho provides an illuminating glimpse into the workings of the Council.

> *The Prince in this Councill used Always first to declare what he was for, and then he Ask'd Every bodys opinion in their turn. Their was one third of the Councill who's principals were that Kings and Princes Can never act or think wrong, so in Consequence they always Confirmed whatever the Prince Said. The other two thirds, who thought that Kings and Princes thought sometimes like other men and were not altogether infallable and that this Prince was no more so than others, beg'd leave to differ from him, when they Could give Sufficient reasons for their difference of Opinion. Which very often was no hard matter to do, for as the Prince and his Old Governor Sir Thomas Sheridan were altogether ignorant of the ways and Customs in Great Britain, and both much for the Doctrine of Absolute monarchy, they would very often, had they not been prevented, have fall'n into Blunders which might have hurt the Cause. The Prince Could not bear to hear any body differ in Sentiment from him, and took a dislike to Every body that did.*

Prince Charles proposed that success at Prestonpans signified they should march on General Wade in Newcastle. He was surprised when the Council advised against the move, arguing that the goal of re-establishing the Stuart monarchy in Scotland had been accomplished. The majority considered the Union to be ended and there was no wish to meddle further with English affairs. It was argued that Prince Charles should consolidate his position in Scotland where there was some chance of maintaining the restored monarchy. Charles was more optimistic and determined to win the throne of England for his father. After much debate, and by exercising his personal authority, the Prince persuaded the clan chiefs to march south, convincing them that help would be forthcoming from English Jacobites. From where this conviction came is not clear. At first sight it seems inconceivable that Charles could contemplate a march into England without being certain of support south of the border. However, there is no documentary evidence of any firm pledges by English supporters and so it seems likely that flushed with the success of the campaign in Scotland the Prince was prepared to throw caution to the wind. He simply believed his cause was just and that the people of England would rally to his banner. He was to be proved wrong and Lord George Murray's aide-de-camp, the Chevalier de Johnstone had no doubts about the matter. '*The enterprise was bold, nay rash, and unexampled. What man in his senses could think of encountering the English armies and attempting the conquest of England with four thousand five hundred Highlanders?*'

John Roy Stewart agreed and allowed himself the luxury of recollection in a letter sent from Boulogne to James Edgar, King James' secretary in 1747. Perhaps relying on the clear vision of hindsight, Colonel Stewart complains that he opposed the invasion of England but as he was not a member of the Prince's inner circle his advice was not asked for.

> *The authors and projectors of that unaccountable scheme, for I must call it so, have much to answer for to God, the King, the Prince and the Country. I was not admitted to their Councilles, being the only Colonel debarred and for no reason I could ever imagine, but that I spoke perhaps too warmly against such a step to John Murray and Sir Thomas Sheridan whom I found both bent upon it to my great surprise. But that did not hinder me from representing upon my knees and tears in my eyes against it. And I appeal to all the principal gentlemen of the army if I did not oppose it with all my soul and but too prophetically and foretold them all that must have happened and what astonished me that the world did not see as plain as myself. To enter into England with*

betwixt three and four thousand men at a time when they had thirty thousand regular troops and all the militia of England to oppose us and when we had no account of a french landing nor no assurance of being joined by the Country, nor not in Correspondence with them.

Lord George suggested that instead of attacking Wade in Newcastle the army should march into north-west England where, it was argued, there was sympathy for the Jacobite cause. The idea was adopted, although the Prince was not enthusiastic. The plan called for the invading force to be split into two in order to confuse General Wade. The first group was to march through Peebles, Moffat and Lockerbie into Carlisle, and the second through Lauder and Kelso, as though it was advancing on Newcastle. The second group was to leave the Newcastle road at Jedburgh and join the other in Carlisle. Lord Strathallan was left in command the troops remaining in Scotland and to organise recruits expected from the Highlands and the Lowlands of the north-east.

The army assembled at Dalkeith and when it marched south on 3 November it was in good shape. The men were rested, well-equipped and fighting fit after the long stay in Edinburgh. The Prince led the group making the apparent attack on Newcastle and the column progressed to Lauder, where Charles stayed the night of 3 November at Thirlestane Castle. The march continued to Kelso where tradition has it that the Prince stayed at Sunlaws, a house three miles south of the town. On 6 November the army crossed the Tweed and turned towards Jedburgh. The march continued through Liddesdale and the army spent the night at a place now called Larriston but named Haggiehaugh in those days. The River Esk was crossed near Canonbie on 8 November and the following day the combined army columns crossed the River Eden to camp at Rockcliff, about three miles outside Carlisle.

Although Carlisle Castle was once a mighty fortress, by 1745 it had fallen into a state of poor repair and was badly defended. The Jacobites had no doubts about their ability take the city and so were able to respond to reports that General Wade was marching towards Carlisle. The Prince moved his troops away from the city in the hopes of meeting Wade in the hills around Brampton, nine miles to the east. However, the reports were false and Wade had not left Newcastle. The Young Pretender remained in Brampton and on 11 November took the opportunity to try and drum up some English support. He wrote a letter to Lord Barrymore, the man who was arguably the most influential Jacobite in England.

> *This is to acquaint you with the success we have had since our arrival in Scotland, and how far we have advanced without repulse. We are now a numerous army, and are laying siege to Carlisle this day, which we are sure cannot hold long. After that we intend to take our route straight for London, and if things answer our expectations we design to be in Cheshire before the 24th inst. Then I hope you and all my friends in that county will be ready to join us. For now is the time or never. Adieu.*

Sadly for Prince Charles, Barrymore was away from home and the letter was handed to his son, Lord Buttevant, who promptly burned it, so frustrating a good chance of turning out some English support.

In the meantime many Jacobite troops returned to Carlisle to resume the siege and by the afternoon of 15 November terms of surrender had been agreed. King James was proclaimed at the market cross and the Mayor later rode out to Brampton to present Prince Charles with the keys to the city. Carlisle was taken for the loss of one man killed and one wounded. In Carlisle coolness between Charles and Lord George Murray broke out into a quarrel affecting their relationship for the rest of the campaign. Lord George was a proud man with more useful military experience and knowledge than the Prince. He was angry when he was ignored in favour of the Duke of Perth as the terms of the surrender were being arranged. He wrote to Prince Charles.

Sir,

I cannot but observe how little my advice, as a general officer, has any weight with your Royal Highness ever since I had the honour of a commission from your hands. I therefore take leave to give up my commission. But as I ever had a firm attachment to the Royal Family, and in particular to the King my master, I shall go on as a volunteer, and design to be this night in the trenches as such.

It seems unlikely that Lord George expected Prince Charles to accept the resignation and was probably surprised when he did. Perhaps the Prince was put out by the reference to his father as the ultimate authority or possibly he was influenced by the Irish contingent amongst his supporters. Sir John MacDonald later wrote of the '*impertinent letter'* from Lord George. *'Strickland and I thought this was a good occasion to get rid of this dangerous man, suspected by all the army except Sheridan and three or four others whom he had persuaded of his ability and honesty.'* Other officers thought differently and voiced their objections to the dismissal of Lord George. Under some pressure but perhaps with relief the Prince asked Murray to resume his position of command. However, the personal damage had been done and from then on there was a tendency for mistrust between the two to come to the surface.

Meanwhile General Wade had at last set off from Newcastle. The seventy-two year old general was reluctant to spend a penny more than absolutely necessary for the well-being of his men and they were in poor spirits throughout the march. The weather was terrible and the roads atrocious. The army ground to a halt in deep snow at Hexham where Wade learned that he was too late to save Carlisle. The Prince took up residence at Mr Highmore's house in English Street where a Council of War determined the next move. Charles was still enthusiastic about advancing towards London whilst others urged a return to Scotland or perhaps a march on Newcastle. Lord George Murray cautioned that further advance into England might be dangerous without more support but eventually bowed to the Prince's authority. On 20 November the Jacobite army left 150 men to defend Carlisle and marched south. Against them were General Wade's 9,000 troops that were slowly marching across country into Lancashire and Sir John Ligonier's force of 10,000 which was in Staffordshire. This latter force was soon to be commanded by George II's son William, Duke of Cumberland.

LANDRANGER MAPS

66 Edinburgh
80 Cheviot Hills & Kielder Forest
73 Peebles & Galashiels
79 Hawick & Eskdale
74 Kelso
85 Carlisle & Solway Firth

Catcune (66)	**NT356599**
Floors Castle (74)	**NT711347**
Stow (73)	**NT460445**
Flex Farm (79)	**NT505124**
Thirlestane Castle (73)	**NT536479**
Riccarton Junction (79)	**NY541978**
Dryburgh Abbey (73)	**NT588316**
Watleyhirst (85)	**NY445784**

I left Musselburgh on the River Esk Walkway. The path passes through lightly wooded countryside and terminates on a road leading to Whitecraig. Here I found a disused railway line transformed into a cycle track and strode south along it to Dalkeith. The Palace, where Prince Charles stayed, (picture p31) stands in grand, impressive grounds to the north of town. It was last used as a private residence in 1918 and today is the Scottish campus for the University of Wisconsin.

The map shows the disused 'Waverley Line' railway track leaving Dalkeith near the Eskbank area of Dalkeith. This line once carried trains between Edinburgh and Carlisle and was to prove a

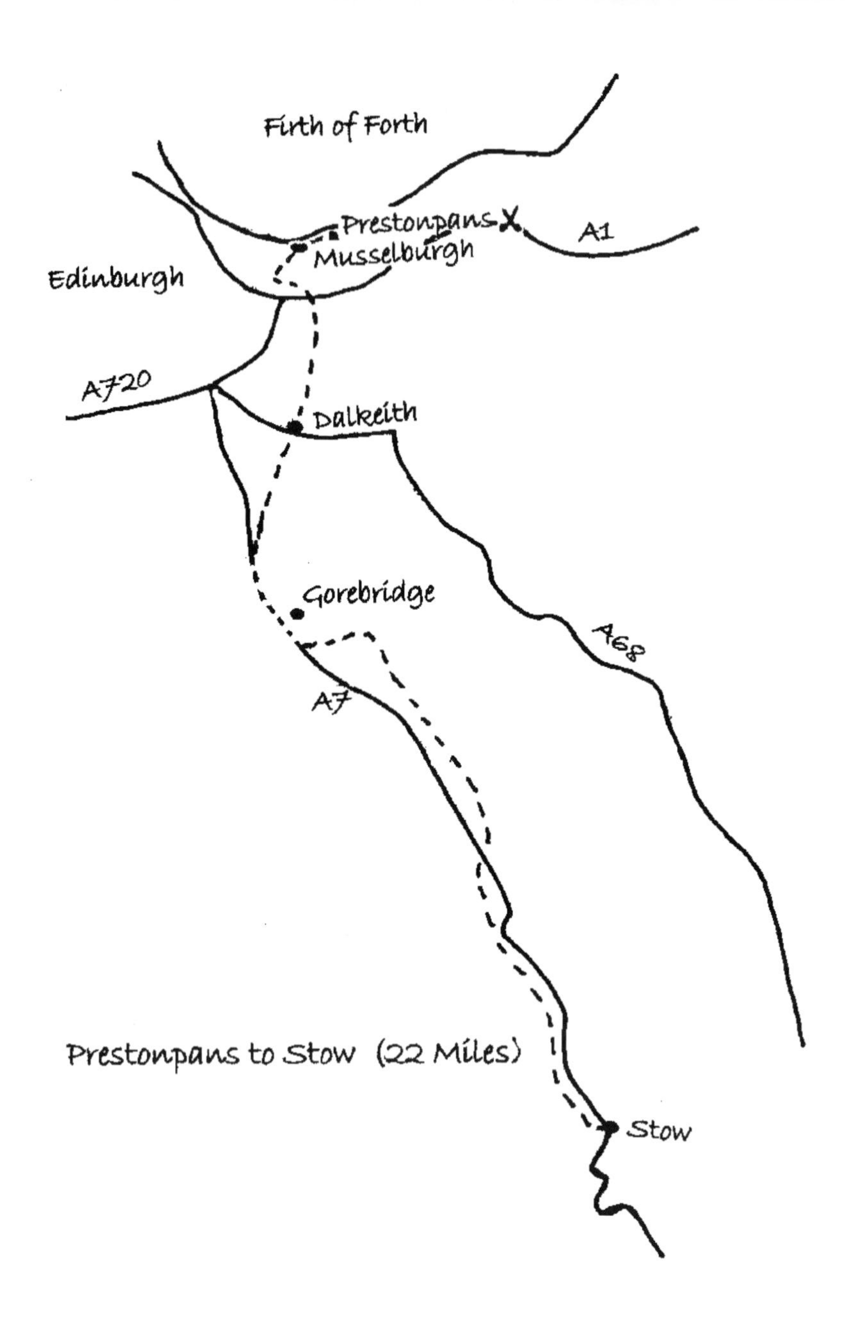
Firth of Forth
Prestonpans
A1
Musselburgh
Edinburgh
A720
Dalkeith
Gorebridge
A68
A7
Prestonpans to Stow (22 Miles)
Stow

useful trail on several occasions on my way south. Unfortunately, breaks in continuity make the line a difficult footpath near Dalkeith and I opted to begin walking about a mile south of Gorebridge, at Catcune. Fences and gates crossed the line every so often but as there are no laws of trespass in Scotland I did not fear prosecution. The absence of such laws leaves walkers in an interesting position. Theoretically walkers may go wherever they wish but this does not mean they are free to ignore the rights of others to farm and maintain proper control over the land. I negotiated barriers with care and no one I met challenged my right to be there or was anything other than helpful. Although the way is clear, the surface is of varying quality. Some parts are firm, dry and clear of undergrowth while others, usually where the track goes through a cutting, are overgrown and often wet and muddy.

As I walked, I mulled over Prince Charles' six-week stay in Edinburgh. Why did he stay so long and what were the consequences of doing so? If a march into England was to take place then the sooner the arrangements were complete the better. Even at this early stage there was serious dissention in the Prince's Council. Those who wanted to invade pointed out that delay allowed the government to better prepare its armies and noted that a long stay in Edinburgh would exhaust the Jacobite coffers. The anti-invasion lobby thought that desertion after Prestonpans had seriously reduced the army's ability to fight and pointed out that there was no sign of help from either English Jacobites or the French. Jacobite failure to capture the castles in Stirling and Edinburgh was also a key factor in the argument not to invade England.

Colonel John Roy Stewart's letter to James Edgar illustrates his thoughts on the Prince's proper course of action and optimistically included the two great Skye chiefs, MacDonald and MacLeod in his plan.

> *It was proposed after Gladsmuir* (Prestonpans) *that in place of going to England there should immediately have been several expresses sent to France to entreat that they should*

send as many men as they conveniently could, with monie and arms and by all means immediately a ship with six pieces of battery cannon, with as many mortars, proper for reducing the Castles of Edinburgh and Stirling which would not resist 3 days on being attackt with proper artillery and that we should in the meantime make proper disposition to rise all the Highlands in the following manner. That Lochiel and Keppoch, with their own men and the Stuarts of Appen, should march straight by Glasgow into Argyllshire. ~~ That the Atholl men at the same time and manner should rise the Breadalbane men, being their neighbours and relations and loyal and willing. Glengarry and Clanranald's men to rise their neighbours and relations, Sir Alex MacDonald's and Mackleod's men, who are second to none in loyalty notwithstanding what happened. ~~ by those means in a Months time we should infallibly have a an army of at least four and twenty thousand good men assembled, to march straight south and chase any army they could spare or venture to send out of England. Then take our two Castles, proclaim the King, call a Parliament and take full possession of all Scotland. Then act according to circumstances. If succours arrived from France tho' not above 3 or 4 thousand, we could march straight to London and I am sure, in that case, would be joined powerfully by the English, but even without them we could really doe the affair. Or in the worst event, that no help came from France, we could always keep Scotland till a more favourable occasion.

The attitude of MacDonald and MacLeod was indeed crucial. Had these two influential men supported the Prince then others would have quickly and willingly followed suit and it is probable that a large invasion force would have been gathered. French and English collaboration might have been more robust and perhaps the Jacobites would have been in London before King George knew what was happening. Nothing is sure of course and as they were unable to call men out to fight as the clan chiefs had done, it is possible that influential English Jacobites would not have rallied to the Standard in even the most favourable of circumstances. Among the general population reaction to the idea of a Stuart restoration was lukewarm. The Hanoverians were foreigners but then, so it could be argued, were the Stuarts.

I left the old railway line at Stow and with some regret took to the road for the relatively easy five-mile walk to Lauder and Thirlestane Castle. The castle was originally built in the thirteenth century as a defensive structure and re-built in the sixteenth as the home of the Maitland family. The family live in a private wing and the rest of the place is open to the public. The 'Bonnie Prince Charlie Room' is complete with the bed in which Charles is reputed to have slept. I left the castle and began to consider my route to Kelso. The most direct route is along the line of the A6089 through the village of Gordon. Unfortunately recognised footpaths do not accompany the road and I concluded that I should instead be guided first by the white thistle waymarks of the Southern Upland Way to Melrose and then the bank of the River Tweed to Kelso. The Way leads south from the Tourist Information Office in Lauder, first passing the golf course and then progressing along a minor road from Fordswell before finally reverting to a footpath for the final stretch into Melrose.

The main attraction of this prosperous town is the beautiful twelfth century Cistercian abbey where the heart of Robert the Bruce is buried. A quiet road behind the abbey leads to Newstead from where I headed for Ravenswood. The area is a confusion of paths, farm tracks and disused railway lines. To complicate matters a recently built road connecting the A7 and A68, was not marked on my map. The omission compounded my disorientation. I knew roughly, but not quite exactly where I was. I was hopelessly studying the map when a gentleman in a Land Rover stopped and offered his help. He farmed the Ravenswood land on behalf of the owner and we whizzed off down the tracks through the estate.

The Land Rover stopped on a grassy bank by the River Tweed and the farmer's parting words were that I was on private land and

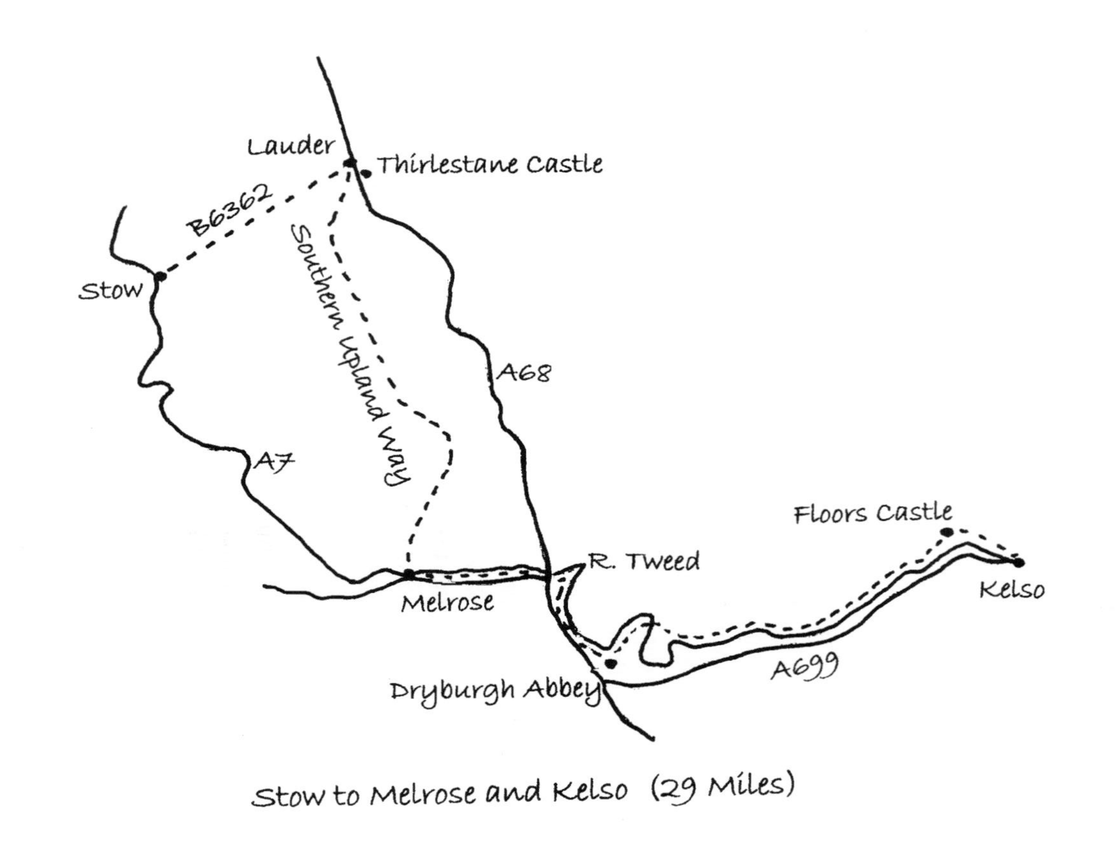
Lauder
Thirlestane Castle
B6362
Stow
Southern Upland Way
A68
A7
Floors Castle
R. Tweed
Kelso
Melrose
A699
Dryburgh Abbey
Stow to Melrose and Kelso (29 Miles)

the ghillie might just chase me off. I scurried along the pleasant riverbank path that started well enough but soon deteriorated into an almost impenetrable jungle of long grass, seed spitting balsam and that huge plant that looks a bit like rhubarb but can grow up to six feet high. There were burns and fallen trees to cross and I became increasingly worried that the muddy path might become impassable. I had long since left the Ravenswood estate and was no longer worried about rampaging ghillies but the thought of having spent several hours and much energy achieving precisely nothing did not fill me with enthusiasm. I persevered and ultimately was able to force my way along the riverbank to Dryburgh Abbey where I joined St Cuthbert's Way.

Following the Tweed took me through the village of St Boswells to Mertoun Bridge where I left St Cuthbert's Way and crossed the bridge to walk around Mertoun House and return to the river on its northern bank. At Old Dalcove the riverbank path ends and I had to follow several minor roads before returning to the Tweed east of Makerstoun House. The route into the centre of Kelso led me past Floors Castle, the seat of the Duke of Roxburgh.

Finding accommodation was something of a problem in Kelso. My visit coincided with the Scottish Rural Women's conference and it appeared that every room in town was taken. The Tourist Information Office was not hopeful but rang a B&B that they said was run by a very helpful fellow who would certainly do his best. Five minutes later I was following instructions to the modest semi-detached house where I was made welcome with tea and biscuits before being shown to my room. I was pleased at having found somewhere to stay and settled in. It was only later that evening that I discovered that my host had generously given up his own room and would be sleeping on the settee downstairs in order to accommodate me. To cap it all, the next morning I was charged at a discount to the already reasonable rate and sent on my way with an excellent breakfast to fortify me throughout the morning.

On a radiantly sunny day I strolled past the elegant eighteenth century courthouse that dominates Kelso's cobbled market square and crossed the bridge over the River Tweed. The A699 guided me for about a mile to a bridge over the River Teviot from where I walked along the riverbank to Roxburgh where I knew the disused Waverley Line would once again make a useful appearance. Another mile or so brought me close to the Roxburghe Hotel that was known until recently as Sunlaws House Hotel. The original Sunlaws House where the Prince is reputed to have stayed was destroyed by fire and it is unlikely that any vestige of the original building still exists.

The railway line is well walked and leads past Ormiston House to Nisbet as part of the Borders Valleys Way. The track continues into Jedburgh but unfortunately two bridges over the river were down, compelling me to cross the Teviot by road at Nisbet and continue the walk along the riverbank. The path follows the Teviot to Jed Water and then I turned south on a minor road parallel to the A68 into Jedburgh. The plaque attached to 'Prince Charlie's House' on Castlegate in the centre of Jedburgh informs that *'Prince Charles Edward Stuart lodged in this house on 6 and 7 November 1745.'*

The route the Jacobites took from Jedburgh might now be described as south-west through remote and lightly populated countryside to Bonchester Bridge and then along the line of the B6357 through Larriston to Newcastleton and Canonbie. I pored over the map for a suitable route through the huge commercial pine forests but found none. The town of Hawick is situated a little south-west of Jedburgh and the good old Waverley Line continues from there to Newcastleton. This was too good to miss and so I left my bed and breakfast accommodation and hopped on a bus. Hawick's economy is based on farming sheep and turning their wool into garments. I hear things are not too good in either branch of those markets, with the result that Hawick could be regarded as a town in a certain decline.

It's twenty miles from Hawick to Newcastleton with not a lot in between except sheep country and forest. Even today this is a little visited part of Britain. The roads are almost empty and there are few places that might afford a walker shelter for the night. The Waverley Line never strays far from the road and so if the walking

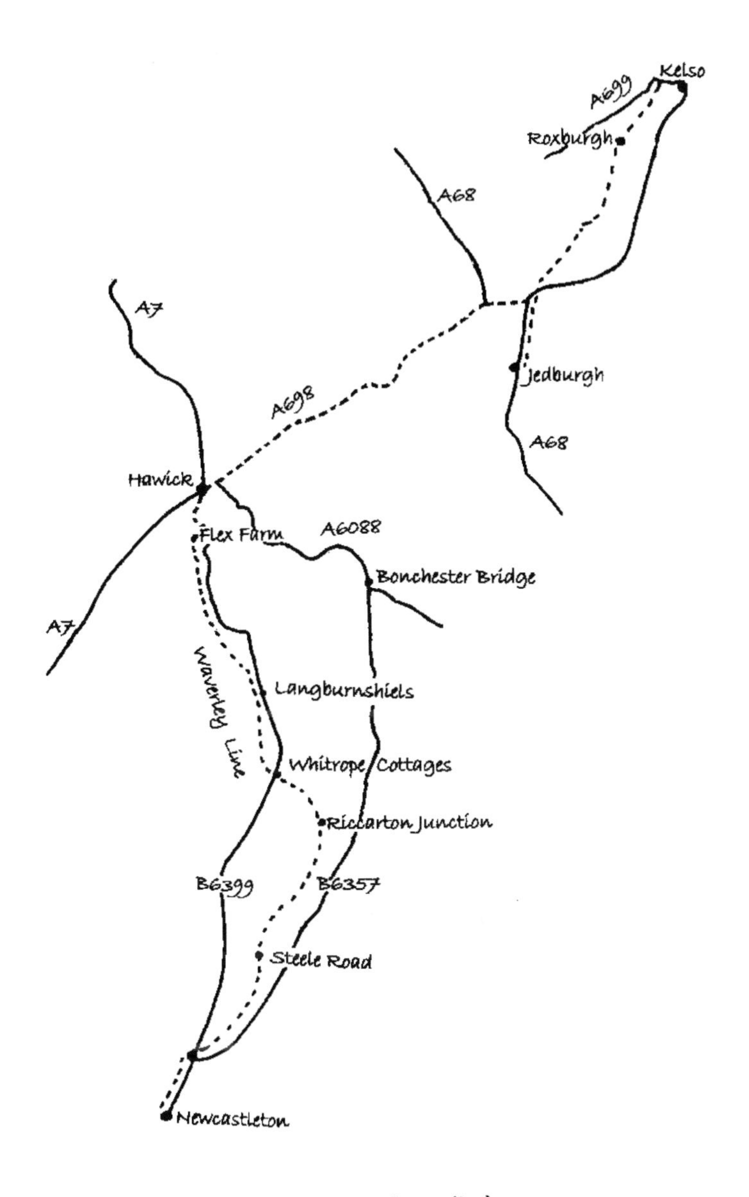

Kelso to Hawick and Newcastleton (42 Miles)

becomes too much, salvation is possible. I walked out of Hawick down Liddesdale Road to Flex farm and the railway line. Half an hour later I arrived at Acreknowe where I ran into a little trouble. The track disappeared; after all it is more than thirty-five years since the trains stopped running. There are lots of criss-crossing paths in the mile or so between Acreknowe and Stobs Castle and I wandered about trying to find my way. At last I was seduced by a well-defined track and, as I failed to check my position frequently, landed up at Barnes Loch. It's a lovely stretch of water and just the job for anglers but unfortunately way off course for me. My irritation was complete when it dawned on me that I would have to backtrack to Acreknowe.

I eventually found Stobs Station House and after a short stretch of road, the railway line re-appeared. The line crosses a viaduct at Shankend farm and veers away from the road towards the forest at Langburnshiels. As it approaches the three-quarter mile long Whitrope tunnel the track descends into a cutting and trees crowd in on both sides. My feet were soaked and the going became increasingly wet, muddy and overgrown. The tunnel is too dark and dangerous to walk through so I climbed over the top. The forest allowed no views of landmarks and I began to lose my bearings but the position of the sun and my compass kept me going in the right direction. I was both relieved and happy when I emerged on the road half a mile south of Whitrope Cottages. It had taken me three hours to negotiate about three miles of forest. Make no mistake, this is no Sunday afternoon stroll. There are many opportunities for picking up a twisted ankle and it might be better to leave the railway line at Langburnshiels and walk along the road to Whitrope.

Forestry vehicles use the old railway line between Whitrope Cottages and Riccarton Junction and so the track is well maintained. At Riccarton I visited 'Will's bothy', a well-equipped shelter for walkers and climbers that was restored and named in memory of Will Ramsbotham who died in a climbing accident in 1993. I took the right-hand fork at Riccarton through forest and then farmland, eventually arriving at the old station at Steele Road. There is no longer a railway bridge over Hermitage Water and it is best to leave

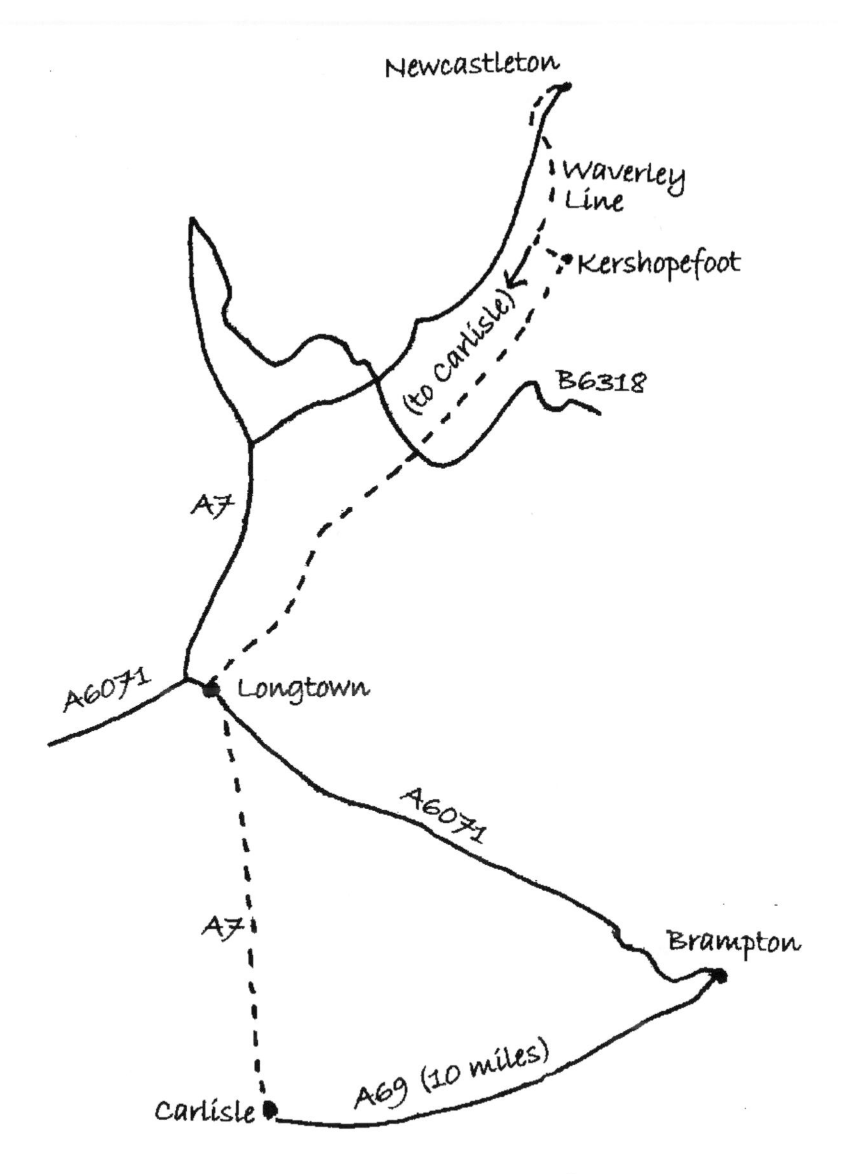

Newcastleton to Carlisle (21 Miles)

the line at Ovenshank Farm and cross by road. The line continues to Newcastleton where I stayed overnight. The village with its two squares connected by a long main street did not exist when the Prince marched through. It was purpose built in 1793 as an early example of a new town.

The following morning it was raining heavily. My hosts were travelling to Carlisle and I was tempted to take a lift but decided to stride out and hope the weather would improve. The railway bridge over Liddel Water south of Newcastleton has gone, necessitating use of the road bridge to a riverbank path. The railway line re-appears at Mangerton farm, a couple of miles north of Kershopefoot and the border with England.

In England footpaths are indicated on Landranger maps by red dotted lines and the railway line south of the border was marked without them. Ludicrously, walking further involved the possibility of prosecution for trespass. No notice at the frontier indicated a disinclination for the landowner to allow access and so despite the missing dots I continued. Half an hour later a fence blocked my progress but in the absence of a ‘Keep Out’ notice I negotiated the barrier and went on. Another half hour brought me to a more robust fence and this time there was no ignoring the large notice, ‘Strictly Private, No Public Access’. Well, nothing could be clearer but what was I to do? Go back and waste two hours getting nowhere. No chance!

There was a smaller fence to the right and this had a taped over barbed wire top, presumably to allow people to cross. I climbed over. I could have returned to the Waverley Line straight away but in the interests of trying to stick to the rules I did not, and soon found myself on a well-used path by the side of the sparkling Liddel Water. Several minutes later I came across a keeper who was just finishing his lunch before doing a bit of fishing. He politely told me that I was on the Kingfield estate and although I did not look like the sort of chap who was going to cause trouble, it might be best if I left. He suggested that I returned to the railway line and join the road near Watleyhirst. I complied, as I had no wish to argue and knew that I was legally in the wrong. The railway line is clear to follow, no one could get lost and there seems to me no good reason why access should be denied. There are game birds being bred but that is so in many places. It is such a shame that after miles of unimpeded walking in Scotland the railway line is not available to walkers in England. Still that's the way it is. At the border an alternative to breaking the law is to turn left along the road to Kershopefoot and then walk south to Watleyhirst and the B6318. There are no public footpaths for much of the way to Longtown and Carlisle and I recommend travelling by car.

Carlisle Castle (picture p31) is under the care of English Heritage and is a popular tourist spot. On the occasion of my visit an exhibition on the top floor of the keep outlined the development and eventual failure of the 1745 rising. The walls of the castle dungeons have some deeply indented stones that collect moisture. These are described as the 'licking stones'. The story goes that prisoners held here after Culloden used them in order to supplement their meagre water rations. A plaque on the facade of Marks and Spencer's in English Street states that the Young Pretender used a house that once stood on the site as his headquarters. A similar and adjacent plaque notes that Cumberland did the same when he took back the city for the government.

On the assumption that General Wade was marching from Newcastle to Carlisle the Prince moved troops to Brampton, a few miles to the east. I decided to pay the little market town a visit. The house in which Prince Charles had his headquarters is in High Cross Street, opposite the White Lion Inn. It is presently being used as a shoe shop and a plaque on the front notes its part in the '45.

Prince Charlie's House
This building dates from 1603
In 1745 'Bonnie' Prince Charlie established his headquarters here during the siege of Carlisle November 12th to 18th 1745.

In 1904 the Brampton Parish Council erected the strangely

named Capon Tree monument a mile south of the village to remember the execution of six of Prince Charlie's men in 1746. The oak tree that formerly grew here was used as a resting and eating-place for itinerant judges. Capons were frequently on the menu and so gave the tree its name. The inscription reads,

> *This stone is placed to mark the site of the ancient Capon Tree under whose shade the judges of assize rested and upon whose branches were executed October XXI MDCCXLVI for adherence to the cause of the Royal Line of Stuart, Colonel James Innes, Captain Patrick Lindesay, Ronald MacDonald, Thomas Park, Peter Taylor, Michael Delard.*

SIX

TO MANCHESTER

'The progress of the rebels was what nobody expected ~ they over-ran one of the united kingdoms, and marched so far into the other, that the capital trembled at their approach.'
John Home ~ The History of the Rebellion in the Year 1745

From Carlisle the Prince's army marched without opposition through Penrith and Shap to Kendal. John Maclean of Kingairloch, a Jacobite officer, kept a journal from August 1745 to April 1746. He notes,

> *Thursday 21, we marched from Penrith, and within a quarter of a mile of it we entered the County of Westmorland and passed through the Town and bridge of Imont, and next through Cliffton, and then through Thrimby and Over a moor to Shap where we quartered that night. 8 miles that Day having frost and Snow. ~ Then into a Glean called Hawsfoot, and then over Highburows bridge, and then into ane other Glean Called Ffassel Forest, Collonell Barkshire Lord of the Manor. And then Came Over Bansden Bridge, and then Over the Keint, which is a beautifull Water & Large too passing through a part of Kendale, which is a Large and handsome Town where we quartered that night. We marched 12 miles that Day having Deep Snow in the Moor passing through Wreaths of Snow and it happened to be a thow.*

In Penrith only one recruit was added to the Jacobite muster roll. The people in Kendal were friendlier but significantly none were prepared to join the Prince. The army passed uneventfully through Lancaster and on 26 November the vanguard arrived in Preston where in 1715 a Jacobite force had been trapped between two government armies and defeated. To avoid superstitious disquiet Lord George marched the men over the Ribble to camp in villages on the southern side. There was no marching further south the following day allowing the rearguard to catch up and so consolidate the army in one place, something that had not been possible since leaving Carlisle. According to O'Sullivan the people of Preston welcomed the Prince ecstatically. *'It can't be expressed with what demonstration of joy the Prince was recd here, bells ringing, bon-fires, all the houses illuminated, such crowdes of people.'*

Great things were expected from the people of Lancashire. Preston had been a Jacobite stronghold in the rising of 1715 and although the Prince's hopes of the area were left unfulfilled some recruits were forthcoming. Notable among these were Francis Townley and John Daniel. Daniel has left us a fascinating account of his adventures up to the moment when he was evacuated on a French ship from Loch nan Uamh on May 4 1746. He joined *'betwixt Lancaster and Garstang'* and was appointed Captain in the Duke of Perth's regiment. Daniel reports that when the army entered Preston it had with it only thirty-nine English recruits. This difficulty in recruiting Englishmen was beginning to sow seeds of disquiet in the minds of those who were already far from home. Lord Elcho notes, '*The Officers of the army began here to doubt of being joined, and to Say they had marched far enough, but upon the Prince Assuring them they would be joined by all his English friends at Manchester, and Monsr de Boyer* (Le Marquis d'Eguilles) *offering to lay considerable wagers that the French were either landed or would land in a week, these discourses were laid Aside.'*

Over the next three days the troops marched through Wigan to Manchester. The city was taken to some cheering and without opposition. Support for the Prince was thought to be strong but the number of new troops joining was much smaller than had been anticipated. A Manchester Regiment of perhaps 300 was formed under the command of Francis Townley. David Morgan, a barrister and William Vaughan, both from Wales, had signed up with Townley and were chosen to be officers in the regiment. According to the Chevalier de Johnstone the credit for the Manchester recruitment drive goes to Sergeant Dickson who went ahead on behalf of the Prince. Dickson, a Scot, had been captured at Prestonpans and come over to the Jacobite side. He entered Manchester accompanied only by his mistress and a drummer. A crowd gathered, intent on taking him prisoner but he successfully defied them with his blunderbuss and was rescued by Jacobite supporters, one hundred and eight of whom enlisted in the Prince's army. The escapade produced jokes against the city to the effect that Manchester had been taken *'by a sergeant, a drummer and a girl.'*

Prince Charles resided in Market Street Lane with John Dickenson, a prominent Mancunian Jacobite. The atmosphere in the town was one of exited anticipation and much talk was heard regarding the proposed advance on London. The troops were happy, and fed off the best that the Manchester taverns could offer. Despite the jollity, Lord Elcho, amongst others, was not satisfied with the progress of the campaign and remarked:

> *The Prince was so far deceved with these proceedings at Manchester of bonfires and ringing of bells (which they used to own themselves they did out of fear of being ill Used) that he thought himself sure of Success, and his Conversation that night at Table was, in what manner he should enter London, on horseback or a foot, and in what dress.*

Landranger Maps

85	**Carlisle & Solway Firth**
102	**Preston & Blackpool**
90	**Penrith & Keswick**
108	**Liverpool**
97	**Kendal & Morecambe**
109	**Manchester**

Lowther Castle (90)	**NY524237**
Natland (97)	**SD514891**
Rosgill (90)	**NY537168**
Hause Foot (90)	**NY552054**
Thorn Cottage (90)	**NY542013**
Johnson's Hillock Locks (102)	**SD591209**

Walking from Carlisle to Penrith involves a lot of roadwork and so I travelled by bus. The Prince's army was not so fortunate and the state of the roads made their journey difficult and slow. In 1745 very few roads had been turnpiked (i.e. greatly improved and paid for by tolls). Roads were usually no more than pitted tracks suitable for packhorses but not convenient for heavy carts. The road from Carlisle to Kendal via Penrith and Shap was particularly bad and drifting snow further hampered progress. The large body of men and equipment could not all leave at the same time and for much of the march the army was strung out over the landscape. It was usual to send out advance cavalry scouting parties, often led by Elcho's Lifeguards, to prepare the way for the main force and so the van was perhaps twenty-four hours in front of the rear.

In Penrith the Prince stayed at The George and Dragon Inn, now The George Hotel in Devonshire Street. The plaque above the gates to the yard reads, *'Prince Charles Edward Stuart stayed here on the night of 22 November 1745.'* Hanoverian informers counted the troops passing over Eamont Bridge, just south of Penrith, and so we know that the Prince's army as it invaded England numbered about 4,500 foot soldiers and 500 cavalry. Prince Charles paused at Lowther Castle for a few hours so I followed the footpath from Eamont Bridge into the castle grounds and then continued along the river to Whale. The path side-steps the farmhouse at Whale and joins the road to Knipe and Bampton Grange where it meets the river again. I followed the stream past Hegdale and Rosgill until I was due east of Shap.

From Shap I took the road south past the Greyhound Hotel and then turned left along the well-marked trail running through the

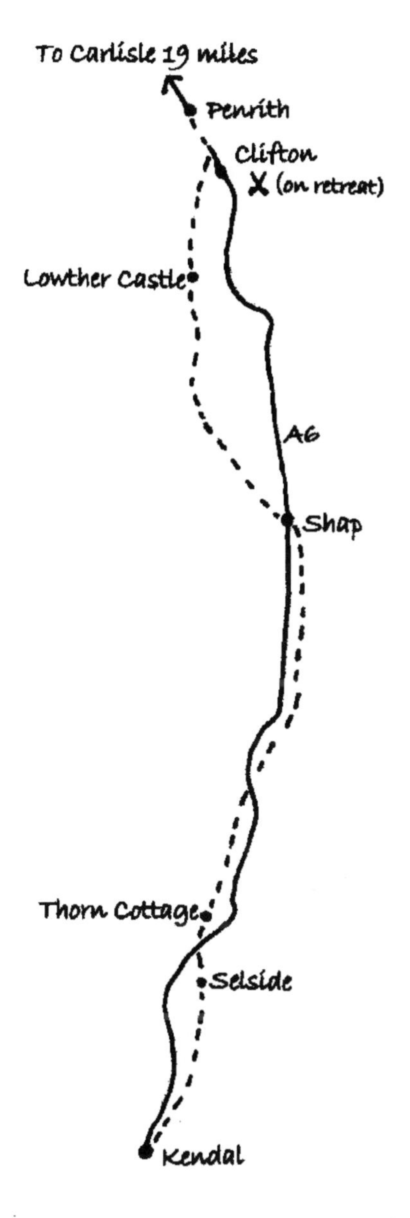

Carlisle to Kendal (44 Miles)

middle of an unsightly concrete pipe factory. Out on the other side and now in reasonable countryside electricity pylons snake across the landscape and provide the path, designated as 'Public Byway, A6', with an additional guide. The path hugs the main road for about five miles before crossing the busy carriageway and disappearing into a morass of wet moorland. After a difficult mile or so, a road so underused it has grass growing in the middle begins at Hause Foot and crosses Borrow Beck at High Barrow Bridge. After two miles, at a junction with the A6, a bridleway on the right snakes uphill and then down again to the little road at Thorn Cottage.

It was difficult to avoid the A6 all together and a few yards further brought me to within twenty yards of the main road. Luckily there is a continuation of the bridleway which is neither well marked nor trodden but led me to a minor road close to the Plough Inn on the A6. At this point I walked off yet another map. The inn is on Map 90 at NY534001 and I was just about to walk onto Map 97 at SD531000. I find something strangely satisfying about changing maps, especially if I have walked from top to bottom. It is a sense of achievement, of real progress. Never mind if there are still dozens, or even hundreds of miles to go, another map is consigned to a plastic bag in the backpack and its successor sees the light of day for the first time. It is a good feeling.

I crossed the A6 and made for Selside. At the junction after the church I turned right, past Selside Hall towards Poppy Farm and then down Dry Lane. The O.S. map marks Dry Lane with red crosses that mean, 'Byway open to all traffic', although I cannot imagine why anyone would want to drive a car here. The road falls away steeply to Otter Bank and it was at the bottom of the hill that I realised I had left my binoculars in Selside Church. My aching feet tempted me to leave them there but I knew the loss would irritate me and so off I trudged. God had kept the binoculars safe but it is a pity He neglected to jog my memory earlier. From Otter Bank I skirted Skelsmergh Tarn on my way to Skelsmergh Hall Farm. The farmyard was six inches deep in evil smelling slurry and I was pleased to have bought such excellent boots. Finding my way to the River Mint for the final mile into Kendal was a struggle, despite the footpath being clearly marked on the map. Prince Charles stayed in the residence of Mr Justice Shepheard. The house, 95 Strickland Gate, bears a plaque on the wall that reads:

> *Built in 1690, this house was owned during the Stuart rebellion of 1745 by Justice Thomas Shepheard. It was slept in by Bonnie Prince Charlie during his advance on London and again during his retreat, when his pursuer the Duke of Cumberland slept in the same bed on the following night. In an exchange of fire with the retreating army a Highlander and a local farmer were shot.*

A riverbank path led me from Natland Road in Kendal to the towpath of the Lancaster Canal. The canal generally follows the route march of the Jacobite army and so it seemed sensible for me to follow it to Preston. At Sedgwick the A590 obliterates the old waterway and I had to make a diversion over the railway line to Stainton and use a footpath along Stainton Beck back to the canal again. Unfortunately, road construction frequently interrupts continuous navigation and until a restoration project is completed boating over any distance is only possible south of Tewitfield locks. Sadly the locks are defunct at present with one pair of gates sitting forlornly on the bank. An information plaque boasts of more important days and relates that the eight locks raised the canal seventy-five feet in half a mile and operated from 1819 to 1942.

A welcome loop away from the M6 takes the canal through Borwick and over the Keer aqueduct. This single span affair, designed by John Rennie, was first used in 1797 and carries the canal thirty-five feet over the River Keer. The canal meets the M6 once again near Carnforth and continues through Bolton-le-Sands and Hest Bank before crossing the River Lune and into Lancaster.

Number 76 Church Street in Lancaster bears a commemorative disc indicating that '*Bonnie Prince Charlie lodged near here in Mrs Livesay's house. 25 November 1745.*' Edward

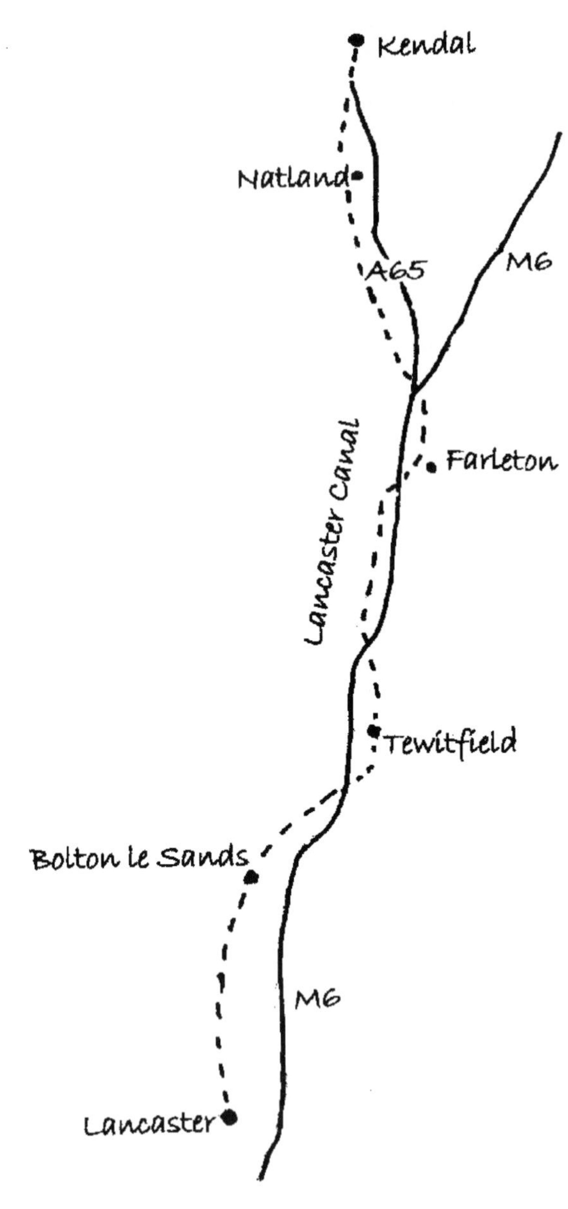

Kendal to Lancaster (23 Miles)

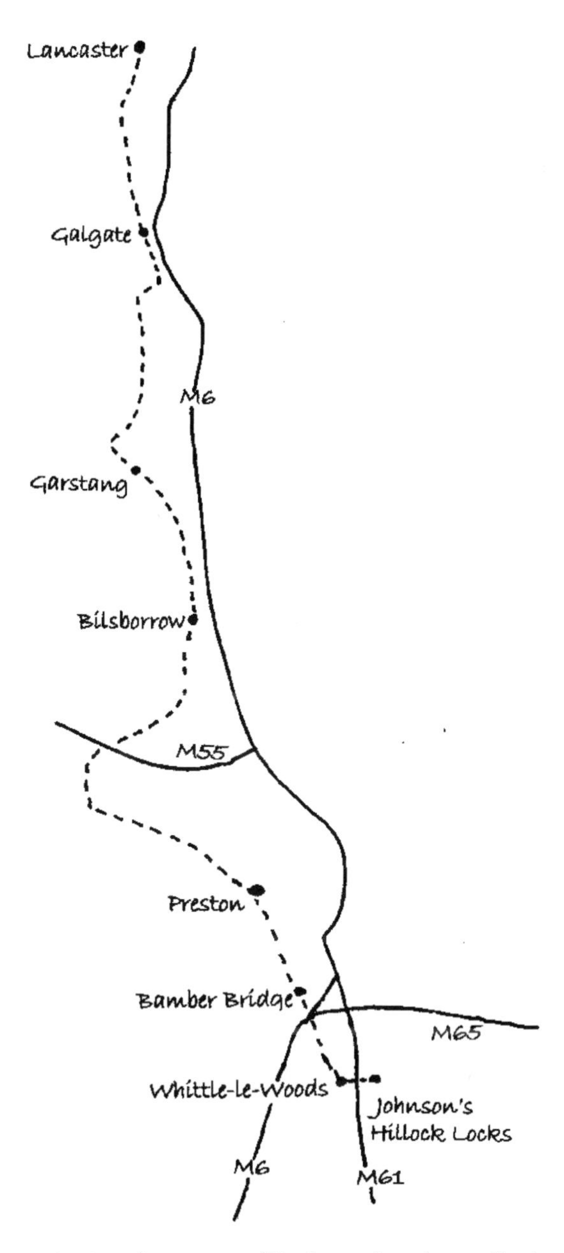

Lancaster to Johnson's Hillock Locks (33 Miles)

Marton owned number 76 in 1745 and as he became MP for Lancaster in 1747 was unlikely to have been a Jacobite. The house was probably requisitioned and it is possible that Lord George Murray and other high-ranking officers stayed there and received the Prince for dinner. It seems that Mrs Livesay's home was to the east of Marton's house. For more than a hundred years number 76 was the home of Lancaster's Conservative Club but is now occupied by a mobile phone software company. I was welcomed into the reception room and shown 'Bonnie Prince Charlie's chair', recently bought to complement the Jacobite history of the house. The chair was originally part of the furniture in Culloden House, where the Prince stayed before his final battle.

Although most communities offered no great enthusiasm for the Jacobites on their march south neither did they provide much opposition and the population of Lancaster was no exception. The marching army usually paid its way and caused little trouble. Meat came from the herds of black cattle that accompanied the army and each man carried a bag containing oatmeal for his daily sustenance. Foraging parties provided additional food and supplies and so looting was rare. The collection of Excise Tax from the towns through which the Jacobites passed provided the finance for the army and this public money was usually acquired without great objection. Tax was levied on candles, soap, leather, malt and ale as well as on victuallers and brewers. Provided receipts were obtained, most town mayors were of the opinion that they could not be compelled to pay the money again to the government in London. Many people cared little who ruled them as long they were left alone to live their usual lives.

I returned to the canal but by now a blister on my right foot was hurting. When a boat crewed by a friendly looking couple and a boy came along I smiled at them and asked for a lift. Stuart, Jane and Scott, who were being bossed about by Dino their boxer dog, kindly stopped and we spent the next couple of hours chatting, drinking beer and trying to stop Dino from jumping into the water. My feet started feeling better at once.

The canal expires without ceremony, close to the centre of

Plaque, Old Bull, Preston

Preston. There is no canal basin with offices, shops and up-market flats although there is surely great potential waiting to be fulfilled from this valuable amenity. I left the canal bank behind me and walked down Fylde Road to Fishergate in the centre of town.

Preston city centre has radically changed since the Prince's visit and Mitre Court in Straight Shambles where Charles is reputed to have lodged has long gone. The oldest inn in Preston is 'The Old Bull' on Church Street. It dates from the 1650s and in 1745 the Jacobites reputedly used the hostelry as their headquarters. From Avenham Park a footbridge crosses the river and joins a disused railway line leading to the junction of the A6 and the B5257, south of Bamber Bridge. From here I followed the Cuerden Valley Park cycle route across the A6 to a modern pedestrian bridge over the motorway. The path crosses the B5256 and continues along Back Lane. I left the cycle track and a hundred yards to the right picked up the footpath through Cuerden Valley Park. Whittle-le-Woods church was soon visible in the distance and keeping the church on my left I emerged on the A6 opposite School Brow. At the Roebuck public house at the bottom of School Brow I turned along Town Lane towards Johnson's Hillock Locks and the Leeds and Liverpool Canal. The canal was to be my companion for most of my journey to Manchester.

The Old Manor House in Bishopsgate, Wigan where the Prince is alleged to have stayed was renamed Walmesley House at some time and was demolished shortly before 1940. Changes in the street plan have done away with Bishopsgate as a thoroughfare and the name now remains only as the postal address of half a dozen buildings opposite the telephone exchange that now stands on the site of Walmesley House. The building can be found close to the entrance the bus station at the end of Hallgate. A plaque reminds readers of the Jacobites' visit.

SITE OF WALMESLEY HOUSE

Where Bonnie Prince Charlie spent the night of December 10th 1745 on the retreat from Derby of the Jacobite rebels. The Duke of Cumberland who was pursuing him spent the following night here.

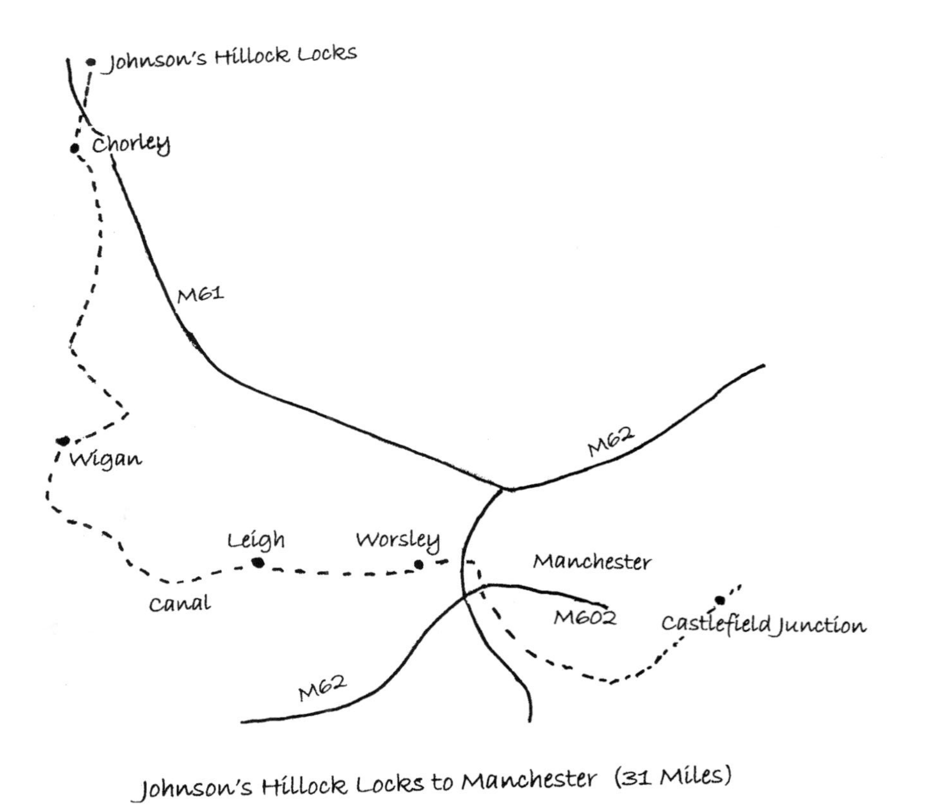

Johnson's Hillock Locks to Manchester (31 Miles)

The wording is interesting. Prince Charles and his army passed through Wigan twice, once on 28 November on their way south and again in retreat on 10 December. For the first occasion there is evidence from James Gib, who kept household accounts for the Pretender, that *'for one night at Wiggan a woman received ten guineas for the use of her house'* but as for the second, even the exhaustive efforts of W.B. Blaikie only result in him noting, *'Dec 10. Marched to Wigan.'*

The Leigh branch of the Leeds and Liverpool canal begins at Wigan and I followed it towards Manchester through a landscape radically altered by industry. The legacy of coal mining is visible everywhere. Even the earth is mixed with coal dust and where mining subsidence has happened the canal sits on an embankment above the level of its surroundings. The view becomes increasingly urbanised as the mill town of Leigh draws closer. At bridge 66, seven and a quarter miles from Wigan, the Leeds and Liverpool transforms itself into the Bridgewater Canal. Francis Egerton, third Duke of Bridgewater, began constructing the canal in 1759. The Bridgewater is wide, has no locks and was a successful enterprise last used by commercial traffic in 1974. At Barton upon Irwell the Manchester Ship Canal forces the Bridgewater into an ingenious steel trough pivoted on a small island. Both ends of the trough can be closed and the whole structure containing 800 tons of water swung parallel to the Ship Canal so that vessels are able to pass.

At Waters' Meeting I crossed bridge 90 and headed towards Manchester. The walk was interesting though not particularly pleasant. Working factories and derelict buildings line the banks and there is much evidence of urban renewal. Castlefield Junction canal basin in the city centre has been magnificently restored and is now a visual feast of Victorian architecture that blends in with new residential development.

Castlefield, Manchester

SEVEN

ADVANCING TO RETREAT

'The question for deliberation was whether we should continue to advance on London, or return to Scotland.'
Chevalier de Johnstone ~ A Memoir of the Forty-Five

The recruitment drive in Manchester had been disappointing but Prince Charles was determined to continue towards London. One piece of good news arrived in a letter from his brother Henry. King Louis XV had decided to provide more help and under the instructions of Antoine Walsh the French were to put together an invasion force of between ten and twenty thousand troops, to be ready before 20 December.

On 1 December the army forded the Mersey above Stockport. On the southern bank a number of supporters greeted the Prince. Among them was old Mrs Skyring, a fervent Jacobite, who had as a child in 1660, witnessed the return of Charles II at Dover. For years she had contributed half her income to the cause and had recently sold all her silver plate and jewellery. Mrs Skyring offered the proceeds to Charles as she was presented to him. It is said that when she heard the news of the retreat from Derby, the shock was too much for her and she passed away.

In Macclesfield the Pretender received news that most of Cumberland's army was in Lichfield in Staffordshire with some troops only seventeen miles away at Newcastle under Lyme. Neither the people nor the government were sure what the Pretender's tactics might be. Would Prince Charles march straight for London or would he advance into Wales in the hopes of finding much needed and hoped for support? According to the newspapers the people of Chester were preparing for the worst. *'Trade is absolutely at a Stop, and I believe most of the Shopkeepers will shut up very soon. The gateways are bricking up and on Monday night there will be no entrance into the City but by two small wickets, one on the bridge and the other at the East Gate.'*

Another report indicates that far from being sympathetic to the rebels, Chester would provide them with hostility and a hard fight.

> *If they come to Chester the Accommodation they will meet with will be Fire and Sword: for the Castle and the City are determined to fight it out to the last Extremity. ~ Their coming here will occasion their being so hemmed in that it will be impossible for them to get out without being destroy'd; for the Duke of Cumberland has sent us word that he will be with us in a Day or two if the City can hold out so long.*

In an attempt to outwit the Duke of Cumberland and so position the Jacobites between the government army and London, Lord George Murray sent troops to Congleton as though the Prince was marching into Wales. The subterfuge worked and the Duke marched his troops through Stafford to Stone to counter such an eventuality. This left the road south unprotected and Lord George's men rejoined the main force for the march through Leek and Ashbourne to Derby.

The first troops arrived in Derby on the morning of 4 December. Prince Charles Edward entered the town on the same evening and lodged at Lord Exeter's house on Full Street. He was now only 125 miles from London and his army had not yet suffered defeat in battle. The news that Jacobite forces were occupying Derby caused panic in London. Shopkeepers put up shutters and the Archbishop of Canterbury said special prayers for divine deliverance. It is said that a run on the Bank of England reduced it to paying out money in sixpences, heated to such a temperature they were difficult to handle. The Duke of Cumberland was ordered to supervise the defence of the capital. Volunteers were recruited, guards were posted in all the main squares and troops stationed on Finchley Common and at Highgate.

The Prince's spirits were buoyed by reports that the men and arms under the command of Lord John Drummond had disembarked from French ships at Montrose and Peterhead and were marching south. The news was received in a different light by many of the army officers. Before Drummond's arrival the commanders had seen no alternative but to comply with the Prince's wishes and somewhat unwillingly continue to press on towards London. The further they marched into England the less possibility they saw of avoiding the enemy should they turn back. The choice seemed to be victory or death on the outskirts of the capital. The news that reinforcements had arrived provided a good reason, or perhaps excuse, for withdrawal so that the two forces could amalgamate, regroup and plan for eventual victory. Charles' enthusiasm was struck a terrible blow when, on the following day, Lord George Murray suggested that such a withdrawal and consolidation was the course the army ought to take. The Prince was outraged and throughout the day an intense argument took place. Sir John MacDonald burst into the room and could not bring himself to even acknowledge Lord George. He wrote,

> *I addressed myself to Locheil, and said to him that I was much astonished that such a gallant fellow as he was, at the head of a troop of brave followers, should think of turning back. ~ that I was very sure that his Camerons like the MacDonalds would follow the Prince to London, that it was absurd to think of making such a long retreat with an undisciplined force like ours, in the face of regular troops in their own country; that if we were to perish, it were better to do so with our faces to London than to Scotland.*

Prince Charles had a few other supporters including Duke William who *'seemed much for going forward,'* and the Duke of Perth who was also in favour of pushing on. Murray of Broughton began by supporting the withdrawal but when it became clear that retreat was almost inevitable changed his mind in order to ingratiate himself with the Prince. Lord George and most of the clan chiefs were unmoved by Charles' desire to march on London. Even O'Sullivan seems to have taken against the idea of marching south with such a small army. While in Manchester he had suggested a retreat as, '*according to all the rules of War and prudence it was the only party to be taken.*'

Firstly, it was argued that the Duke of Cumberland had 12,000 men at Stafford and that General Wade was marching south with a similar number. There were tales of another large force being formed to defend London, making total government numbers of around 30,000 troops, against which the Jacobites had only 5,000. The clan chiefs argued that although the Highlanders could win a battle against Cumberland, this could not be achieved without substantial losses, leaving them in no position to march against the army supposed to be defending London.

Secondly, Captain Dudley Bradstreet provided information about the number and position of troops ranged against the rebels. He was hailed as an English Lord who had come to help the Jacobite cause and was brought before the Prince. In fact he was a government spy sent to infiltrate the Prince's camp and spread what malicious talk he could. His objective was to delay the advance of the Jacobite army by twelve hours. His tales were believed and his invention of an opposing army of some 8,000 men waiting to meet the Highlanders at Northampton in effect delayed them forever.

The final argument was that English Jacobites had provided the campaign with few men and little money and despite continuing rumours of greater French involvement, not much help had materialised from that direction either. The Highlanders had done their best but were now a long way from home and could not be persuaded to continue the march south.

Landranger Maps

109 Manchester
119 Buxton & Matlock
118 Stoke-on-Trent
128 Derby & Burton upon Trent

Marple Locks (109)	**SJ963887**
Quixhill Bridge (128)	**SK102414**
Raven's Clough Farm (118)	**SJ922637**
Osmaston Park (128)	**SK206431**
Nether Burrows (128)	**SK270393**
Markeaton Church (128)	**SK321378**

At Castlefield Junction in central Manchester I crossed the modern suspension bridge and found Duke's lock where the Rochdale Canal begins. The Rochdale was an ambitious project begun in 1794 and completed ten years later. However, the canal gradually fell into disuse and was closed in 1952 except for the short stretch of nine locks connecting the Bridgewater to the Ashton Canal in central Manchester. An ambitious restoration plan has recently been completed and the Rochdale reopened for through navigation in the summer of 2002.

Between Princess Street and Minshull Street, Canal Street replaces the towpath. The area is bustling with shops and restaurants and makes an interesting change from the usual canal bank scenery. An office building has been constructed over the canal and the whole of Piccadilly Lock is under it. Darkness reigns down here. It is remarkable experience to see and hear the water forcing its way through the gaps in the underground lock gates but I was pleased to blink my way back into the daylight at the other end. At Ducie Street bridge I left the Rochdale and began my journey on another of these great eighteenth century waterways. The Ashton Canal was opened in 1799 and was last used for commercial traffic in 1957. It was derelict by 1961 and remained useless until restoration work started in 1968. The towpath took me past the smart residential accommodation of Piccadilly Village, a fine example of rejuvenation. Next came Ancoats locks, the first three in a flight of eighteen spread out over several miles culminating at Fairfield Junction from where the surroundings gradually become more rural. The junction with the Peak Forest Canal is at Portland Basin, where the formerly industrial area has been transformed into an attractive place to live and visit.

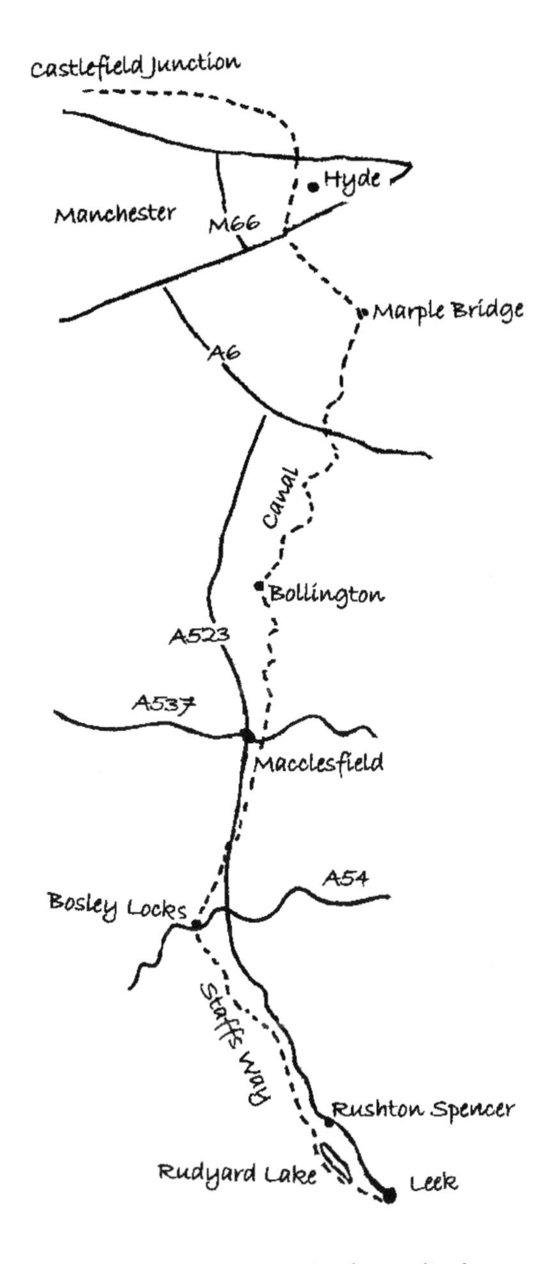

Manchester to Leek (35 Miles)

The Peak Forest runs high above the dashing River Tame, along a rural corridor between Denton and Hyde. The canal reaches Woodley tunnel and the light that can be seen at the far end produces the impression that it is quite short. This is an illusion. The tunnel is 176 yards long and the middle so dark it was impossible to see the ground. I had no flashlight to help me and although the towpath was mostly dry and not slippery I was pleased to find a handrail to help steady my footsteps until I emerged thankfully into the sunlight again. I had not walked much farther when another tunnel entrance loomed in front of me. After my disconcerting experience at Woodley I was pleased to note that the footpath is alongside Hyde Bank tunnel, as it has no towpath through its 308 yards of darkness. In the days of horsepower the animals were unshackled from the narrowboats and the boatmen progressed from one end to the other by using their feet against the tunnel sides and 'legging' the boats through. The three-arched Marple aqueduct carries the canal a hundred feet above the River Goyt and brought me to the sixteen-lock Marple flight, not built until 1804, four years after the rest of the canal was opened. £27,000 was needed to build the locks and until the money was raised, cargo had to be laboriously transported between the two levels of the canal by horse and cart.

I found the Macclesfield canal at the top of the Marple flight and all that was required of me for the next seventeen miles or so was to follow it. Macclesfield still has elegant Georgian buildings that reflect the town's past glories in the silk industry. Prince Charles stayed in Jordangate, in the centre of town. The house was later occupied by the Duke of Cumberland and subsequently named after him. The building is currently used a health centre.

Two hundred yards past the last lock of twelve at Bosley an aqueduct carries the water over the River Dane and at the next bridge I forsook the canal in favour of a river leading to the road and Cloud House. In another mile I arrived at Raven's Clough Farm on the Staffordshire Way. This footpath was to be my companion for the next twenty-three miles. Shortly after passing Raven's Clough the track follows a disused railway line to Rushton Spencer and the northern end of Rudyard Lake. The lake is artificial and was constructed in order to feed the Caldon Canal. Its main claim to fame is in the naming of one of Britain's best-known authors. Mr and Mrs John Kipling visited the lake before the birth of their son and were so taken with its beauty they named him after it. It's true, honest!

The path stays to the right of the lake and passes Cliffe Park House near the Hotel Rudyard. I walked down to the dam at the end of the lake and entered Longsdon Wood Nature Reserve. Near the end of the parkland I turned right into fields and emerged on the A53 Leek to Stoke-on-Trent main road at Longsdon. A detour from the Staffordshire Way took me into the centre of Leek where tradition has it that Prince Charles stayed in Mr Mills' house on the north side of the Market Place. The building still exists as 2-4 Church Street and the ground floor is used as a shop. Contemporary accounts describe the main part of the Jacobite army as a sorry looking band of men. *'The greater part were such poor, shabby, lousey, diminutive creatures. Grey beards and no beards; old men fit to drop into the grave, and young boys whose swords were nearly equal to their own weight.'* The sight of soldiers dressed in kilts seems to have been the cause of some confusion if not amusement and derision; one observer describing the Highlanders as *'men with petticoats on.'*

Once back on the Staffordshire Way at Longsdon I walked along Mollats Wood Road to Wood Road at Horse Bridge. Once over the Leek arm canal bridge I picked up the towpath of the Caldon Canal to Oakmeadow Ford Lock and then Consallforge, a place that was once the site of a mighty water-powered iron works. A little further on is Cherryeye Bridge, taking its name from the inflamed eyes of the industrial workmen who used to cross it. Shortly the Staffordshire Way leaves the canal and heads off to the short squat tower of St. Werburgh's church in Kingsley. Some way further is Hawksmoor nature reserve and I left these woods on Oakamoor Road following the route to the Rambler's Retreat Café and from there to Alton.

In Alton I walked along Malthouse Road towards the Wild Duck Inn and St Peter's church to Town Head and the beginning of Back Lane. Fields lead to Saltersford Lane and I enjoyed an easy ramble along this wide, green road for about three quarters of a mile. The waymarks brought me to the B5032 near Denstone and then Quixhill Bridge where the Staffordshire Way parts company with the direction of the Prince's route. The Way turns right to Rocester but I continued into Ellastone and down Dove Street towards Norbury and the farm road to Calwich Abbey.

After a mile and a half a path led me to a weir on the River Dove. I followed the river for a while and then headed for Mayfield, a village certainly visited by the Jacobite army in retreat and probably on the way south as well. John Maclean of Kingairloch notes that his brigade was '*billeted in a Countrey place Called upper Mayfield in a Nook of Staffordshire.*' The guide to Mayfield's St John the Baptist Parish Church comments that as the Jacobites passed through they shot a local innkeeper and Mr Humphrey Brown who refused to hand over his horse. Some of the terrified population took refuge in the church and although the rebels did not break down the church door they did fire a number of shots at it. The bullet holes in the west door are still visible. From Mayfield I found my way to St Oswald's hospital in Ashbourne and then along Belle Vue Road to the centre of town. A plaque on the Town Hall reads, *'At Ashbourne on December 3rd 1745 Charles Edward Stuart declared his father James, King of England, Wales and Scotland.'*

Ashbourne Hall is in the centre of the town on Cokayne Avenue but has been significantly altered since Jacobite days. One half of the building has a modern, ugly, rendered addition to the front and is currently being used as the town's library. Fortunately the other half is rather more elegant and is used as a restaurant. In 1995 the Ramblers' Association developed an eighteen-mile waymarked walk from Ashbourne to Derby to celebrate their sixtieth birthday and commemorate the 250th anniversary of the Jacobite advance. It begins at the Market Cross and, then using St. John's Street and Church Street, heads south-east to Osmaston. Other villages on the route

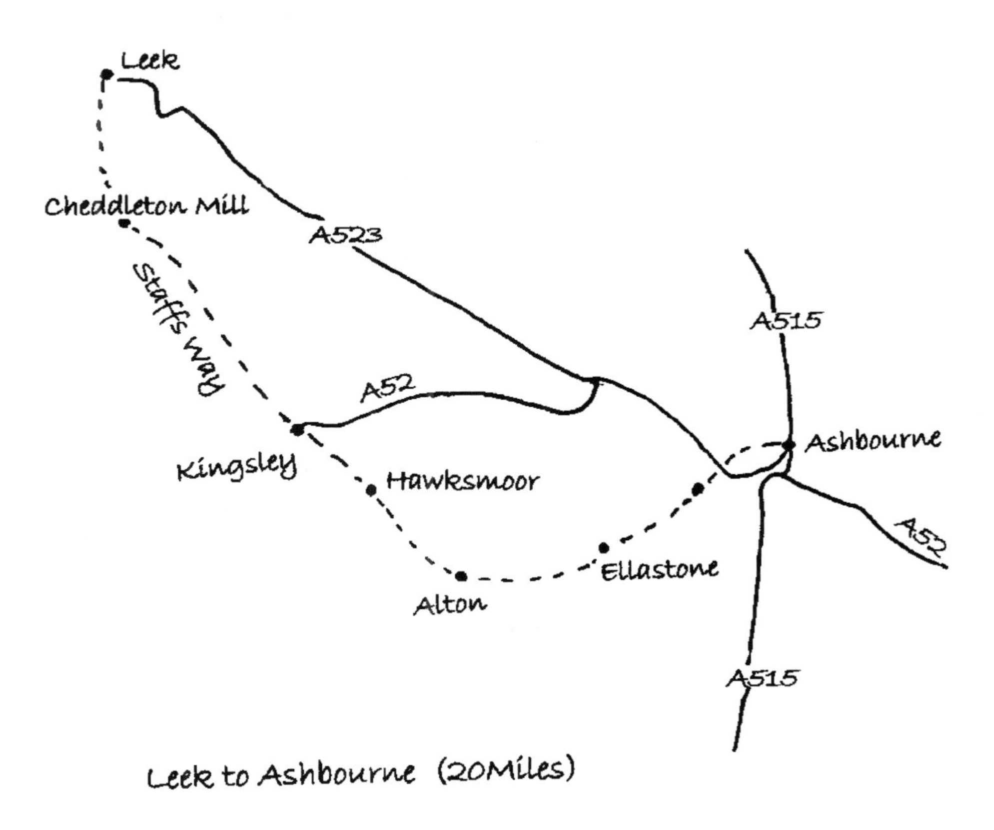
Leek
Cheddleton Mill
A523
Staffs Way
A515
A52
Kingsley
Hawksmoor
Ashbourne
A52
Ellastone
Alton
A515
Leek to Ashbourne (20Miles)

are Shirley, Longford, Osleton, Radbourne and Mackworth. The path follows the general direction of Prince Charlie's army but, useful as its waymarks may be, I declined to follow it in its entirety. The journal of John Maclean of Kingairloch mentions Mackworth and Brailsford on his route from Ashbourne to Derby.

Wednesday the 4 December we marched from Ashburn & passed through Brilsford a Countrey Long Town and at severall houses we saw White flags hanging out Such as Napkins and white Aprons, and in the Gavels of Some houses white Cockades fixed. After that we passed ane other town called Macwith and they had a Bonefire in the Middle of the Town, and as oft as a Captain of a Company passed by the Whole Croud of the town who were gathered about that fire Gave a huza and the men waving their hats.

The commemorative walk goes through Mackworth but regrettably not Brailsford. I followed the walk as far as Shirley and then, managing to resist the temptations of the Saracen's Head, journeyed east using Derby Lane and a footpath past Ednaston Hall to the Yew Tree Inn. My path crossed Brailsford Brook to the square tower of the isolated church of Brailsford Green. From Brailsford there are many footpaths leading towards Derby but I chose the minor roads, footpaths and tracks through Over Burrows, Nether Burrows and Langley Common to Mackworth with Markeaton Church where I rejoined the official path for the remainder of the journey into Derby.

The Derby Mercury of December 12, 1745 provides us with a description of the Jacobites' arrival in town.

The next morning (Wednesday) about eleven o'clock, two of the rebels' van-guard rode into the town, and at their entrance gave a specimen of what we were to expect from such villains, by seizing a very good horse, belonging to young Mr. Stamford; after which, they rode up to the George, and there inquiring for the magistrates, demanded billets for 9,000 men or more. In a short time after the van-guard rode into town, consisting of about thirty men, clothed in blue, faced with red, most of 'em had a scarlet waistcoat with gold lace, and being likely men, made a good appearance. They were drawn up in the market-place, and sat on horse-back two or three hours: at the same time the bells were rung, and several bonfires made, to prevent any resentment from 'em that might ensue on our showing our dislike to their coming among us. About three in the afternoon Lord Elcho, with the life-guards, and many of their chiefs, also arrived on horseback, to the number of about one hundred and fifty, most of them clothed as above; these made a fine show, being the flower of their army. Soon after their main body marched into the town in tolerable order, six or eight abreast, with about eight standards, most of them white flags ands a red cross. They had several bag-pipers, who played as they marched along; and appeared in general to answer the description we have long had of them: viz't. most of their main body a parcel of shabby, pitiful looking fellows, mixed up with old men and boys; dress'd in dirty plaids, and as dirty shirts, without breeches, and wore their stockings made of plaid, not much above half way up their legs, and some without shoes, or next to none, and numbers of them so fatigued with their long march, that they really commanded our pity rather than our fear.

Exeter House, where Prince Charles set up his headquarters, was demolished in 1854 and the site is now occupied by a police station. Fortunately the oak panelling from the house was saved and stored in the cellars of the Derby Assembly rooms. In 1879 the panelling was used to line the walls of a room in what is now the Museum and Art Gallery. The 'Bonnie Prince Charlie' room was opened in 1995 to mark the 250th anniversary of the Prince's arrival in the city and contains several period pieces including the iron

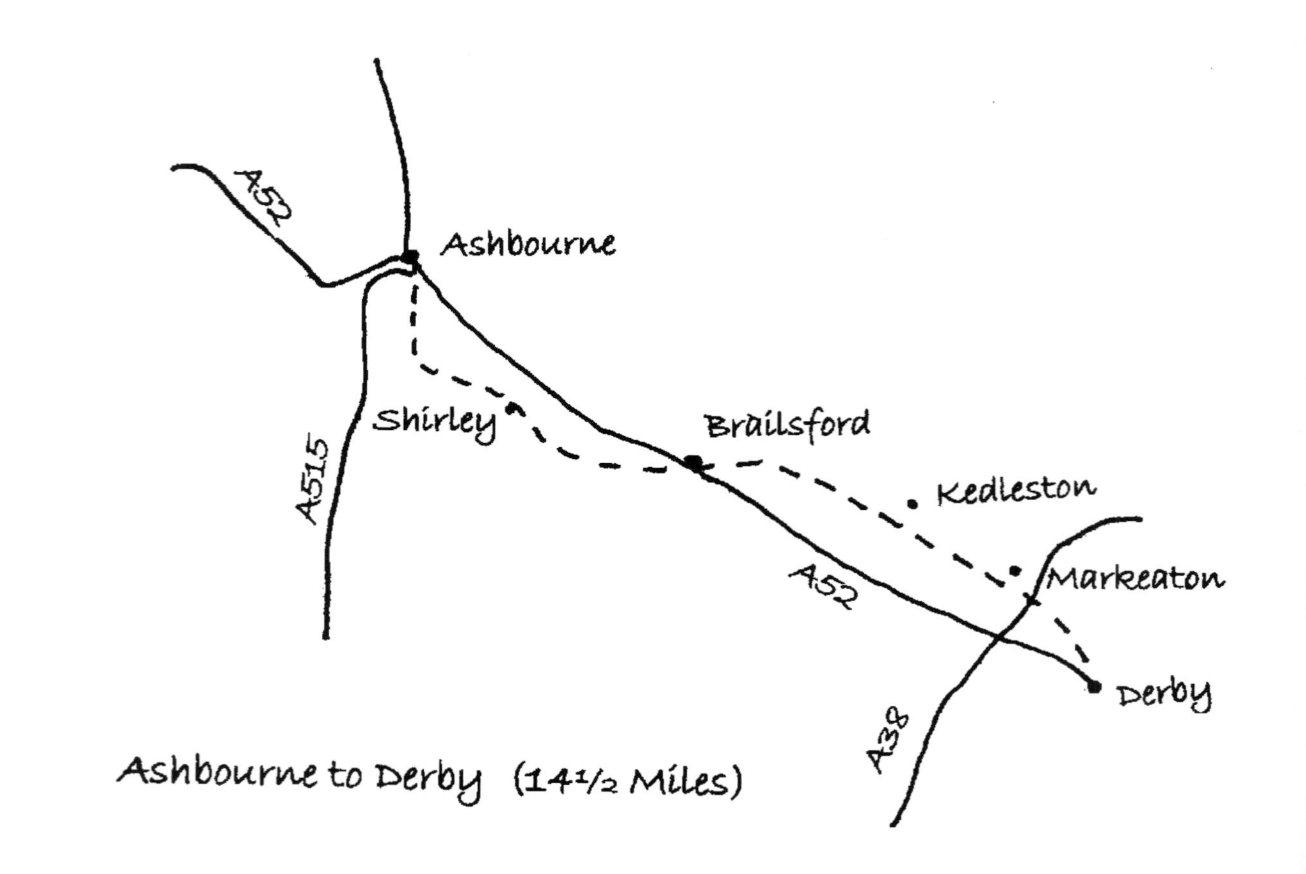

Ashbourne to Derby (14 1/2 Miles)

Armada chest with its seven-way lock in which the Prince kept money. There is a display of medals struck to commemorate the rising, a letter from Edinburgh dated 22 October written by the Prince to his father addressed simply *'To the King'* and several contemporary newspaper articles commenting on the occupation of Derby. The city boasts the only statue (picture p32) of Bonnie Prince Charlie in the world. The Prince is on horseback and the statue is just off Irongate, behind the cathedral at the end of the appropriately named Amen Alley. Irongate boasts the eighteenth century public house, called 'The George' at the time, where Jacobite troops were billeted. The Crewe and Harpur Arms at the northern end of Swarkestone Bridge, six miles from Derby, has a cairn in the garden marking the Jacobite army's furthest point south.

What might have happened had the Jacobites decided not to retreat but to continue their march south? They were heavily outnumbered, hundreds of miles from home and had concluded that additional help was unlikely. On the other hand they had been so far successful by a mixture of luck, good decision-making and government incompetence. Perhaps they had been too successful. If the rebels had ever been in serious difficulty, Lord Barrymore, Sir Watkin Williams-Wynne and other supporters in England and Wales might have come to their aid with more than merely promises.

General Wade's army was slow moving and Charles' forces had already outwitted it several times. The eighteen-stone Duke of Cumberland had proved to be a poor commander in encounters against the French and there was no reason to believe he would do better against the Jacobites. It is arguable that the rebel army, having come so far, should have taken the ultimate risk and marched on London. However, in order to achieve a Stuart restoration to the throne several events needed to happen quickly. The rebels had to out-manoeuvre Cumberland again and reach London before needing to fight. Scouting parties had to establish that the supposed army waiting at Northampton was fictitious. The ragbag of hastily trained volunteers defending London had to run away, be defeated or come over to the Jacobite side. Finally there needed to be swift action by the French to reinforce the Jacobite army. If Charles had entered London it is just possible that English Jacobites would have rallied to a winning side and installed Charles as Prince Regent. What would the Hanoverian armies have done then? The whole course of British history could have moved onto a different tack. On the other hand Britain was prosperous and although the Hanoverian line was not English, neither was the Stuart. Many people had no great interest in who ruled the country and the Stuarts had not been the luckiest of dynasties. The British were intermittently at war with the French who actively pursued their interests in the War of Austrian Succession throughout the Forty-Five. How the majority of the British people would have reacted to the French enemy putting ashore thousands of troops in an attempt to remove the incumbent king was something we shall never know.

EIGHT

WITHDRAWAL TO SCOTLAND

'The Prince's Council judged it more proper to retire back into Scotland without risking a battle, and there to await the arrival of foreign Succors.'
John Daniel's Progress with Prince Charles ~
Origins of the Forty-Five

As expected, Prince Charles was totally opposed to the idea of retreat and said, *'Rather than go back, I would wish to be dead and buried twenty feet underground.'* However, on this occasion he could not change a sufficient number of minds and on 6 December the Highlanders began the march north. The significance of the withdrawal was not lost on Sir Thomas Sheridan who was heard to remark, *'All is over. We shall never come this way again.'* The Prince spent the first night of the bitterly disappointing withdrawal at Ashbourne Hall and the next day the army continued the march back to Scotland following the route they had so recently taken south. It was at Ashbourne where lawyer David Morgan deserted. He was a bitterly disappointed man. Morgan had enlisted in a flush of enthusiastic fervour with William Vaughan at Preston, eleven days before on 26 November. The withdrawal from Derby made Morgan see the escapade in an entirely different light. *'Damn me Vaughan',* he said, '*they are going to Scotland..' 'Wherever they go',* Vaughan replied, *'I am determined, now that I have joined them, to go along with them.'* Morgan was not to be persuaded, saying, *'By God, I had rather be hanged than go to Scotland to starve.'* His wish was granted as the Staffordshire militia captured him almost at once. He was executed in London on 30 July 1746. An eyewitness described the return of the Jacobite army to Ashbourne at the beginning of the withdrawal.

> *On the following Friday, the whole body returned to Ashbourn (which put the inhabitants in the utmost confusion.) They stayed all night; and on Saturday morning, to our great joy, they marched towards Leek. The Prince and his retinue, quartered at Ashbourn Hall, on their return from Derby. There were many fine men among them, (especially in the vanguard,) which had a very fine appearance. They had with them fifteen field pieces, each about three inches diameter, and about fifty covered carts, containing ammunition &c. As the rebels went through, they behaved better than was expected; but as they came back, they were insolent and impudent.*

In retreat the Jacobites found that the population was not so pleased to see them and instead of cheering crowds and pealing bells they were greeted with disdain, anger and stone throwing. John Daniel thought the enemy were circulating a story that the rebels had been defeated and commented, '*This report was believed in many of the towns: great rejoicings were made, and every man thought himself capable of knocking out a Rebel's brains with a club or staff. Then you might see heroic valour displayed among cocks that never crowed but among hens upon their own dunghill.'* Charles was anxious that the withdrawal should not turn into headlong flight and hence a stop for a day was made at Preston. Dudley Bradstreet, the Hanoverian spy, was still with the army and had sufficiently ingratiated himself for Murray of Broughton to send him south to report upon the movement of the enemy armies. He did not return.

The Jacobites reached Lancaster on 13 December and once again Prince Charles ordered a halt to show his enemies that he *'was retiring and not flying.'* General Wade and the Duke of Cumberland were closing in, prompting Lord George Murray and Colonel O'Sullivan to find a suitable battlefield south of the town should fighting become inevitable. The conflict never happened as Charles changed his mind the next day and decided to march on. Unknown to the Prince, the Duke of Cumberland was distracted from the chase by an urgent message that French forces were about to sail from Dunkirk. Cumberland was required to march south with the majority of his troops in order to defend the capital. Scarcely had this message been received when another arrived, proclaiming the first to be a false alarm. The French invasion fixed for 15 December had been postponed after considering the strength of the Royal Navy and news of the Jacobite withdrawal from Derby. The Duke renewed his pursuit of the rebels who had taken advantage of the confusion to gain a twenty-four hour advantage. Charles arrived in Kendal on 15 December with the enemy in hot pursuit. In contrast to the Jacobites' trouble free southbound march through Kendal, skirmishes occurred in Finkle Street and Highgate and it was clear the Jacobites were unwelcome.

Bad weather had turned the road to mud and the journey north was difficult. The Prince had ordered that neither artillery nor ammunition should be abandoned and so progress was extremely slow. Despite his objections Lord George Murray found himself responsible for the artillery and hence the difficult task of dragging the cannon over Shap Fell. Infirmity amongst the horses and breakdowns of the wagons carrying the baggage and ammunition reduced Lord George to offering sixpence to each man prepared to carry a cannon ball the four or five miles over the pass. The front of the column soon left Lord George's men behind and he decided that his troops should spend the night in Shap village about twelve miles from Penrith. The next day, 18 December, as Lord George arrived in Clifton, he encountered a troop of government cavalry. In the subsequent skirmish the government dragoons were beaten and driven off by the ferocity of Lord George's men. The Duke of Cumberland lost forty or fifty dead and wounded and five Highlanders were killed.

The Jacobite army straggled into Carlisle and despite the advice of almost everyone the Prince determined to keep the town as a foothold in England as he was sure he would return. Colonel

O'Sullivan agreed, *'Some people were for leaving no garrison at all, wch wou'd be the most unreasonable thing in the world.'* Francis Townley's Manchester Regiment, and two hundred Highlanders commanded by Colonel John Hamilton were left as a garrison. Most of the artillery that Lord George had so laboriously dragged over the atrocious roads was left in Carlisle to help in what proved to be an act of self-delusion on the part of the Prince. Defending the castle for any length of time was impossible as the Jacobites had demonstrated on the way south. Charles really had no idea when or even if he would return to Carlisle and so left the garrison to their fate. The Chevalier de Johnstone is in no doubt when he comments, *'We must draw a veil over this piece of cruelty, being altogether unable to discover the motive for leaving these four hundred men at Carlisle, or to find an excuse for it.'*

On Charles' birthday, 20 December, the army crossed the Esk at Longtown. John Daniel provides a vivid account of the conditions and although the army crossed successfully considers himself lucky not to have drowned.

> *The deepness and rapidity of the river, joined to the obscurity of the night, made it most terrible: but the good Prince, here, in particular, animated the men; and how noble it was to see these Champions, who had refused him nothing now marching breast-deep, one supporting another, till wonderfully we all passed safe. ~ But at this river I narrowly escaped drowning; for in crossing it, and being very near the middle of the stream I perceived two women (tho' never was an army known with so few) rolling down it and in imminent danger of perishing if I did not guide my horse in order to stop them.*

Once safely over the river, six battalions under Lord George marched by Ecclefechan, Lockerbie, Moffat, Douglas and Hamilton to Glasgow. The remainder, under the command of the Prince, followed by way of Annan and Dumfries. On 22 December the Prince stayed at Drumlanrig Castle as the unwelcome guest of the Duke of Queensberry. During the Jacobites' stay they defaced portraits of William of Orange and did a considerable amount of other damage. After leaving Drumlanrig the Prince marched up Nithsdale and over the Mennock Pass through Leadhills to Douglas Castle where he halted for the night of 23 December.

Letting Lord George carry on to take possession of Glasgow the Prince spent Christmas Eve and Christmas Day shooting at Hamilton Palace and at the beginning of January Charles entered a largely undefended city and reviewed his army on Glasgow Green. Charles remained in the city for ten days, staying in the Trongate at Mr Glassford's residence, Shawfield House. The Jacobites were not popular in Glasgow and persuading the population to provide food, arms and clothing was difficult. Many Highlanders resented the attitude of the city and wanted to treat it and its citizens harshly. The personal influence of Lochiel prevented the looting that might otherwise have occurred and so began a tradition that whenever the Chief of Clan Cameron visits Glasgow the bells are rung in recognition of this act of compassion. During the Prince's stay in Glasgow he received the news that Carlisle had fallen to the Duke of Cumberland on 30 December. The garrison was taken prisoner and many of the soldiers paid the price of supporting the Jacobite cause with their lives. Francis Townley was executed on Kennington Common, London on 30 July 1746. He was thirty-eight years old.

By 3 January the Jacobite army had been re-equipped. Prince Charles marched towards Stirling, buoyed by the thought that he was back in friendly territory where he could look forward to more support. The army marched through Kilsyth to Bannockburn, where Charles stayed at Bannockburn House as the guest of Sir Hugh Paterson. The Prince had a bad cold and was nursed by Sir Hugh's niece, Clementine Walkinshaw, who was named after Charles' mother. Years later this young woman became Charles' mistress and it is just possible that a sexual relationship developed between them at Bannockburn. However, no direct evidence exists to substantiate the idea and throughout the campaign Charles showed no inclination to take sexual advantage of his position.

Recent recruits had strengthened the army and now Charles had 9,000 men under his command. His next objective was to take the town and castle of Stirling. On the evening of 5 January a drummer was sent to demand a surrender. The town was surrounded and defended by only 500 badly trained men and so offered itself to the Prince's mercy three days later. Major General William Blakeney who commanded the castle garrison had no intention of capitulating and hence the Prince's army laid siege, apparently without much thought as to the castle's strategic importance. Monsieur Mirabel de Gordon, sometimes called The Marquis de Mirabelle, was put in charge as he came to the Prince with a reputation of being one of the finest engineers in France. It was soon discovered, *'that his knowledge as an engineer was extremely limited, and that he was totally destitute of judgement, discernment and common sense.'* Colonel O'Sullivan describes him as, *'a headstrong ignorant fellow that wou'd go on his own way, and follow no mans advise.'* Mirabelle sited his gun batteries in ineffectual positions, with the result that the castle remained in government hands and the rebels wasted several weeks to no useful purpose.

Desertion was still occurring and morale was low. Charles began to increasingly rely on advice from a select number of favoured people, to the point that the clan chiefs became worried. Lord George presented the Prince with a letter outlining the major concerns, including specific criticism of the disastrous decision to leave a garrison at Carlisle. *'Had a Council of War been consulted as to leaving a garrison at Carlisle, it would never have been agreed to, the place not being tenable, and so many brave men wou'd not have been sacrificed, besides the reputation of His Royal Highness's arms.'* The letter also requested that Councils of War comprised of all the leaders should take future decisions. The Prince was affronted and his reply indicated that he did not intend to fight the campaign by committee. *'When I came to Scotland, I knew well enough what I was to expect from my Enemies, but I Little foresaw what I meet with from my Friends. I came vested with all the Authority the*

King could give me, one chief part of which is the Command of his Armies, and now I am required to give this up to fifteen persons.' Prince Charles reserved for himself the final right to take or countermand decisions and ended his letter by saying, '*I ~ shall only tell you that my authority may be taken from me by violence, but I shall never resign it like an ideot.'* The resentment shown in this exchange of letters is illustrative of the deteriorating relationship between the Prince and many of his officers since the withdrawal from Derby. The problems would not be resolved satisfactorily and proved deleterious to the remainder of the campaign.

General Wade retired from military service during the siege of Stirling Castle. He was replaced by Lieutenant-General Henry Hawley who was rumoured to be the illegitimate son of George I and had a reputation for cruelty. Hawley at once moved troops from Newcastle towards Edinburgh in anticipation of a Jacobite attack on the city that was once again in government hands.

The rebel army was now in two groups, one under the command of the Prince at Bannockburn and the other with Lord George Murray at Falkirk, nine miles away. Having heard that government supplies were being accumulated at Linlithgow Lord George moved south in an attempt to destroy them. The venture proved unsuccessful and, after returning to Falkirk, the troops joined the Prince at Bannockburn the following day.

Hawley reached Edinburgh on 6 January and re-equipped his army. Nine days later he marched on Stirling with the primary intention of lifting the siege of the castle. On the way the Royal army camped in a field a little to the west of Falkirk. Only a few miles now separated the opposing armies and the Jacobites took the view that they were in imminent danger of attack. After some manoeuvring they took up a position on Plean Muir, south-east of Bannockburn but the attack never came. Lord George suggested that rather than wait they should take the initiative and accordingly moved off to confront the government positions.

The Battle of Falkirk took place on 17 January. Both sides mustered about 8,000 troops, as the Jacobites had decided to leave

1,000 men laying siege to Stirling Castle. Both armies possessed some artillery, although this played little part in the battle as most of the guns did not make it to the battlefield before the conflict was over. General Hawley spent the night before the battle at Callendar House, where Lady Kilmarnock, whose husband commanded a troop of Jacobite cavalry, entertained him. Hawley was an arrogant man and had no great belief in the Jacobite army's ability to fight. The bravery of the Highland clans he recognised and perhaps respected but described the rest, in words he would soon regret, as *'lowlanders and arrant scum'* and *'the most despicable Enimy that are.'*

The Prince's army crossed the River Carron and made for the top of Falkirk Hill. On the right of the front line were the MacDonald regiments and on the left the Stewarts of Appin and Cameron regiments. Macphersons, Mackenzies, Mackintoshes, Frasers and Farquharsons occupied the centre ground. In the second line stood the Atholl Brigades and the regiments of Lords Lewis Gordon, Drummond and Ogilvy.

The Hanoverian forces marched up Falkirk Hill using the road known as Maggie Wood's Loan. The cavalry arrived at the top first and were slowly followed by the infantry and then the artillery. Colonel Francis Ligonier led the cavalry and his brother General Sir John Ligonier, commanded an infantry regiment. Price's, Cholmondley's, Wolfe's and Pulteney's regiments made up the remainder of the front line. Behind them were Barel's, Battereau's, Fleming's, Munro's and Blakeney's with Howard's Old Buffs further back in reserve.

By the time the armies were within range of each other the light was failing, as it was 4 p.m. and pouring with rain. General Hawley was becoming impatient and rashly ordered Ligonier's dragoons to attack. Lord George Murray who commanded the MacDonalds on the right flank waited until his enemy was no more than ten yards away before giving the order to fire. The musket volley tore into the cavalry charge and stopped it in its tracks with perhaps eighty troopers falling dead and many of the rest fleeing in disarray. Having successfully repelled the charge the MacDonalds were ordered to stand their ground but could not be prevented from

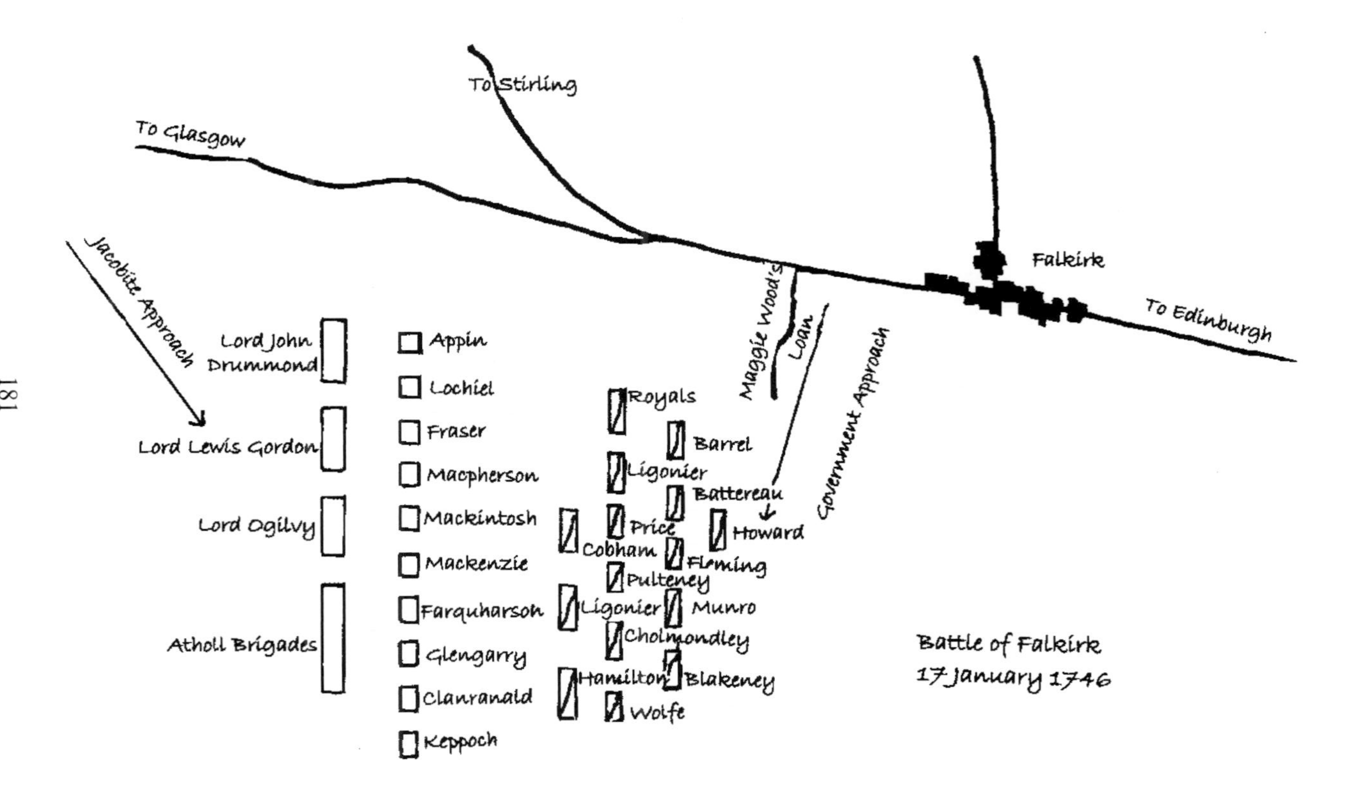

To Stirling
To Glasgow
Falkirk
To Edinburgh
Jacobite Approach
Maggie Wood's
Loan
Government Approach
Lord John Drummond
Lord Lewis Gordon
Lord Ogilvy
Atholl Brigades
Appin
Lochiel
Fraser
Macpherson
Mackintosh
Mackenzie
Farquharson
Glengarry
Clanranald
Keppoch
Royals
Barrel
Ligonier
Battereau
Price
Howard
Cobham
Fleming
Pulteney
Ligonier
Munro
Cholmondley
Hamilton
Blakeney
Wolfe
Battle of Falkirk
17 January 1746

chasing the fleeing dragoons. For these Highlanders at least, the battle appeared to be won. On the left of the line the situation was a little different. No one seemed to be in overall command, although some assumed that Lord John Drummond, who was unfortunately not present when the fighting began, had that responsibility. Lack of decisive action allowed some government dragoons to rally and ride back up the hill to outflank the Jacobite left and perhaps even capture Prince Charles. Fortunately for the Prince, the left of the line at last received some orders and successfully drove the enemy back.

The battle was over and had lasted no more than twenty minutes. It ended in victory for the Prince, with fewer than fifty of his men killed. Several hundred of Hawley's soldiers were killed, wounded or taken prisoner. The Jacobite army profited from a huge amount of abandoned equipment. Tents, muskets, cannon and gunpowder were carried away. Only one rebel soldier was captured. Major MacDonald of Tiendrish mistook enemy troops for Lord John Drummond's regiment and was taken prisoner. He ended his days at the end of the hangman's noose in Carlisle on Saturday, 18 October 1746.

Despite success, the Jacobites could not look upon the victory without some regret. The Prince's army was now scattered over the surrounding countryside, with the men more intent on looting than returning to camp. Much discussion took place regarding what to do next. Some were for pursuing the fleeing redcoats and perhaps retaking Edinburgh. Others, including Prince Charles were for continuing the siege of Stirling Castle. The unfolding story can be told no better than in the words of the Chevalier de Johnstone.

> *The friends of the Prince exhorted him to repair with all haste to the capital, to disperse this wreck of an English army and resume possession of that city. This in the opinion of everyone, was the only sensible course which the Prince could adopt, but it was soon seen that it is much easier to gain a victory than to know how to profit by it. The gaining a battle is very often the effect of pure chance, but to reap*

all the advantages of which a victory is susceptible, requires genius, capacity, and superior talents, and it is in turning a victory to account that we particularly discover the great soldier. ~ On the 19th, when the weather became favourable, it was natural to think we should take the road to Edinburgh. But ~ what fatal blindness! ~ instead of pursuing a vanquished and routed enemy, the Prince resolved to return to Bannockburn to continue the siege of Stirling Castle. This determination was the result of a consultation with Monsieur Mirabelle, the senseless individual already mentioned, who promised to reduce it in the course of forty-eight hours. The possession of this petty fort was of no essential importance to us; on the contrary, it was of more advantage to us that it should remain in the hands of the enemy, in order to restrain the Highlanders, and prevent them from returning, when they pleased, to their own country, for, whenever they got possession of any booty taken from the English, they were constantly going home to secure it.

London was placed into further worry with the news of another lost battle, even though it was against recent evidence of Jacobite retreat. Hawley was relieved of command and replaced by His Royal Highness, The Duke of Cumberland. Hawley was not pleased at having command taken away and took his revenge in the aftermath of the Battle of Culloden later in the year.

LANDRANGER MAPS

85 Carlisle & Solway Firth
71 Lanark & Upper Nithsdale
84 Dumfries & Castle Douglas
64 Glasgow
78 Nithsdale & Annandale
65 Falkirk & Linlithgow

Nivenhill Farm (85)	**NY283664**
Priest's Pool (71)	**NS863199**
Portrack House (78)	**NX939829**
Douglas West (71)	**NS821310**
Keir Mill (78)	**NX860931**
Canderside Toll (64)	**NS769483**
Drumlanrig Castle (78)	**NX851993**
Kilsyth (64)	**NS736774**
Meadowfoot (71)	**NS864137**
Battle of Falkirk (65)	**NS874791**

What can the Prince's men have thought of the retreat from Derby? They were certainly apprehensive about marching on London and many would have been happy to remain in Scotland. Some had no interest in the campaign at all and were only there out of loyalty to their clan chief. Everyone was deeply disappointed in the lack of response from their English friends and the French. The march south had been long, cold and arduous but they had come through with flying colours and morale was undoubtedly high as the army entered Derby. The Chevalier de Johnstone wrote that the Highlanders were *'animated, on that occasion, to the highest pitch of enthusiasm and breathing nothing but a desire for the combat. They were to be seen, during the whole day, in crowds before the shops of cutlers, quarrelling about who should be the first to sharpen and give a proper edge to his sword.'* To turn tail and run without being defeated in battle was not their style. However, the withdrawal was never planned to be a short tactical manoeuvre but was intended to take the army all the way back to Scotland. No matter what reasons are given it is difficult to see the withdrawal as anything but a full-scale retreat. The chances of further recruitment from England and Wales were shattered by the decision. The British government took heart and as Horace Walpole succinctly put it, *'No one is afraid of a rebellion that runs away.'*

The prime mover for turning back was Lord George Murray

who is usually depicted as the Prince's most able commander. Prince Charles, who supposedly had ultimate authority, was first amongst those few who were all for pressing on. Who was right? The short answer is that we shall never know. Support for the rising had not materialised in the manner required for a successful Stuart restoration and the Jacobite army found itself stranded in the middle of England, unsure of what course to take next. Lord George had concluded that pressing on meant certain destruction. He was the man to whom the clan chiefs looked for leadership. If George Murray said withdrawal was the only sensible option then so be it. In coming to his decision Murray must have known that although there was a chance of building a new campaign after a period of consolidation in Scotland the prospects were not good. He cannot possibly have imagined that the British army would allow the men to melt back into the glens for the winter only to rise again the following year. In retreating Lord George knew that the game was up but had no choice but to soldier on.

The Young Pretender could not believe what was happening. Retreat, after all the hardships his brave Highlanders had gone through, was unthinkable. Prince Charles truly believed his cause was just and in Derby he still believed he was infallible. If only his army would march south the people of England would rise up and smite the Elector of Hanover and the French would send ships full of arms and men when they saw a Stuart Prince in London. The possibility of defeat never entered his head.

I was able to sympathise with the Jacobite army as I stood on Swarkestone Bridge (picture p32) and contemplated my own journey north. Fortunately for my feet, the march back to Carlisle covered the same ground as the southbound journey and so I drove. On the way I stopped in Clifton, a couple of miles south of Penrith. There is a memorial stone just inside the church gate '*in memory of the troopers of Bland's regiment who lie here, killed at Clifton Moor 1745.*' A stone in the village centre commemorates the skirmish and on 18 December 1995 the Earl of Lonsdale planted a tree in the adjoining field to mark the 250th anniversary of the battle that was the last to be fought on English soil. An almost forgotten and somewhat neglected memorial marks the grave of the Highlanders killed on that day. The small headstone is in a fenced triangular enclosure under an old, bent and knotted tree on the right-hand side of a track running towards the railway line from the George and Dragon inn. *'Here lie buried the men of the army of Prince Charles who fell at Clifton Moor 18 December 1745.'*

It is difficult to follow the Prince's route all the way from Carlisle to Dumfries on footpaths and so I travelled to Gretna by car. At Nivenhill Farm, half a mile west of Rigg on the Gretna to Annan road, there is a track to the beach. At first the coastal path was excellent but later deteriorated so badly I began to wonder if it was worth the effort. The sticky mud and sand clung to my boots and drove me up the beach to equally difficult scrubby grassland peppered with hundreds of tiny pools and rivulets. I struggled past Dornock Cottage and came gratefully at last to Battlehill and a road into the red sandstone built town of Annan.

Plodding along the road from Annan to Dumfries was not my idea of a good time and as I could not find a footpath the car once again came to my rescue. Prince Charlie's house is in Dumfries' High St. It was once the County Hotel but is now used as a fashionable clothing shop. A trail leads north from Dumfries along the bank of the River Nith but after a couple of miles I was back on the road again. I chose the single-track road to Portrack House, crossed the A76 and followed the signpost to Merkland past Milliganton Farm. From Merkland the road travels past Gateside to Glenmidge and Keir. At Keir Mill I crossed Scar Water, a tributary of the Nith, and joined the A702 at Burnhead about a mile from Thornhill. The walk took me past Tibbers farm and on to Drumlanrig Castle, the seat of the Dukes of Buccleuch and Queensbury. The castle was built for the first Duke of Queensbury in 1680 and is open to the public during the summer months.

Several woodland paths lead north from Drumlanrig but I chose to stay on the minor road past Alton Farm and Crairiehill to Burnmouth. From here the road continues alongside the A76 to Mennock from where it is possible to use the B797 to Leadhills. I

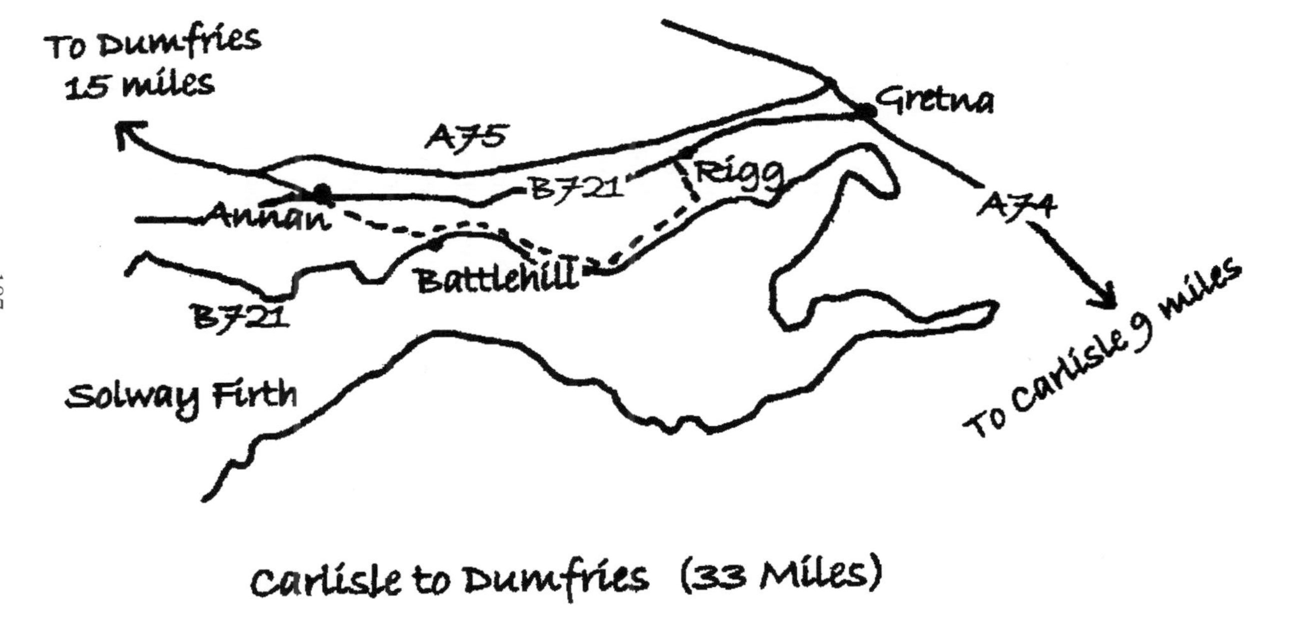

Carlisle to Dumfries (33 Miles)

declined this motorised route over the Mennock pass and continued on the narrow road, past Eliock Grange, to Goose Hill Farm and Ulzieside and into the small town of Sanquhar. The town has a 'Historic Walk' that includes Baronscourt where Jacobite troops were housed in 1745. From Sanquhar there is a useful section of the Southern Upland Way to follow. The path has white thistle waymarks and leaves Sanquhar at Leven Road on the way to Wanlockhead. At Meadowfoot I left the Southern Upland Way and hiked off to Leadhills.

When I jumped into bed that night the weather outside my window was cold but clear. As I drew back the curtains the following morning I was greeted with the sight of a blanket of snow over the heather moors and a sky which promised more to come. After taking advice from my hosts and keeping in mind that Leadhills is one of the two highest villages in Scotland I decided to continue my walk and hope the weather would improve. The air was fresh and the snowy heather crunched under my feet as I strode out along the path to Snar Head. I followed the course of Snar Water as it gurgled past Priest's Pool and Snar Farm before disappearing into Duneaton Water. The day became warmer and the snow vanished. At the junction with the B740 near Liscleugh I took the road to Glespin. A lift would have been welcome but the road was almost deserted and during my two-hour walk to the A70, a couple of miles west of Douglas, I saw not a single car. A pleasant route took me through Windrow Wood to the ruins of Douglas Castle. Only one tower now stands and even that is nothing like complete. Except to be able to say I have been there it was hardly worth the effort.

From Douglas West a disused railway line heads off past an open cast coal mine towards the M74. The track drops down onto the pit approach road and reappears just before Poniel farm to continue north alongside the motorway to Cairnhouses and Lintfield Bank. A short diversion is needed where the track crosses Coal Burn as the bridge is down. The railway line comes very close to the B7078 and passes through a woodland park as it enters Lesmahagow. In October 1745 Donald MacDonald of Kinlochmoidart was captured

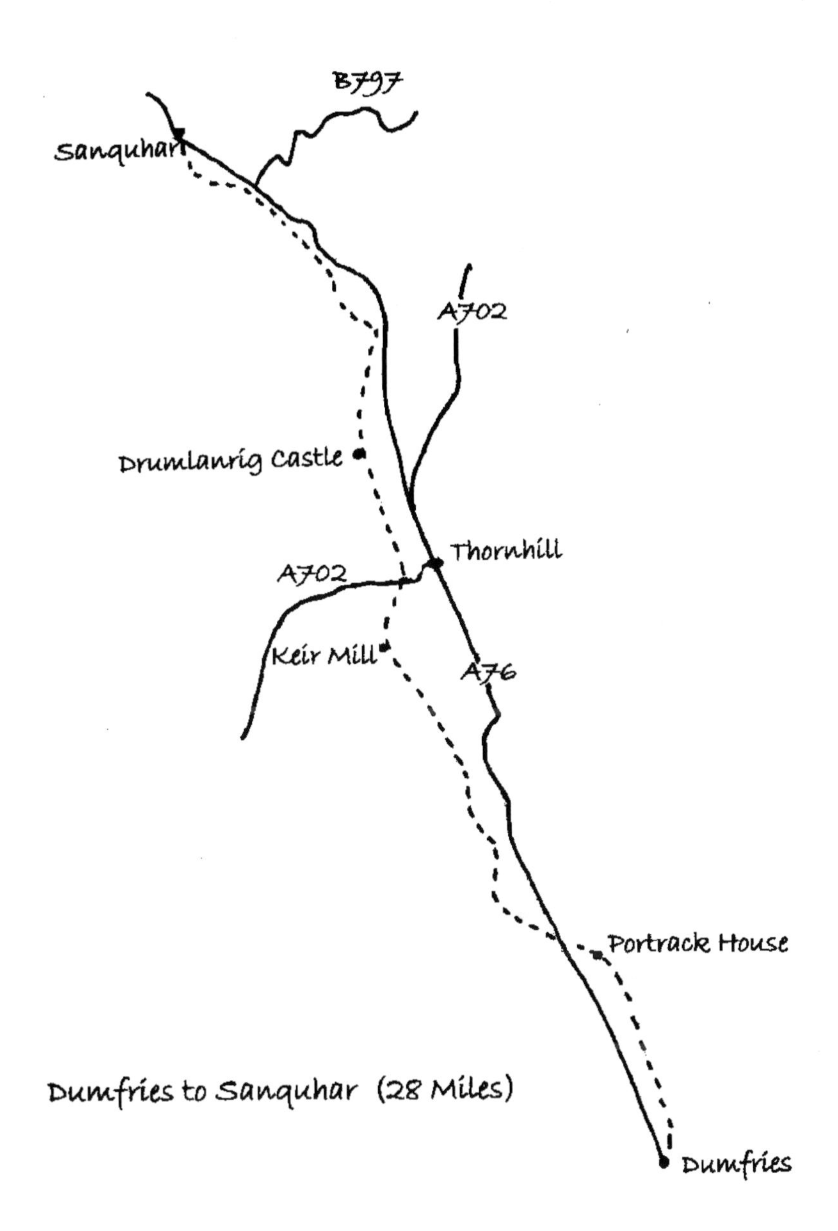
B797
Sanquhar
A702
Drumlanrig Castle
Thornhill
A702
Keir Mill
A76
Portrack House
Dumfries to Sanquhar (28 Miles)
Dumfries

and sent to Edinburgh by the townspeople of Lesmahagow. Kinlochmoidart had been sent north in a largely unsuccessful attempt to rouse the less enthusiastic clan leaders and was apprehended on his way back to Carlisle. In response Jacobite soldiers plundered the small town as they withdrew northwards. Kinlochmoidart was executed in Carlisle on 18 October 1746.

An uninspiring walk along the road took me to the northern side of Blackwood and a welcome return to the railway line. At Stonehouse it was back to the road and I struggled along the A71 hoping to find a footpath on the bank of the Avon Water. I gave up at Canderside Toll roundabout and hopped on a bus to travel through an increasingly urban area to Larkhall and Hamilton. Resisting the temptation to ride when I knew I should be wearing out my boots I steeled myself to alight at the entrance to Chatelherault Country Park and walked into town.

Before continuing my journey into Glasgow I made a detour to find the monument to the memory of Jenny Cameron who is notorious for supposedly becoming Prince Charles' mistress after she raised a few men for him at Glenfinnan. After the rebellion was over Jenny settled in East Kilbride where she bought the Blacklaw estate, renaming it Mount Cameron. She died on 27 June 1772. After the old house was pulled down, new ones were built and Mount Cameron Drive named in Jenny's honour. Her grave is in the St Leonard's area of town in a children's park on a street named Glen Dessarry. In 1959 the East Kilbride Development Corporation planted a tree in her memory. A plaque commemorates her life.

> *Site of the grave of Mrs Jean Cameron who died in 1772. Her zealous attachment to the house of Stuart and the active part she took to promote its interests in the year 1745 made her well known throughout the country. The house occupied by Jean Cameron which stood nearby was demolished in 1958 when this Horse Chestnut was planted.*

Another bus brought me to the centre of Glasgow and the corner of

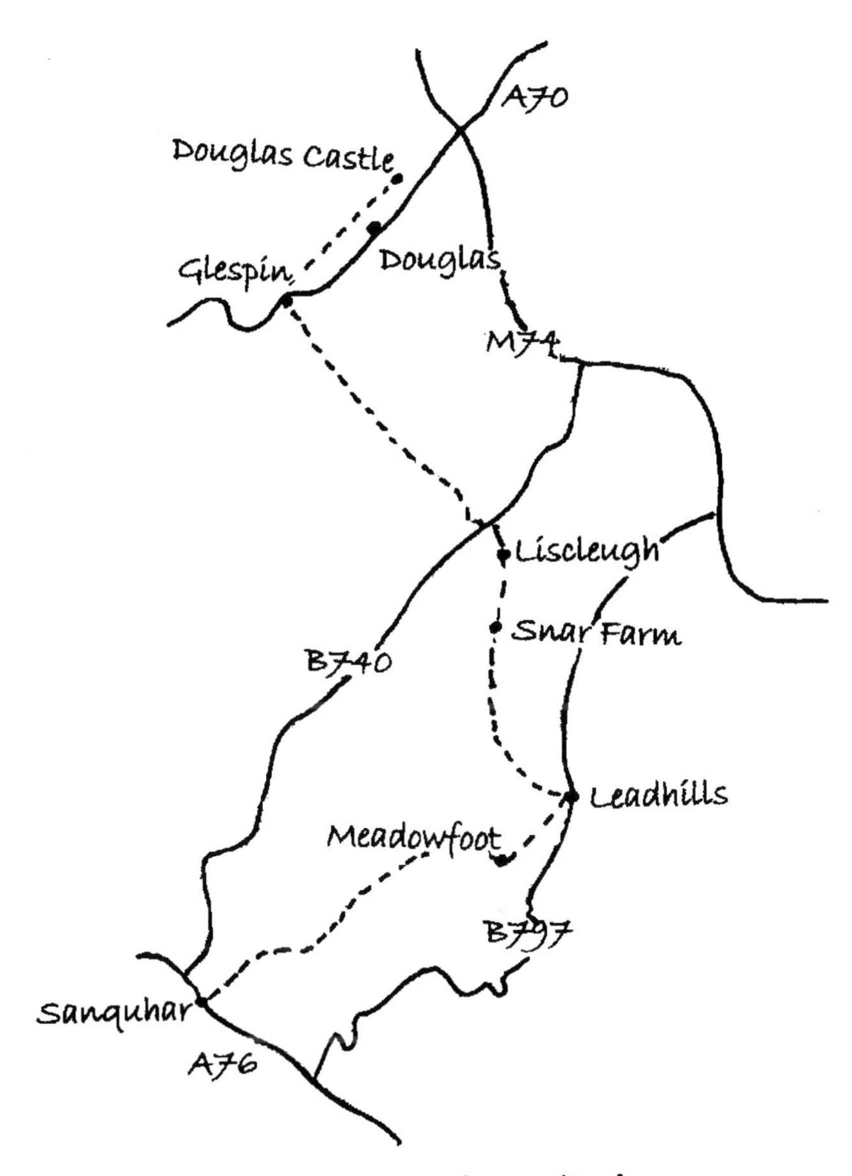

Sanquhar to Douglas (20 Miles)

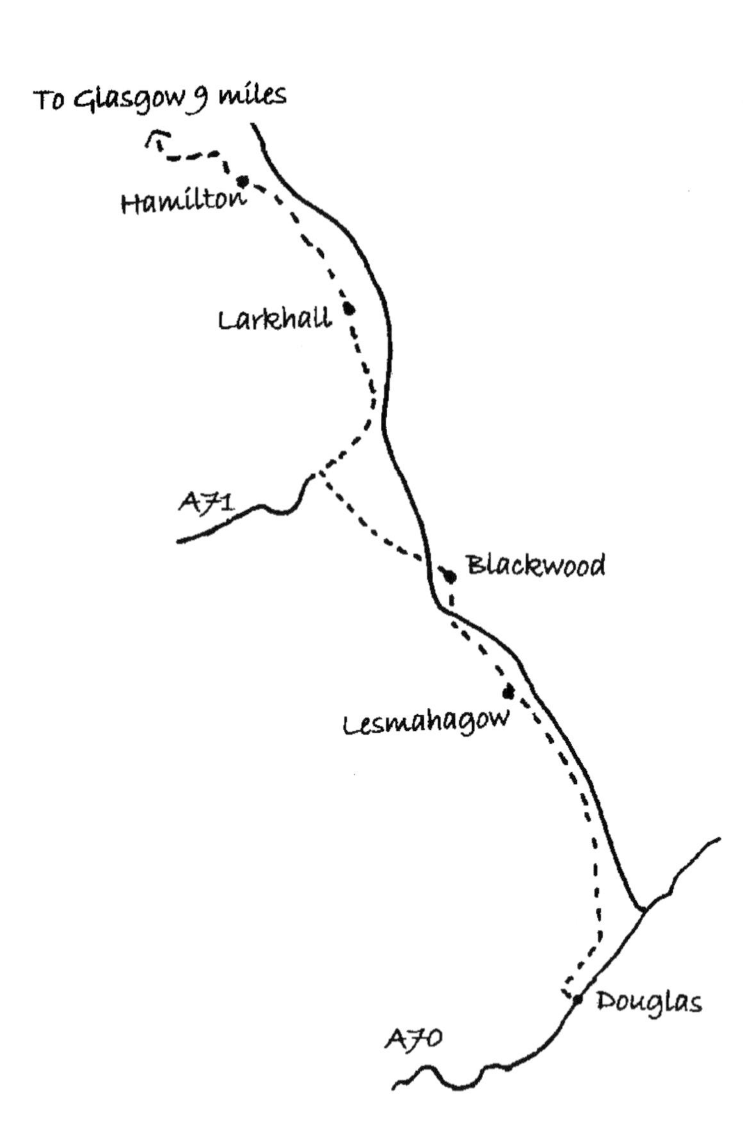

Douglas to Glasgow (27 Miles)

the Trongate and Glassford Street. A brass plaque on a building reads, '*On this site stood the Shawfield Mansion where Prince Charles Stuart resided in 1745.*'

I began to walk again at Kilsyth on the towpath of the Forth and Clyde Canal. The canal stretches all the way to Falkirk and was opened in 1790, serving as a main route for goods for a hundred and fifty years. Competition from both road and rail forced its closure in 1963, since when it was seriously neglected until its recent renovation as part of the Millennium celebrations.

In 1927 the Duke of Atholl unveiled the rocket-shaped monument (picture p33) that marks the battle of Falkirk. Unfortunately there is nothing to inform visitors of troop deployment, progress of the battle, or even which side won. The inscription on the monument reads, '*The Battle of Falkirk was fought around here 17 January 1746.*' One real piece of understanding I gained from my visit was why the cannon did not reach the field before the battle was over. The hill up from town is steep! I made my way down Maggie Wood's Loan into Falkirk and paid a visit to the Howgate shopping centre where three remarkable, large, stained-glass windows (picture p33) depicting Prince Charles Edward, Lord George Murray and Lord John Drummond are displayed. They originally adorned South Bantaskine House, a building that was close to the battlefield but is now demolished. After being in storage for more than forty years the windows recently underwent an eighteen-month restoration and provide a colourful reminder of a significant event in the history of Falkirk. At the bottom of each panel is a verse and that attributed to Lord George reads,

Murray, the first to lead in battle fray,
On Falkirk muir thy courage won the day;
Far in the van was ever heard thy cry,
"Follow me, men, we conquer or we die!"

Falkirk Parish Church is across the road from the shopping centre. The graveyard contains two impressive tombs of men who

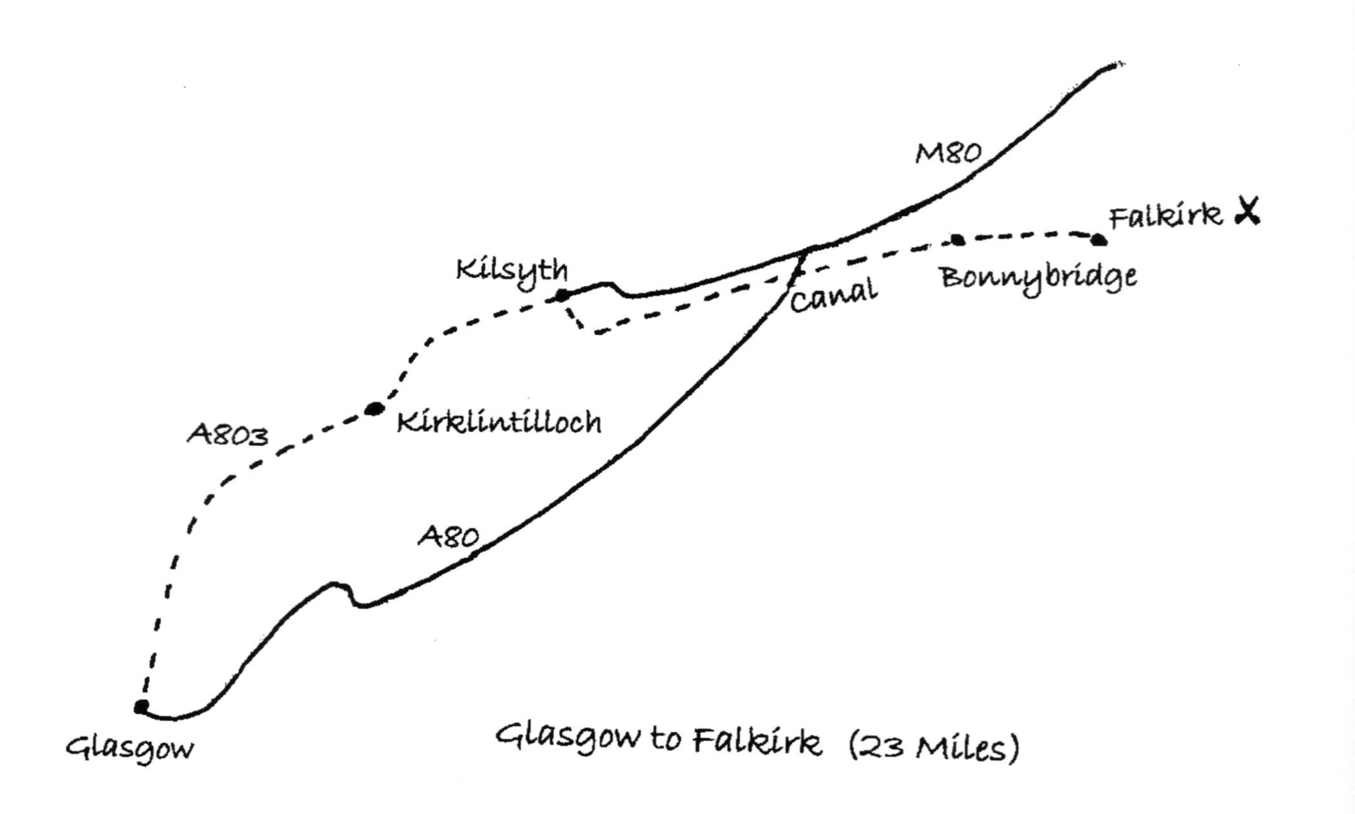
M80
Falkirk X
Kilsyth
Canal
Bonnybridge
Kirklintilloch
A803
A80
Glasgow
Glasgow to Falkirk (23 Miles)

fell on the government side in the battle. One is the grave of Robert Munro, Chief of Clan Munro, who commanded the Black Watch at the battle of Fontenoy. The inscription is suffering from some erosion but is nonetheless impressive.

> *Here lyes interred the body of Sir Robert Munro of Foulis, Colonel of a Regiment of Foot. The life he had spent in the Parliament and Camp with honour he lost in the cause of liberty and religion near Falkirk on XVII of January MDCCXLVI aged 42. As long as history narrates the battle of Fontenoy his courage and conduct on that day in the command of the Highland Regiment will be remembered. Sincere and active in the service of his friends, humane and forgiving to his enemies, generous and benevolent to all, his death was universally regretted even by those who slew him.*

The other tombstone is inscribed, *'In memory of William Edmondstoune of Cambuswallace, Captain Lieutenant in the 27th Regiment of Foot who bravely fighting in defence of his King and of the liberties sacred and civil of his country, fell in battle near Falkirk, the 17th day of January 1746 aged 32 years.'* I wondered about the location of Cambuswallace and discovered in a booklet entitled 'Doune Historical Notes' that it is the old name for Doune Lodge, a house that belonged to the Edmondstoune family before it was sold to the Earl of Moray in 1809

NINE

CULLODEN

'In short, never was more improper ground for Highlanders than that where we fought.'
Letter from Lord George Murray to Prince Charles, 17 April 1746

On 19 February Charles returned to the various comforts of Bannockburn House. The Lowland regiments marched with the Prince and resumed the siege of Stirling Castle. Lord George Murray and the clans continued to occupy Falkirk and were subjected to a demoralising and unhappy incident. One of the Clanranald MacDonalds was examining an enemy musket found on the battlefield. The man knew the piece was loaded and extracted a ball before pointing the weapon out of a window and firing to clear it of powder and wadding. Disastrously the gun had been double-loaded and the remaining musket ball fatally wounded Colonel Aeneas MacDonald of Glengarry. Before he died he pleaded that no harm should befall his unwitting assailant, but in an indignant and angry mood the Glengarry officers demanded the man's life. Young Clanranald was summoned and, mainly to avoid a clan feud, agreed to the execution of the unfortunate offender. The Highlander was taken out forthwith and died at the hands of a firing squad that included his father who took part in an attempt to make his son's death as instantaneous as possible.

By 29 January Stirling castle still showed no sign of yielding, despite the assurances of M. Mirabelle. Indiscipline in the Highland army was rife as the men had little to do. Morale was low and desertion high. Lord George and the principal clan chiefs wrote to Charles arguing that the army was in no fit state to fight again.

If yr R.H. should risque a Battle and Stirling Castle not in your hands, we can forsee nothing but utter destruction to the few that will remain, considering the inequality of our numbers to that of the enemy. For these reasons we are humbly of opinion, that there is no way to extricate yr R.H. and those who remain with you out of the most imminent danger, but by retiring to the Highlands, where we can be usefully employed the remainder of this winter, by taking and mastering the Forts in the North.

John Hay of Restalrig, who was acting as Secretary to the Prince, was charged with presenting the letter to Charles but it was first shown to Murray of Broughton who took it to O'Sullivan. '*The Prince went to bed very cheerfully,'* Broughton commented, *'but this will set him mad, for he'l see plainly, yt it is a Caballe and yt Ld George has blinded all these peoples.'* The Prince and O'Sullivan opposed further withdrawal and argued that the army should not be so despondent just twelve days after defeating Hawley. On 30 December Prince Charles composed a reasoned reply but accepted that without majority support he had no choice but to accept the proposal to withdraw.

Is it possible that a Victory and a Defeat shou'd produce the same effects, and that the Conquerors should flie from an engagement, whilst the conquer'd are seeking it? Shou'd we make the retreat you propose, how much more will that raise the spirits of our Ennemys and sink those of our fellow People? Can we imagine that, that where we go the Ennemy will not follow, and at last oblige us to a Battel which we now decline? Can we hope to defend ourselves at Perth, or keep our Men together there, better than we do here? We must therefore continue our flight to the Mountains, and soon find our selves in a worse condition than we were in at Glenfinnen. What opinion will the French and Spaniards then have of us, or what encouragement will it be to the former to make the descent for which they have been for so long preparing, or the latter send us any more succors? ~ For my own Part I must say that it is with the greatest reluctance that I can bring my self to consent to such a step, but having told you my thoughts upon it, I am too sensible of what you have already ventured and done for me, not to yield to yr unanimous resolution if you persist in it.

A meeting between the Prince and the clan chiefs was held at Bannockburn. Quite what happened is not clear but that the arguments were furious is certain. The following day the Prince wrote a final despairing appeal in an attempt to have the chiefs see the situation from his point of view. The letter shows Charles' exasperation at the situation and, although accepting the inevitability of withdrawal, disowns all responsibility for what he sees as the potentially disastrous consequences.

I doubt not but you have been informed by Cluny and Keppoch of what passed last night and heard great complaints of my Despotick temper, I therefore think it necessary to explain my self further to you. I can't see nothing but ruin and destruction to us all in case we should think of a retreat. Wherever we go the Ennemy will follow, and if we now appear afraid of them their sprits will rise and those of our men sink very low. ~ After all this I know I have an Army that I cannot command any further than the chief Officers please, and therefore if you are all resolved upon it I must yield; but I take God to witness that it is with the greatest reluctance, and that I wash my hands of the fatal consequences wch I foresee but cannot help.

On 1 February the withdrawal began. All the troops except those besieging Stirling Castle marched north towards the River Forth and the Fords of Frew. The retreat quickly deteriorated into a full-scale flight with Lord George and O'Sullivan at loggerheads, each blaming the other for the disorder. According to O'Sullivan, Prince

Charles was dining when Lord George, *'Spook to the Prince after the most disrespectfull & impertinent manner. Teling him before all the Compagny, yt it was a most shamefull & courdly flight, yt they were a persel of Villans yt advis'd him to it; as if he had never consented, nor had any share in it. So I leave yu to judge of Ld George after that behaviour.'*

Cumberland's troops left Edinburgh on 31 January and spent the night at Linlithgow where many of the men were housed in the ancient palace of the Stuart kings. Either by accident or design a fire broke out and the palace was reduced to ruins. The Duke continued in hot pursuit of Prince Charles but by the time the Hanoverian army entered Falkirk the Jacobites were long gone. The redcoat army marched to Stirling on 4 February and arrived in Perth two days later only twenty-four hours behind the Prince. However, Cumberland wanted to consolidate his position and so spent the next two weeks in Perth gathering supplies and sending out raiding parties to harass Jacobite supporters. On 8 February his brother-in-law, Prince Frederick of Hesse, landed at Leith with 4,000 German soldiers. There were other new recruits most notable of whom were men from Argyll, under the command of Major-General John Campbell of Mamore. Cumberland briefly returned to Edinburgh on 15 February where a Council of War concluded that the campaign was all but over. The Prince was in retreat and there was little left to do but root out any remaining Jacobite support from the Highlands. Cumberland was determined that when the rebellion was finally defeated there would be no possibility of a Jacobite recovery. The Duke having re-equipped his army set out with his main force, by way of Montrose, to Aberdeen.

The Prince passed the night of 1 February at Drummond Castle, leaving most of his army in some confusion ten miles to the rear at Doune and Dunblane. On 2 February the Highland regiments travelled north to Crieff where the Prince stayed at Fairnton, Lord John Drummond's house. At a Council of War held in the Drummond of Perth's Arms in Crieff, differences between the leaders once more emerged and the Jacobite campaign continued to lose direction.

Ruthven Barracks

When the Prince discovered that recent desertions from the army were nothing like the levels previously estimated he was angry and disappointed at the idea of further retreat. Lord George was still furious at the way his planned withdrawal had turned into headlong flight but eventually the wrangling ended and some thought was given to the route to be taken north. Even here agreement seemed impossible but at last it was decided that the Highland regiments, led by the Prince, would take a direct route north and the rest of the army with Lord George would take the coast road via Aberdeen towards Inverness.

Meanwhile in France, activity supporting the Jacobite cause had resumed and attempts were made to land more Irish troops with a remarkable lack of success. A combination of the Royal Navy and bad weather defied the best efforts of the French and only forty men and a little money were brought ashore.

The Highland army crossed the River Tay at Aberfeldy on 4 February and Prince Charles spent a couple of nights at Menzies Castle. A day later he arrived at Blair Atholl, where he broke his journey as the guest of Duke William. On 10 February Charles marched to Dalnacardoch where he spent two more nights while his men went on to Ruthven. The small government garrison was still commanded by Terrence Mulloy who had been promoted to Lieutenant after successfully repelling a Jacobite attack the previous September. This time Mulloy was outnumbered and surrendered to the rebels who destroyed the barracks with gunpowder. The withdrawal continued towards Inverness.

Charles left Ruthven on 15 February and was received with a less than enthusiastic welcome at Inverlaidnan House, the home of Grant of Dalrachny. The next morning as the band of men departed Grant's wife was moved to comment, *'What a pack ye are. God lat me never hae the like of you in my house again.'* The following day a more effusive welcome was provided for the Prince at Moy Hall, the home of 'Colonel' Anne Mackintosh, a loyal Jacobite whose husband was in the government army.

Lord Louden, the Hanoverian holder of Inverness, was

interested in the reward of £30,000 that was on the Pretender's head and the kudos to be gained from his incarceration and so resolved to capture Charles. Louden marched towards Moy with 1500 men intending to take the Prince by surprise. However, his Lordship had not reckoned on the response of Colonel Anne's mother, Lady Mackintosh, who lived in Inverness. According to James Gib, the Master of the Prince's Household, when Lady Mackintosh heard of Louden's plan she dispatched a young clansman, Lachlan Mackintosh, through the government cordon to her daughter's house to warn Charles. On hearing the news Colonel Anne sent five men, including the Moy blacksmith, to keep a look out for the arrival of Louden's men. When they saw the advance guard approaching the men fired their weapons and filled the air with war cries and chants. Believing that the whole Jacobite army was about to descend on them the terrified attackers panicked and fled back to Inverness in disorder.

The 'Rout of Moy' produced only one casualty, the MacLeod hereditary piper, Macrimmon, who had prophesied his death in the lament 'Cha til me tuille' which translates as 'I'll return no more'. However, the ignominious rout demoralised the garrison in Inverness and two hundred men deserted the following day. The arrival of Jacobite troops at the outskirts of Inverness on the morning of 18 February encouraged many more to withdraw across the ferry at Kessock to Ross and Cromarty to await the arrival of the main force of Cumberland's army and Prince Charles captured the town without a shot being fired. Two days later the castle surrendered and was destroyed under the supervision of a French artillery sergeant who unfortunately blew himself up in the process. It might appear from these successes that the Hanoverians were under pressure but it was the rebels who were running out of steam. The Prince was short of almost everything needed to keep an army in the field and desertion was once again common. Even so, reinforcements still arrived from time to time and all was not yet lost.

The French had still not completely given up their increasingly feeble attempts to bring succour to the Pretender. Le Prince Charles, once in British service as the Hazard, sailed with 12,000 guineas for the Jacobite army. It was hoped that she might be able to slip into harbour somewhere on the Moray Firth as Montrose, Peterhead and Aberdeen were in government hands. The venture failed and to the delight of the Royal Navy the ship was captured in the Kyle of Tongue. Lord Cromartie sent his 1500 men north in a hopeless attempt to recover the treasure with the result that these men were absent from the forthcoming battle, where their presence was to be sorely missed. The financial loss was a serious blow to Jacobite hopes. The money would have fed and equipped the army and perhaps produced a situation where the battle could be postponed until the Prince was at full strength. The warriors would have fallen upon their enemy with the confidence and vigour a full belly brings instead of a suicidal desperation brought about by hunger and exhaustion.

Prince Charles set up his headquarters at Culloden House, a few miles from Inverness. He also spent some time in town with Lady Mackintosh in Church Street. Culloden House belonged to the Lord President, Duncan Forbes, who had escaped with Louden the previous day. Troops under the command of Lord George Murray and Duke William of Atholl joined the Prince's forces two days later and the majority of the army was now concentrated close to Inverness. A force under the command of Brigadier Walter Stapleton turned its attention to Fort Augustus. After ten days and partially by the good fortune of a shell landing in the castle's powder magazine, the garrison surrendered. This was the final success the Jacobite army was to have and the slide towards the debacle of Culloden gained momentum.

The next target was Fort William. Lieutenant-General Alexander Campbell, in whom Cumberland had no great faith, commanded the garrison and Captain Caroline Scott was dispatched to bolster its defence. Scott was a fiercely anti-Jacobite Lowlander and developed a fearsome reputation for his ruthless and brutal operations throughout the campaign in the Highlands. The captured guns from Fort Augustus were brought into the Jacobite attack but to no avail. Fort William was still holding out at the end of March and on the night of 2 April the siege was abandoned. Several skirmishes took place with varying degrees of success for both sides, with the

Prince's forces eventually falling back on Inverness.

Meanwhile, Blair Castle had fallen into government hands and was garrisoned by 500 men commanded by Lieutenant-General Sir Andrew Agnew of the Scots Fusiliers. Lord George was anxious to wrest the castle back and Prince Charles gave permission for the attempt. 700 of the Atholl Brigade marched south and were joined near Ruthven by others including Macpherson of Cluny and 300 of his clan. On 17 March headquarters were established at McGlashan's Inn. A message was sent to Sir Andrew calling on him to surrender. The note was carried by a serving girl from the inn as she, *'being rather handsome, and very obliging, conceived herself to be on so good a footing with some of the young officers, that she need not be afraid of being shot.'* The demand seems to have caused hilarity rather than fear and was ignored. The Jacobites had no luck with their bombardment: their artillery was not powerful enough to make much impression on the castle walls. They tried to set the building on fire by firing red-hot cannon balls at the roof with an equal lack of success. By the end of March 3000 German mercenaries with 300 English cavalry arrived in Dunkeld. This uncomfortable fact coupled with the arrival of a message from Prince Charles indicating that the Duke of Cumberland would soon be on the march persuaded Lord George to call off the siege and return to Inverness, leaving Cluny Macpherson to once again guard the passes in Badenoch.

After spending a month in Aberdeen, Cumberland moved north through Old Meldrum and Banff. When he arrived at Cullen the Duke found himself only twelve miles from a Jacobite force commanded by the Duke of Perth that was occupying the far side of the River Spey. Cumberland drew up his men on the riverbank and prepared to cross. The men found the swollen river had *'loose stones at the bottom, which made it very difficult for Man or Horse to step without falling; the Water Belly-deep, and very rapid.'* James Ray, a volunteer in the Duke's army clearly expected the enemy to attack and notes, *'In this Situation, had the Rebels stood us here, it might have been of bad consequence to our*

Army.' To his amazement the Jacobites withdrew in order to *'draw our Army over, and further into their country, from whence (in their Imagination) we were never to return.'* The exact reason for the withdrawal is not clear but it lost the Jacobites the opportunity to inflict heavy casualties on their enemy or at the very least delay their advance. Possibly Perth's orders were to retire unless supported by others of the Prince's army who were thirty miles away. The Chevalier de Johnstone considered the affair to be a serious mistake and offers general thoughts regarding commanders of high birth. '*It is astonishing that persons of illustrious houses, destined by their birth to command armies, to fill the highest offices in the state, and to act the first parts in the kingdom, should not apply themselves with keenness and assiduity to the study of military affairs, in order to enable them to discharge their duty with honour and distinction, to the advantage of their king and country.'*

Once over the river, the road to Inverness was wide open for the Hanoverian forces and they reached Nairn on 14 April. On the same day the Jacobite army marched out of Inverness and camped for the night at Culloden House. Prince Charles and Colonel O'Sullivan chose the battlefield where they would meet their enemy. Lord George Murray was not happy about the site, preferring a position reconnoitred by Brigadier Stapleton and Colonel Ker of Graden where *'the hill ground on the south side of the Water appeared to be steep and uneven, consequently much properer for Highlanders.'* The next day someone at the Council of War came up with the idea that perhaps a pre-emptive strike during the night could be a smart move. The Prince and his closest aides liked the idea. Even Lord George, mainly to do anything to avoid a daylight battle in what he considered an unsuitable position agreed. *'I was with many others for a night attack,'* he wrote, '*but that was only of the two evils to choose what we thought the least. We thought it was better than to fight upon that plain muir. I was for it provided it could be done before two in the morning so as to surprise the enemy.*' An additional, but as it turned out forlorn hope was that as the 15th was Cumberland's birthday his troops would *'all be as drunk as beggers.'*

The Prince's army was short of food and many troops were out foraging for supplies. The march towards Cumberland's camp at Balblair on the outskirts of Nairn did not begin until eight in the evening. It soon became clear that this had not been such a good idea after all. The columns of men were being stretched too thinly, with those at the front marching more quickly than the rearguard. With the leading troops perhaps as far forward as Kildrummie a discussion between Lochiel, Lord George and the Duke of Perth decided that they would not be able to reach Cumberland's camp in darkness and the men were turned back. Before Perth could inform Prince Charles, John Hay of Restalrig found the Prince and portrayed the decision as deliberate disobedience of Royal orders. Never one to pass up the chance of challenging Lord George Murray's authority and soldiering skills, Colonel O'Sullivan questioned Murray about the decision to withdraw. *'Yu know the Scituation the Prince is in, neither money nor vivers. If yu retire yu discourage your men who suffer enough already, you loose all yr advantages, & give over to yr enemy; if they come upon yu in battle, superior as they are in horse & foot, & their Artillery, can yu resist them?'*

Sir John MacDonald agreed and noted, *'I heard afterwards that Lord George maintained that there was still too far to go, and that it was too late. As he was already marching back with the column, it was certainly too far away when day dawned, but when he turned round he was near enough to have defeated the enemy before they were drawn up before their camp; several enemy officers told us so, afterwards.'*

Captain Maclean provides a report of the event. He is not too good at sentence construction and his spelling leaves something to be desired but he presents us with an immediacy not found in the accounts of others, most of which were written with hindsight some years afterwards.

Next morning 15th we marched ½ a mile to the Mure and Encamped there. We marched from that about Nightfall to surprise the Enemy near 12 miles of Very Dirty Rod but Did not meet with them and Cam back next Morning very Much fatigued with sleep and hunger and travelling to the above mentioned parks where we continued not above one Hour when we were Alarmed with the Enemys Aprotch.

Charles was not pleased with the withdrawal and took the Duke of Perth to task over the matter. On hearing that Lord George had ordered the return the Prince furiously commented, '*What does he mean? We were equal in number, and would have blown them to the devil. Pray Perth can't you call them back yet? Perhaps he has not gone far yet.*' After further debate Prince Charles seemed to accept the decision and shouted out, *'There is no help for it my lads; march back to Culloden House.'* At six o'clock in the morning on 16 April, 1746 the Highlanders were back where they had started on Drummossie Moor and, according to Lord Elcho,

Every body seemed to think of nothing but sleep. The men were prodigiously tired with hunger and fatigue, and vast numbers of them went into Inverness, and the villages about, both to Sleep and to pick up what little nourishment they Could gett. The principal officers went all to the house of Culloden and were so much tired that they never thought of calling a Councill what was to be done, but Every one lay'd himself down where he Could, some on beds, others on tables, Chairs & on the floors for the fatigue and the hunger had been felt as much amongst the officers as Soldiers.

At eight o'clock news arrived that King George's army had been sighted marching towards the Highlanders' position. Under these difficult circumstances Lord George, Lochiel and others called for withdrawal to the field south of the Water of Nairn. Here the impending battle might just be postponed for a few hours if not a whole day, allowing perhaps two thousand additional troops to assemble and fight. Even the Marquis d'Eguilles tried and failed to persuade the Pretender to retreat and regroup. He wrote to King Louis of his exasperation. *'In vain I represented to him that he was still without half his army; that the great part of those who had returned were without their targets — a kind of defensive armour without which they were unable to fight to advantage; that they were all worn out with fatigue by a long march on the previous night and for two days many of them had not eaten at all for want of bread.'*

It was recognised that Cumberland was not going away and that there was not enough food to sustain the men for another march. Battle was now inevitable. Drums beat and the pipes played the call to arms, to which only about 5,000 men immediately responded. It soon became clear that they were outnumbered and outgunned by Cumberland's 2,400 horse and 6,400 foot soldiers. By midday the Jacobite army was drawn up in battle order. To the right and left were fields enclosed by stone walls that the commanders hoped would give the troops some protection. The MacDonalds of Keppoch, Glengarry and Clanranald were on the left of the front line. They were disgruntled and insulted at having been deprived of their traditional position on the right by the Atholl Brigade. These warriors, although pleased at being granted the position of honour, were already complaining of the restrictions imposed by the stone walls and turf dyke of the Leanach enclosure. The centre of the line consisted of Macleans and MacLachlans, John Roy Stewart's regiment, Frasers, Stewarts of Appin, Farquharsons, Lochiel's Camerons and others including the loose alliance of clans that made up Clan Chattan. Prince Charles was in overall command with control of the front line falling to Lord George Murray on the right, Lord John Drummond in the centre and his brother, the Duke of Perth on the left. There was an odd assortment of artillery of varying calibre positioned in the centre and on the flanks of the front line. It was handled by badly trained men and was all out of action within ten minutes of the battle starting.

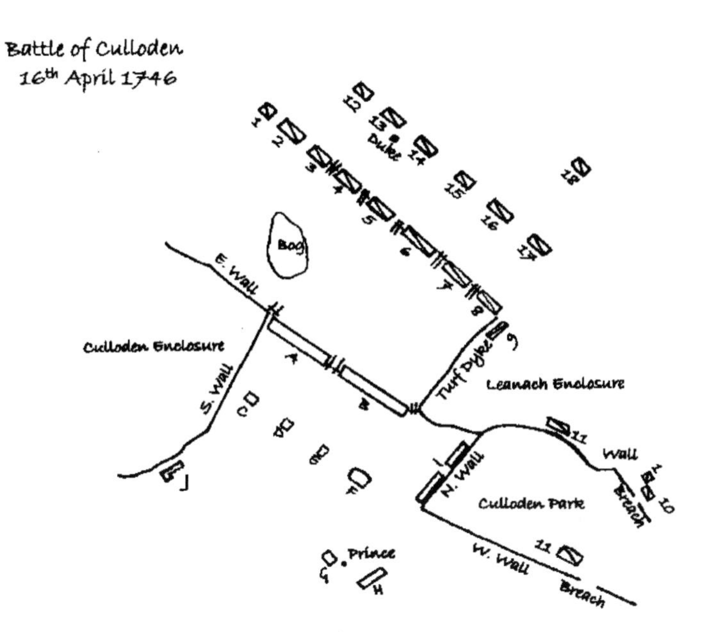

<u>Jacobite Army</u>

A (left to right)
Glengarry
Keppoch
Clanranald
Duke of Perth
Glenbucket
John Roy Stewart
Farquharson
Maclean/MacLachan

B (left to right)
Mackintosh
Fraser
Stewarts of Appin
Cameron
Atholl Brigades

C Irish Piquets
D Royal Scots
E Foot Guards
F Lord Lewis Gordon
G Balmerino's Life Guards
H Lord Elcho's Lifeguards etc.
I Lord Oglivy
J Hussars, Perthshire Horse etc.

<u>Government Army</u>

1 Cobham's Dragoons, Kingston's Light Horse
2 Pulteney
3 Royal Scots
4 Cholmondley
5 Price
6 Royal Scots Fusiliers
7 Munro
8 Barrel
9 Wolfe
10 Lord Mark Ker's Dragoons
11 Campbells
12 Battereau
13 Howard
14 Fleming
15 Bligh
16 Sempill
17 Ligonier
18 Blakeney

The second line, commanded by Brigadier Stapleton, was composed of Lord Lewis Gordon's, Lord Ogilvy's, Lord John Drummond's and the Duke of Perth's regiments. These together with the Royal Scots and the Irish Piquets made up the majority of the foot soldiers. The cavalry numbered only about 150 and some of these were unmounted. They were under the command of Lords Balmerino, Pitsligo and Strathallan. Despite the overwhelming superiority of the Duke of Cumberland's forces and the fact that the Jacobite troops were weak from hunger and fatigue the Prince seemed convinced of their invincibility. He rode along the lines rallying flagging morale. '*Here they are comeing my lades, we'l soon be with them. They don't forget, Glads-mur, nor Falkirk, & yu have the same Armes & swords, let me see yours. Il answer this will cut off some arms & heads today. Go on my Lads, the day will be ours & we'll want for nothing after.*' His speech over, Prince Charles stationed himself to the rear of the second line and was escorted by horse soldiers from Balmerino's and FitzJames' regiments.

Five hundred yards away William Augustus, the Duke of Cumberland, was ready. In the front line were Pultney's, the Royal Scots, Price's, Cholmondley's, Munro's and Barrel's regiments flanked by Cobham's Dragoons and the Duke of Kingston's Light Horse. The second line contained Battereau's, Howard's, Fleming's, Bligh's, Sempill's and Ligonier's regiments. Behind them were the reserves commanded by General William Blakeney. James Wolfe's regiment was taken out of the second line and placed at right angles and to the left of the front line where it would later be used with fearsome effect. The Campbell Militia was further forward and to the left of the front line. Artillery was positioned between the front line regiments and the firepower was greatly superior to that in the Jacobite lines. The gunners were well trained and could fire each of the ten three-pounders every fifteen seconds. Additional cannon and some mortars were positioned further back.

The two armies were not directly opposite one another. The Atholl Brigades were nearest the redcoats and the MacDonalds furthest away. The Prince's army was wedged between the walls of the Culloden enclosures with barely enough room to stand, making correct deployment during the battle impossible. The opening shots were fired by the Jacobite artillery and a minute or two later the enemy guns replied with devastating effect. The deadly round shot sailed over the moor ripping huge holes in the Jacobite lines. Colonel Belford who commanded the government artillery spotted Prince Charles' Royal Standard and the small group of horsemen surrounding it. Two cannons were trained on the target and balls fell all around. The Prince's horse was hit and his groom was killed. Charles slunk away to safety in the steadings of Culchunaig Farm, to the rear and right of his original position.

Colonel Belford now changed tactics and loaded his cannon with grapeshot, causing more havoc in the Jacobite ranks. The Highlanders stood their ground in the face of this withering fire waiting in vain for the shout of 'Claymore' that would signal their customary charge. With all the Jacobite artillery out of action the government lines were suffering no casualties and Cumberland was happy to wait and watch as Belford's gunners thinned the enemy ranks. If the Highlanders were to have any chance at all a charge must be ordered quickly. Prince Charles was slow to make the decision but at last the instructions were dispatched to both flanks of the army. Lachlan Maclachlan was to take the message to Lord George but was decapitated by a cannon ball on his journey. The orders eventually reached the commanders but not soon enough for Clan Chattan at the centre of the line. The Mackintoshes, MacGillivrays, MacBeans and others broke rank and surged towards the guns of the Royal army. The clans on the right followed suit but the MacDonalds on the left were still in a surly mood and held their position, either ignorant of the orders or reluctant to join the battle.

The Athollmen were restrained from forward movement by the Leanach dyke and veered slightly left to become jumbled with the men of Clan Chattan who, perhaps to avoid the worst of the boggy ground, had shifted to their right. Despite the confusion the combined thrust of this screaming throng of Highlanders drove deep into the left of the enemy lines. Barrel's and Munro's regiments took the full force of the charge suffering perhaps two hundred casualties between them. Highland charges relied on surprise and the ability to instil fear and panic in the hearts of the enemy and the tactic had worked well enough in the past. This time the wall of red coats and white gaitered legs stood firm, and the muskets and artillery kept firing. The Hanoverian front line was penetrated at tremendous cost to the clan regiments. The Campbell Militia, together with Cobham's and Lord Mark Ker's dragoons had broken down the walls to the right of Jacobite positions and outflanked Lord George's men. Wolfe's regiment, still positioned at right angles to the government front line, poured volley after volley into the right of the Prince's advancing clansmen. The charge was suicidal. Athollmen fell in huge numbers and of the twenty-one officers in Clan Chattan, eighteen were killed. Stewarts, Frasers and Camerons fared no better and of those who lived long enough to fight through the enemy front line many were bayoneted to death by soldiers in the second. Lochiel survived the charge but was felled by grapeshot and wounded in both ankles.

The MacDonalds on the left were now in an impossible position. The Duke of Perth and his brother did their best to motivate the men but by the time they were prepared to advance, the right of the line was already retreating. Many MacDonalds saw no action at all to the dismay of their chiefs. Keppoch fell to enemy bullets in a gallant but fatal attempt to rally his men. The battle was all but over and had lasted less than an hour. The Highlanders fled, pursued by enemy cavalry and the retreat became a panic-stricken rout. John Maclean of Kingairloch was killed on that fateful day and the last entry in his journal sums up the whole unfortunate and bloody business in a few well-chosen lines.

When all that pleased or was able to follow ther Collours marched out and was Drawn in order of Battel about 2 musket shot from the Enemy they was waiting us in very good order with their Artilary befor them and the wind and snow in ther Backs. After a short stay and all the Disadvantages an Army could meete with as to ther numbers they Doubled or tripled ours and all advantages of Ground and wind and weather our Cannon began to play upon them and they upon us. After we stayed about 10 minutes we wer ordered to march hastily to the Enemy which we did Boldly. They began a smart fire of their Small Guns and Grape Shots from there Cannons till we wer Beat Back with Great Losses our Right wing was flanked and surrounded by the horse which did Great Execution.

Once again O'Sullivan places much of the blame for the disaster on Lord George Murray's shoulders. *'Ld George says yt he lost a great many officers. Really I cant tell but he never lost one nor a man before yt day, & if he had marched & attacked the enemy the night before, all this misfortune wou'd be avoided.'* There were just three set piece battles in the Forty-Five and Culloden was the only one in which the rebels were defeated. However, they were so badly beaten that all realistic hope of a Stuart restoration from this campaign was lost. How many were killed in the battle and its aftermath is not accurately known. The Duke of Cumberland probably exaggerated the number when he commented in his official report, *'By the best calculations we can make, I think we may reckon the rebels lost 2,000 men upon the field of battle and in the pursuit.'* John Home comments, *'As to the number of men in the rebel army killed at Culloden, it seems impossible to ascertain what it was. The newspapers and magazines, published at the time, make the number amount to 2000 or 3000. Other accounts make the number to be less than 1000.'*

It is probable that about 750 rebels were killed in the battle but many of the wounded were slaughtered in its aftermath and so a total of between 800 and 1200 Jacobite dead seems about right. Government casualties were much smaller. John Home lists the official total as 50 dead, 259 injured and 1 missing. These numbers seem only to include regular army casualties with perhaps another fifty from the Campbell Militia and other volunteers. The disparity in casualties between the protagonists illustrates the scale of defeat suffered by the Prince's army but in truth it could have been much worse. The battle so quickly turned into a rout that although there were 14,000 men on the field no more than 3,000 were engaged in the fighting. Many men were not able to fire their muskets and several regiments on both sides saw little or no action.

Landranger Maps

65 Falkirk & Linlithgow
35 Kingussie
57 Stirling & The Trossachs
36 Grantown & Aviemore
58 Perth to Alloa
27 Nairn & Forres
52 Pitlochry to Crieff
26 Inverness & Strathglass
42 Glen Garry & Loch Rannoch

Bannockburn House (65)	**NS808889**
Ruthven (35)	**NN765998**
Drummond Castle (58)	**NN845181**
Sluggan Bridge (35)	**NH870220**
Castle Menzies (52)	**NN837497**
Moy Hall (27)	**NH768357**
Trinafour (42)	**NN728646**
Culloden (27)	**NH743451**

I left Falkirk by bus and as Bannockburn House is in private hands and closed to the public I made my way to St Ninian's church, (picture p34) less than a mile to the south of Stirling. The rebels had been using the kirk as an arsenal and for some reason the place blew up on 1 February 1746 destroying the main body of the church but leaving the tower intact. The clock keeps good time and chimes the hours to this day. The storyboard tells that *'the Jacobites had been using the building as a store for gunpowder which they deliberately exploded.'* However, it is likely that as men attempted to remove the gunpowder an accident occurred. The fearsome explosion happened just as a chaise containing Lochiel and Mrs John Murray of Broughton was passing. '*The horses startled and threw Mrs Murray on the street, where she lay speechless till she was taken up by some of the men.'* Maclean of Kingairloch offers his views on the destruction of St Ninian's:

> *That Day there happened Ane Accident. The most of our ammunition was Lodged in the Church at St Ninians and that morning Every One was ordered to take Ammunition as wanted it, which they did. And a little after that I happened to goe up to the Church to gather Our Men who was there upon Guard, and as I was Coming Back by the walls of the Church the Blast was Given, but thanks to God Almighty who preserved me safe in such Eminent Danger.*

The unsuccessful siege of Stirling Castle lasted from 8 January to 1 February. For all that time and several days previously, Charles slept at Bannockburn House. So what of the idea that it was here that Charles and Clementine Walkinshaw first became sexually involved? It seems possible. Perhaps Clementine distracted the Prince into making foolish decisions, for he certainly wasted time, effort and resources in failing to break the castle garrison's resolve. Generally accepted tradition has it that Clementine looked after him while he was ill and perhaps His Royal Highness fell for the charms of his nurse.

If Charles and Clementine were lovers at Bannockburn then maybe there was a child born. Such a happening would have been difficult for the Walkinshaw family and efforts probably made to conceal the event. Several claims over the years have offered theories and possibilities regarding the fate of a love child born to Clementine and Charles. My favourite is the story of the Finsthwaite Princess. Finsthwaite is a tiny village in the Lake District near the southern tip of Lake Windermere. A woman named Clementine Johannes Sobiesky Douglass is buried in St Peter's churchyard. The grave is marked with a simple cross and the inscription tells us she died on 16 May 1771 but offers no indication of her date of birth. The grave was unmarked for a long time but in 1913 the canon of Carlisle Cathedral, Charles Townley, who was descended from a family of Lancashire Jacobites, raised the money to erect the cross that stands there today. Although the Prince did occasionally use the name Douglas as an alias there is no proof of the woman's identity. Sometime about 1897 Miss A.M. Wakefield reported that the oldest inhabitants of the village remembered their elders talking of a young woman known as 'The Princess' arriving in about in the middle 1740s accompanied by two servants. If this is the person buried in the grave then clearly she is too old to be the child of Clementine and Charles.

I believe the grave is that of the daughter of a Jacobite sympathiser and not the offspring of Prince Charles. The Prince was quite indifferent to the women he met during the campaign. He rarely danced and seems to have flirted not at all. If the Finsthwaite Princess was Charles and Clementine's daughter and she was cast out from the family until the day she died, why on earth would she have been given such a provocative name? The only scrap of evidence that Charles and Clementine were lovers at Bannockburn comes from Lord Elcho when he offers his opinion that Charles *'made the acquaintance of Miss Walkinshaw, who forthwith became his mistress.'*

I declined to repeat my journey over the River Forth at the Fords of Frew and so enjoyed a pleasurable train ride from Stirling to Dunblane. Footpaths are notable by their absence between Dunblane and Crieff and so I continued to rest my feet and travelled by car. For the determined there are minor roads that are not too bad for walking. The first of these leaves Dunblane as the B8083 to Braco. The road joins the A822 for a mile or more before an old military road forks to the left in a straight line to Muthill. From Muthill there seems to be little option but to rejoin the A822, past the entrance to

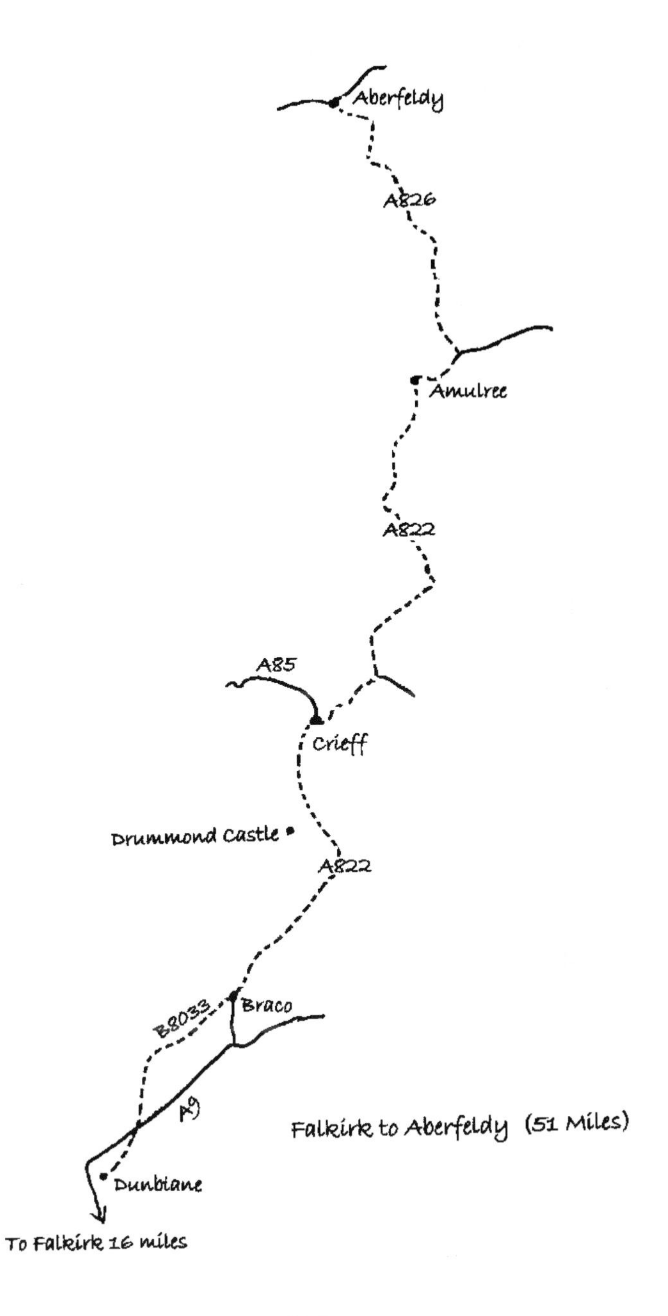
Aberfeldy
A826
Amulree
A822
A85
Crieff
Drummond Castle
A822
Braco
B8033
A9
Dunbiane
To Falkirk 16 miles
Falkirk to Aberfeldy (51 Miles)

Drummond Castle and into Crieff. The castle is privately occupied but between May and October the grounds are open to the public for a modest entry fee. The original hostelry accommodating Prince Charles in the centre of Crieff has been demolished and a newer building stands there now. A plaque on its wall informs the reader that this is, '*The site of the inn known as the Drummond of Perth's Arms where Bonnie Prince Charles Edward Stuart held his final War Council in February 1746 before reviewing his army and marching north to his eventual defeat at Culloden.*'

The A822 from Crieff to Aberfeldy closely follows a Wade military road. It snakes north through Sma' Glen, over the hills to Amulree and then through Glen Cochill to the River Tay at Aberfeldy. I began at the Hydro in Crieff and walked over the golf course where, close to the fourteenth tee, the ruins of Lord John Drummond's house stand as a desolate reminder of the past. The main house was demolished decades ago and derelict stables and servants' quarters are all that remain until they too are finally removed. My walk continued north for a couple of miles to the Shaggie Burn and Monzie where I had little choice but to join the modern road. A good walking path begins at Newton Bridge and continues to Milton just north of Amulree where it might be best to rejoin the A822. The old road re-emerges at White Cairn and crosses the Cochill Burn before losing itself in modern forestry operations and a return to the modern road seems to be the only reasonable option. Just south of Aberfeldy, the military road provides a footpath past the hospital into town.

General Wade built the impressive Tay Bridge with its four obelisks. It is a tribute to its construction that the structure is able to cope with modern traffic. A stone tablet is inscribed with the words:

> *At the command of His Majesty King George II, this bridge was erected in the year 1733. This, with the roads and other military works for securing a safe and easy communication between the Highlands and the trading towns in the low country, was by His Majesty committed to the care of Lieutenant General George Wade, Commander in Chief of*

the forces in Scotland who laid the first stone of this bridge on 23 April and finished the work in the same year.

Castle Menzies is across the river from Aberfeldy. Until 1918 the castle was the seat of the Menzies of Weem but after that date it gradually fell into disrepair. The Menzies Clan Society acquired the building in 1957 and serious work to save the castle began in 1972. It is now sound and open to the public. There is the room where Charles Edward slept and a number of interesting artefacts including a bronze copy of the Prince's death mask. From Castle Menzies I followed the B846 north of the Tay to Tummel Bridge and then along the edge of Tummel forest to Trinafour. Here another stretch of military road goes to Dalnacardoch Lodge. The original building no longer exists but the new inn built by the government in 1774 is used as a shooting lodge today and bears a stone inscription testifying to its completion.

The Drumochter Pass took me to the whisky distillery in Dalwhinnie and the start of a few miles of quiet military road running parallel to the A9. Near Crubenmore the Wade road crosses the dual carriageway and continues as a footpath almost all the way to Ruthven Barracks. First I came to little Loch Etteridge and then crossed the Wade bridge near Lochan Dabhaich before skirting Lochan Odhar to Milton Burn. Perhaps there was once a bridge here but no trace of it now remains. The water was a couple of feet deep and about twelve wide. Wading was the only way so I changed my boots for a pair of lightweight old shoes and soothed my midge ravaged ankles for a few seconds in the cold water. I am told there is an easier crossing point about a quarter of a mile upstream for those without extra footwear.

The barracks at Ruthven is one of four identical garrisons built to discourage further rebellion after the rising of 1715. Ruthven was constructed between 1719 and 1721 and is much in the same state today as the Jacobites left it in 1746. The most interesting way to walk from Ruthven Barracks to Aviemore is to follow the B970 south of the River Spey and take some of the adjacent forest paths.

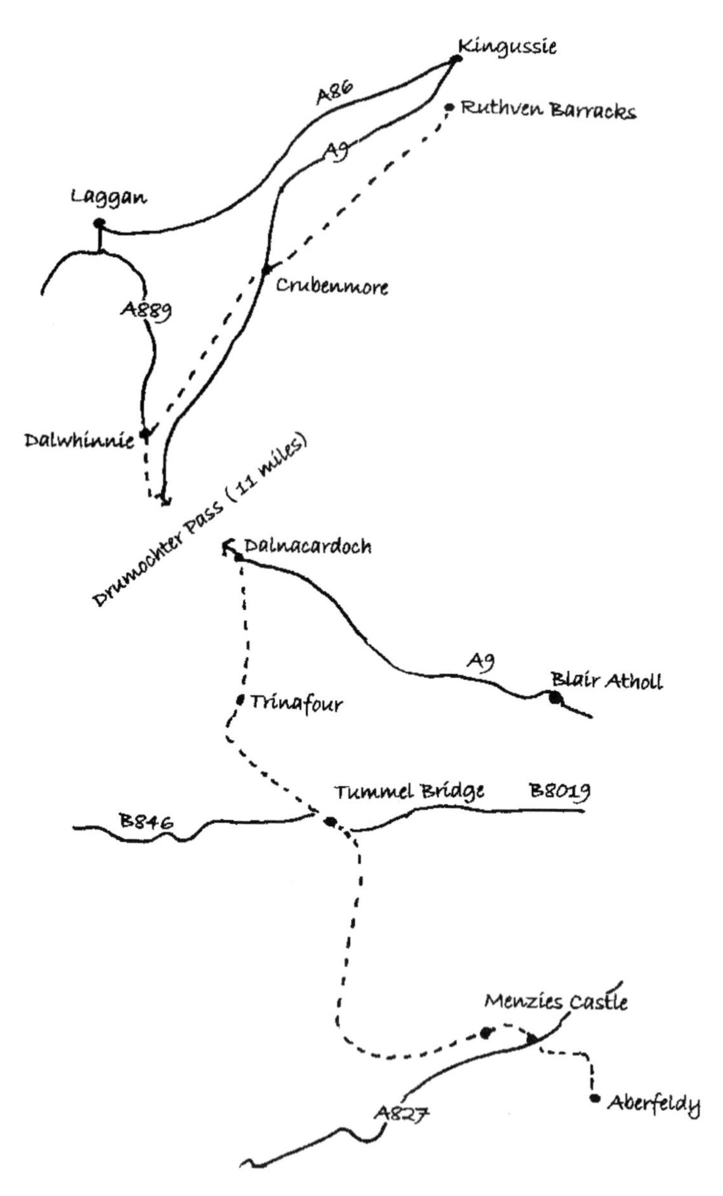

Aberfeldy to Ruthven Barracks (44 Miles)

Sluggan Bridge

From Aviemore there are a number of woodland paths running northwards to Kinveachy Lodge and then a Wade road, north-west over the Feith na Doire to Sluggan Bridge. A two-arched Wade bridge once stood here but it was swept away by floods a long time ago. The existing Sluggan Bridge is a remarkable sight. Built over the River Dulnain, it seems to not have been touched since its completion and is a beautiful yet fragile creation carrying the green road high over the fast flowing stream. A short mile south-west of Sluggan Bridge are the desolate remains of Inverlaidnan House where Prince Charles spent the night with Grant of Dalrachny and his inhospitable wife. The building has been in a state of complete ruination for more than a hundred years. I carried on to the isolated farmstead at Insharn and found the woodland road and bubbling burn that lead to Slochd on the A9.

The military road continues parallel with the A9 to Tomatin and Moy. After Culloden 'Colonel' Anne Mackintosh continued to live with her husband Aeneas at Moy Hall. Aeneas died in 1770 and Anne moved to Leith near Edinburgh where she died at the age of 64 in 1787. Colonel Anne is buried in a cemetery in Coburg Street, North Leith where a plaque close to the entrance commemorates her life. The precise site of her grave is unknown.

Leading off to the left opposite Moy there is a trail all the way to Inverness. It starts well but at Lynemore deteriorates into a boggy heather morass. Fortunately General Wade's road reappears, driving north across the Midlairgs Burn and into a large and visually unpleasant sand and gravel works. It is so big I had to ask a truck driver for directions to get me out of the place. He suggested I jump into the cab and we drove down to the B851 close to Faillie and the Wade bridge over the Nairn. The military road continues, first as a modern forestry track and then as a minor road heading for Inverness. It finishes on Stevenson Road about a mile and a half from the city centre.

The exact location of Lady Macintosh's house in Church St, Inverness is not known and so sadly nothing is marked. Culloden House was badly damaged by fire in 1753 but was rebuilt after being

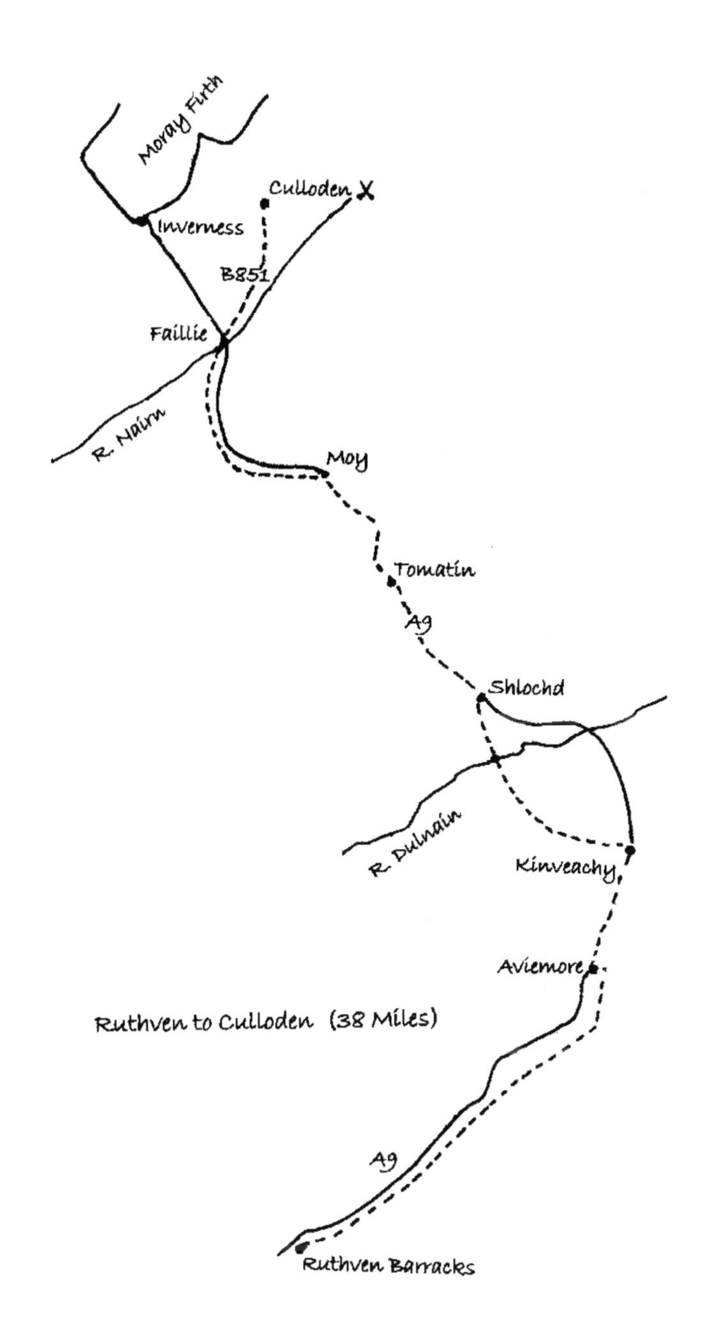
Moray Firth
Culloden
Inverness
B851
Faillie
R. Nairn
Moy
Tomatin
A9
Shlochd
R. Dulnain
Kinveachy
Aviemore
Ruthven to Culloden (38 Miles)
A9
Ruthven Barracks

derelict for nearly twenty years. It stayed in Forbes' family hands until 1897 when death duties forced the sale of both house and contents. In 1975 the property was converted into the Culloden House Hotel. The hotel has a catalogue of the 1897 sale and it makes fascinating reading. The bed in which the Prince slept sold for £750, a huge sum especially when compared to the £30 realised from a painting by Titian. Balblair House, where the Duke of Cumberland had his headquarters, is half a mile to the west of Nairn. The house there today is set back amongst trees in extensive grounds but is not old enough to have been there in 1746. I walked out to Meikle Kildrummie perhaps the most forward point the Jacobites attained on that fateful night of 15/16 April. John Home recounts that *'the place where the Highland army halted, is called the Yellow Know (Knoll), the name of a small farm-house belonging to Rose of Kilravock, which is above three miles from Nairn.'* Quite where this might be found is not clear but there is a house named Rosefield marked on the modern map, south of the river about a mile from Kildrummie.

We shall never know what would have happened if the clans had continued the night march and rushed upon the British army in the early hours of the morning. Did they have any chance of victory? Did anyone think it through? The answer to both those questions is, 'probably not.' The Jacobite army had marched about six miles in about six hours and at two in the morning were still four miles from their enemy with the columns of men stretched out way behind those in the van. By the time the whole army was in position to attack it would certainly have been daylight, the element of surprise would have been lost and Cumberland would have been prepared. Nevertheless, with hindsight we can see that the outcome of a night attack could not have been worse than the consequences of turning back were to prove.

John Daniel has his own opinion of what went wrong during the night march. The army either lost its way or was deliberately misled and marched '*over double the ground that was necessary.'*

We began our March about seven o'Clock leaving great fires burning in our camp: but by some strange infatuation or misfortune the road was not rightly taken, either through the ignorance or treachery of Lord George Murray's guide. This still remains doubtful, but this I can say, that with the little knowledge I had of the country I could have conducted them much better and sooner.

The army straggled back to Drummossie Moor in some disarray. The men were exhausted and famished and the right course of action would have been to retreat, regroup, rest, eat and prepare for battle on another day. The Prince perhaps frustrated by yet more advice to withdraw would have nothing to do with such ideas and simply hoped that Cumberland would not attack immediately. The Jacobites' last hope was for a day of respite, the delivery of provisions and the chance for Cluny Macpherson's men and others to join the ranks. They were to be disappointed.

I caught the bus from the centre of Inverness to Culloden field. On a bright April morning, two hundred and fifty-three years and four days after the battle that ended Stuart chances of a return to the throne, I stood gazing at the monument (picture p34) commemorating the event. It is difficult if not impossible to imagine how the ordinary clansmen or their officers felt before the battle began. They were almost defeated before a shot was fired. Perhaps they knew they would be beaten. Perhaps they were too tired and hungry to care. That they would fight to the end was sure. They had no choice. Quite how Prince Charles felt is even more difficult to imagine. He was probably still unrealistically optimistic. He believed passionately in his cause and his divine right to the throne. He was sure his Generals had let him down and was furious with Lord George for having ordered the withdrawal the night before. Nevertheless he had the memories of Prestonpans and Falkirk to encourage him and with his invincible Highlanders and God on his side the Young Pretender could continue to pretend. The fury of the cannonade seemed to paralyse the Prince and that he allowed his lines to be blasted to pieces for so long is inexcusable. At last the orders to charge were given but it was all too little and too late. The consequences were inevitable.

The battlefield is relatively unspoiled and efforts are being made to bring it even closer to the conditions that prevailed at the time. The positions of the opposing regiments are marked and the visitor centre contains numerous period pieces and details of the campaign. The choice of the Chief of Clan Cameron, Colonel Sir Donald Cameron of Lochiel to open the centre on 19 July 1984 was a fitting tribute to his predecessor without whose support the campaign would probably never have begun.

Duncan Forbes, the tenth laird of Culloden erected the memorial cairn in 1881. In 1944 Hector Forbes, the thirteenth laird, presented it to the National Trust for Scotland.

THE BATTLE OF CULLODEN
was fought on this moor
16th April, 1746.
The graves of the gallant highlanders
who fought for
SCOTLAND AND PRINCE CHARLIE
are marked by the names of their clans.

Much has been made over the years of the cruelty meted out to the rebel army immediately after the battle, and to the Highland way of life in the succeeding years. The government was certainly determined to stamp out sympathy for the Jacobite cause and took the view that if this involved the destroying of the clan structure in the most fearsome way, then so be it. The discovery of a forged letter purporting to be signed by Lord George Murray and instructing the Prince's army *'to give no quarter to the Elector's troops on any account whatsoever,'* served only to enrage Cumberland's men. Whether the Duke used this letter as an excuse to order severe treatment of Highlanders is not certain. The handwriting is not the

Duke's nor any of his closest aides, neither is it that of Lord George Murray. Lord Balmerino who commanded a troop of the Prince's personal lifeguards insisted, in a speech immediately before his execution on Monday, August 18 1746, that no such orders were given.

Lord President Duncan Forbes sought to ameliorate the worst of the atrocities by mentioning to the Duke of Cumberland that Highlanders suspected of being involved in the rebellion ought to treated according to the laws of the country. Cumberland would have none of that, retorting, *'the laws of the country my Lord! I'll make a brigade give laws by God!'* Contemporary accounts are full of reports of looting, killing and house burning. Captain Caroline Scott, Major Lockhart, General Hawley and Captain John Ferguson who commanded HMS Furnace are just a few of the notorious men who ordered the most brutal treatment.

William Augustus, Duke of Cumberland was born on 15 April 1721, the second son of the future King George II. He died at the age of 44, on 31 October 1765 and is buried in nave of The Lady Chapel in Westminster Abbey. He was a Major-General at the age of 21 and was wounded at Dettingen in 1743. The Duke went on to command the army in 1745 at Fontenoy where the French defeated him. Sustained musket and cannon fire tore into the ranks of his men, teaching Cumberland a tactical lesson he was to use with good effect at Culloden. The Duke's life involved attempts to reform the army and he directed the course of the Seven Years War. Many of the events of his life and his efforts in the realms of princely public service do not indicate that he was a barbaric or unusually cruel man. However, because of the murders, rapes, lootings and burnings visited upon the Highlanders in the aftermath of Culloden, he has been dubbed 'Butcher Cumberland' ever since.

A notable incident occurred when Hawley noticed Charles Fraser of Inverallochy, the commander of Clan Fraser, wounded and defenceless on the ground. Hawley asked him to whom he belonged and received the reply, *'To the Prince.'* Brigade Major James Wolfe was instantly ordered *'to shoot the insolent scoundrel,'* an order that to his credit he refused to obey on the grounds that the King's commission did not include the requirement for him to become an executioner. Not to be denied Hawley ordered an ordinary soldier to do the dirty work and thus had his way.

Captain Caroline Scott hanged three men near Glenevis despite the fact that they had come to him to give up their arms. Scott told them that as others had not surrendered they were to hang. The men could not believe he was serious and even as the ropes were put about their necks were laughingly of the opinion that Scott simply meant to frighten them. *'But they were mistaken; for instantly they were hang'd and had not so much time as to beg God to have mercy upon their souls.'*

Another insight into redcoat behaviour after the battle can be found in John Maclean's journal. Donald Maclean continued the chronicle after his kinsman's death. *'In this Battell the greatest Barbaritys was Committed that ever was heard to be done by Either Cristians turks or Pagan, I mean by our Enemies who gave no quarters Kild our men that was wounded in cold blood and continued so doing for three or four Days or any others they could Catch.'*

Highlanders were often killed wherever they could be found and prisoners treated according to the laws of treason. The high-ranking were beheaded or hanged and more than a thousand others were transported to America. Additionally 3471 men, women and children were imprisoned in Britain and around 600 of these died in custody. Some Jacobites who managed to escape capture fled to the continent to live permanently in exile. 'Hangman' Hawley, as he was known, was of the opinion that if, '*the parliament would give the men a guinea and a pair of shoes for every rebel's head they brought in I would still undertake to clear this country.'* He bragged of seven thousand houses already burned and that there were still many more to be destroyed. John Daniel recorded some observations made of the privations suffered in the Highlands while travelling through Lochaber on his way to the coast and escape to France.

> *On the road I was overtaken by about forty women, half starved to death who were wandering up and down for safety. Some of them, who spoke English, told me, they had been driven out of their houses by the soldiers who were sent out from Fort William to ravage and burn and plunder all before them and now it was that the most heart-rending scenes of misery began to present themselves; for many of these poor creatures with children in their arms, lay extended in the clefts of the rocks half covered in snow, dead and a-dying in the most piteous manner.*

Even the wearing of tartan was proscribed. The Act for the Abolition and Prescription of the Highland Dress was passed after Culloden and the West Highland museum in Fort William has a copy of the oath that suspects had to swear.

> *I swear as I shall answer to God at the great Day of Judgement I have not and I shall not have in my possession any gun, sword or arms whatsoever and never use tartan plaid or any part of the Highland garb and if I do so may I be accursed in my undertakings, family and property. May I never see my wife nor children, nor father, mother or relations. May I be killed in battle as a fugitive coward and lie without Christian burial in a foreign land far from the graves of my forefathers and kindred. May all this come upon me if I break this oath.*

The Act was not repealed until 1782 but as the years passed it seems not to have been enforced rigorously. By the time Thomas Pennant made his 1769 tour of Scotland he was able to record the sight of *'a most singular group of Highlanders in all their motley dresses.'* He continues:

The fillebeg, i.e. little plaid, also called kelt, is a sort of short petticoat reaching only to the knees, and is a modern substitute for the lower part of the plaid, being found to be less cumbersome, especially in times of action, when the Highlanders used to tuck their brechan into their girdle. Almost all have a great pouch of badger and other skins, with tassles dangling before. In this they keep their tobacco and money.

TEN

ESCAPE TO THE ISLANDS

'Let every one seek the means of escape as well as he can.'
Message from Prince Charles to his troops at Ruthven
Chevalier de Johnstone ~ A Memoir of the Forty-Five

In the confusion after the battle the men of FitzJames' Horse led Charles across the River Nairn at the Ford of Faillie to relative safety. It was here that Lord Elcho was reunited with the Prince and *'found him in a deplorable state.'* The Prince was in shock and could not believe that his beloved Highlanders had failed to put the enemy to flight in the same way as they had at Prestonpans and Falkirk. The Pretender seemed to think that treason was the foundation of the defeat and, according to anecdotal evidence recorded by Sir Walter Scott many years after the event, Elcho, *'appeared to be afraid of the Scotch as a whole, thinking that they would be capable of giving him up to the Duke to obtain peace and the £30,000 sterling that the King had offered for his head. He appeared to be concerned only about the lot of the Irish and not at all about that of the Scots.'* Lord Elcho asked if his Prince had orders for him and was less than impressed by the reply.

> *He told me that I might go anywhere I liked; as for himself, he was about to leave for France. I told him that I was surprised at a resolution so little worthy of a Prince of his birth, that it was unworthy to have engaged all this people to sacrifice itself for him, and to abandon it because he had possibly lost a thousand men in battle; that he ought to remain and out himself at the head of the 9,000 men that remained to him, and live and die with them. But these reasons made*

no impression on him. He told me he was determined to seek safety in France: whereupon I left him, thoroughly resolved never to have any more to do with him.

So began Charles' long journey, running and hiding, until at last, and quite amazingly, he escaped into France and a life of exile. The Prince's party included Thomas Sheridan, John William O'Sullivan, Lord Elcho, Alexander MacLeod, Ned Burke, and Captain Felix O'Neil. The men fled down the shore of Loch Ness through Tordarroch, Aberarder and Farraline to Gorthleck, fifteen miles south-west of Culloden. Fraser of Gorthleck offered the men shelter and supper despite the fact that his clan chief Lord Lovat, who had no desire to become involved with the Prince, was visiting the house.

The fugitives could not afford to stay long and were soon on the run again. They halted briefly at Fort Augustus where the Prince perhaps hoped to rendezvous with what remained of his army. Felix O'Neil recorded that *'previous to the battle the Prince ordered the chieftains in case of a defeat, as the Highlanders could not retreat as regular troops, to assemble their men near Fort Augustus.'* However, it appears that the Pretender, perhaps unable to countenance defeat, had not made the orders clear to all his officers and there was confusion regarding the rallying point. Lord Elcho, who had supper with the Prince twenty-four hours before the night march to Balblair reports that the Prince was overly optimistic in anticipating the result of the forthcoming battle and refused to countenance the need for a muster station in the event of a beating. *'The Prince was so far from thinking of retreating that he would have taken it much Amiss if any body had doubted so far of a Victory as to have ask'd him where the army Should rendezvous in Case of a defeat.'*

When the battle was lost most of the troops and those prominent Jacobites who were not with the Prince had made for Ruthven under the command of Lord George Murray. Whether Prince Charles meant to rally his troops and continue the campaign, or had accepted defeat and was concerned only with escaping capture and sailing to France is debateable. We have an insight in the form of a letter written to Cluny Macpherson by Alexander MacLeod, who was Charles' aide-de-camp, on the evening after the battle.

> *You have heard no doubt ere now of the ruffle we met with this forenoon. We have suffered a good deal; but we hope we shall soon pay Cumberland in his own Coin. We are to review tomorrow, at Fort Augustus, the Frasers Camerons, Stewarts, Clanranald's and Keppoch's people. His R.H. expects your people will be with us at furthest Friday morning ~ for God's sake make haste to join us.*

This does not sound like a letter from a man whose commander-in-chief has accepted defeat. The letter was passed to Lord George Murray and his comments written on the back of it indicate that he was in the dark regarding the rallying point, *'I observe the rendezvous was to be as yesterday at Fort Augustus, but those who came from there last night, say H.R.H. was gone for Clanronald's country.'* Clearly Lord George was of the opinion that Prince Charles did not intend to rally his troops at Fort Augustus, Ruthven or anywhere else. Some explanation for the Prince's apparently contradictory positions may be found in a letter written by Lord George to Charles on 17 April. It is a long, scathing and bitter letter of resignation which comments on Prince Charles' conduct of the campaign in general and places the blame for defeat at Culloden squarely on the shoulders of Colonel O'Sullivan.

> *It was surely wrong to sett up the Royal Standard without having posetive assurance from his most Christian Majesty that he would assist you with all his might ~ As for what regards the management of your Army, we were all fully convinced that Mr O'Sullivan, whom yr R.H. trusted with the most escential things in regard to your operations, was exceedingly unfit for it, & committed gross Blunders on many occasions. ~ In short never was more improper ground for*

Highlanders than that where we fought. Our Athollmen and others on the right lost half their officers and men. Happy had it been for us that Mr. O'Sullivan had never got any other charge or office in our army then the care of the Baggage and equipages, which I'm told he had been brought up to and understood.

This letter perhaps contributed to Charles' growing realisation that all was lost and influenced his decision to flee. Charles never forgave Lord George for writing in such a manner and the letter ended the already difficult relationship between them. The two men were never to see each other again. The Chevalier de Johnstone was of the opinion that the Pretender had given up too easily. He points out that the Jacobites still held all the passes between Ruthven and Inverness and that Cluny Macpherson's clan and others who were not at Culloden had joined them at Ruthven.

Our numbers increased every moment, and I am thoroughly convinced that, in the course of eight days, we should have had a more powerful army than ever capable of re-establishing without delay the state of our affairs and of avenging the barbarous cruelties of the Duke of Cumberland. But the Prince was inexorable and immoveable in his resolution of abandoning his enterprise.

The Prince and his small group crossed the River Oich near Aberchalder and followed the shore of Loch Oich to Invergarry Castle where they arrived in the early hours of the next day. The castle was deserted and the group took some welcome rest. After a breakfast of salmon caught by his servant Ned Burke, Charles marched south-west along the northern shore of Loch Lochy and then west to the head of Loch Arkaig and the house of Donald Cameron of Glenpean. On 19 April the fugitives marched *'by the cruelest road yt cou'd be seen'* to Meoble in South Morar to spend the night in a small house in a wood. By six o'clock in the morning on

20 April they reached Arisaig by way of Glen Beasdale. Once again the Prince took up residence in Angus MacDonald's house at Borrodale and he remained there for five days. An idea of the adversity suffered during the journey can be had from Captain Daniel's account.

> *And now it was that I began to be truly miserable, and to endure hardships which I had thought impossible for human nature to support, for in that most hideous place I was deprived of every thing that could give me comfort. ~ Though I was fat and strong at the battle of Culloden, I was now quite emaciated and reduced to so miserable a state, that, if I had had another day to walk, I am sure I must have died; for I was not only starved with hunger and cold, but frightfully covered with vermin, which bit me all over my body so that there remained not one whole place in my skin.*

It is difficult to believe but it seems that Prince Charles had it in his head to sail to Skye where he imagined help would be forthcoming from MacLeod of MacLeod and MacDonald of Sleat. Prince Charles met sixty-eight year old Donald MacLeod of Galtrigill on Skye *'in a wood, all alone'* and asked him to take a message to the two great Skye chiefs adding, *'for I am really convinced that these gentlemen for all they have done, will do all in their power to protect me.'* For the Prince to consider such a crazy plan is indicative of the dire straights in which he found himself. MacLeod was clearly flabbergasted at the idea and straightforwardly refused the mission. *'What,'* said Donald, *'does not your excellency know that these men have played the rogue to you altogether, and will you trust then for a' that? Na, you mauna do't.'* Charles was eventually convinced and after discovering that Galtrigill was a fine pilot, changed his plans hoping to be carried *'safely through the islands, where I may look for more safety than I have here.'*

On the evening of 26 April the Prince, Colonel O'Sullivan, Captain Felix O'Neil, Father Allan MacDonald, Donald MacLeod,

Ned Burke and several boatmen set out to sea from the shore of Loch nan Uamh. The weather was terrible and the boat began to fill with water. Even MacLeod who knew the seas well thought all was lost. The sailors prayed for deliverance, prompting the Prince to comment that while the clergyman who was with them ought to pray, the rest would be better employed bailing out the water. Next morning they struggled into a creek at Roisinis on the north-east point of Benbecula.

On 30 April, just four days after the Prince had escaped from the mainland, two French ships, Le Mars and La Bellone put into Loch nan Uamh and engaged in a fierce battle with the 24-gun Greyhound and two smaller vessels. Le Mars was badly damaged but La Bellone got the better of the British ships and they withdrew. The French vessels brought weapons and brandy as well as 35,000 louis d'or, of which Murray of Broughton used 5,000 for current expenses and buried the rest. Very few people knew the location of the 'Treasure of Loch Arkaig', possibly not even the Prince. What to do with the treasure became the source of much argument in years to come and it is possible that some of the gold remains hidden to this day.

The crews of Le Mars and La Bellone were told that the rebellion was effectively over and on 4 May the ships picked up the Duke of Perth, Lord John Drummond, Lord Elcho, Sir Thomas Sheridan and dozens of other Jacobite supporters. Had Prince Charles not made off for the western isles it is likely that he too would have been on board so avoiding the hardships and difficulties of the next few months. John Daniel sailed on La Bellone and his comments throw light on the conditions on board.

> *In the ship I was in, there raged a contagious distemper, which carried off sixty-seven in twenty-five days; and about the tenth day of our voyage, I saw the body of my friend and patron the Duke of Perth, thrown over-board; which afflicting sight, joined with my violent sickness, I expected would have put an end to my life. But what I thought would*

have killed me, perhaps contributed to save my life in that pestiferous ship; as my continual vomiting may have hindered any thing noxious from taking effect on me. But what is very surprising, for twenty-two days I had not one call of nature, which I affirm upon honour.

Despite the absence of their Prince, the clan chiefs had not yet quite given up hope of further resistance. On 8 May, at Muirlaggan on Loch Arkaig the chiefs made a number of precise resolutions that show a willingness to carry on the struggle.

To raise in arms, for the interest of His Royal Highness Charles Prince of Wales, and in defence of our country, all the able-bodied men that all and every one of us can command or raise within our respective interests or properties. We hereby promise and agree that the following Clans, viz Locheil, Glengary, Clanronald, Stewarts of Appin, Keppoch, Barrisdale, Mackinnon, and Macleods, shall rendezvous on Thursday next the 15th instant, at Auchnicarry, in the braes of Lochaber. ~ Never to lay down our arms, or make a separate peace, without the general consent of the whole. And in case any one engaged in this association shall make separate terms for himself, he shall be looked upon as a traitor to his Prince, and treated as an enemy.

Whether this determination was inspired by a unanimous consensus that a viable fighting force could be assembled is not clear. Quite how their Prince was reacting to the defeat at Culloden was unknown. The situation was desperate and it is possible that the clan chiefs felt that the choices were either to fight on or to surrender to the harsh reality of redcoat mercy. Arranging the gathering scheduled for the 15th was proving difficult. On 13 May Lochiel wrote to Cluny Macpherson and his opening words, *'I have nothing new to acquaint you of,'* perhaps sum up the position. The letter expresses hope that '*a summer campaign*' might be mounted but the admission that *'I have scarcely a sufficiency of meal to serve myself and the gentlemen who are with me, for four days and can get none to purchase in the country'* is indicative of the terrible conditions even the commanders of the rising had to bear.

Several days later Cluny received another letter written by Murray of Broughton on 19 May. He says, *'It has not been possible for numberless reasons to keep the time fixed upon at our meeting; neither will the ammunition be here before Friday night, by which time I hope we may have many more men than have yet appeared.'* The proposed clan rendezvous had to be postponed for a few days and when at last it took place fewer than 500 men turned up. By 25 May even Lochiel had to admit that the game was up. He wrote to the chiefs expressing his disappointment at the poor response to the gathering.

> *Our assembling was not so general nor hearty as was expected, for Clanronald's people would not leave their own country, and many of Glengary's have delivered up their arms; so that but few came with Lochgary to Invermely on Tuesday last, where he staid but one night and crossed Locharkaik with his men, promising to return with a greater number in two days, and that he would guard the passes on that side; neither of which was done. ~ Your people should separate, and keep themselves as safe as possible, and keep their arms. ~ We have great expectations of the French doing something for us.*

Prince Charlie's life was becoming a series of unplanned escapes from danger. Ships of the Royal Navy swarmed over the Minch and travelling by day was risky. On the evening of 29 April the Prince's party was again at sea making for Stornoway on the Isle of Lewis. Just before daybreak they went ashore on Scalpay, at the entrance to Loch Tarbert where they stayed for four nights with MacLeod's friend Donald Campbell. It is not likely that Campbell was a confirmed Jacobite but when approached by a boatload of armed men anxious for the £30,000 reward on the Prince's head, he remembered his duty as a host and threatened the potential captors who slunk off without a fight.

Clearly the Prince's whereabouts were either known or strongly suspected, and MacLeod was sent to Stornoway to hire a vessel to take Charles Edward to France. A suitable brig was found and initial negotiations secured its hire for £100. However, the ship's master suspected the nature of the voyage and withdrew from the bargain, prompting MacLeod to offer to buy the vessel for £300. Not one to miss out on a desperate customer the owner demanded £500 and having no choice Donald promised the sum. Three days later Charles received the message that a ship had been found and so sailed to the head of Loch Seaforth on Lewis and then walked to Stornoway, accompanied by O'Sullivan, O'Neil and Burke. The journey was difficult. The guide was not familiar with the path and took the party through swamps and bogs in pouring rain. Charles lodged himself with Mrs Mackenzie of Kildun House who was kind enough to supply provisions for the proposed sea voyage. While finalising arrangements Donald MacLeod encountered a party of armed Mackenzies who suspected that the Prince was on the island and were fearful of redcoat reprisals. They eventually forced Donald to admit that the Prince was nearby. The men intended no harm to Charles but left Donald in no doubt that they would be delighted if he left their part of the Hebrides. To make matters worse the ship's captain reneged on his bargain and no other suitable vessel could be found. There was no choice but to leave Stornoway and return to Scalpay.

As the fugitives' little craft ploughed a southerly course it was spotted by the Royal Navy and compelled to flee. The tiny island of Eurin (now called Eilean Iubhaird) provided relative safety and the Prince and his companions spent four days there. They took shelter in a tiny hut and were sustained by a stock of dried fish, hurriedly left behind by local fishermen who had scattered at their approach. The journey to Scalpay was resumed on 10 May but on arrival the group discovered that Donald Campbell was no longer there. He had preferred to leave home temporarily rather than risk the wrath of the redcoats by offering hospitality to the Prince.

The party put to sea again and hugged the coast towards Benbecula. Captain John Ferguson commanding HMS Furnace spotted them off Finsbay on Harris. Low water in an ebbing tide prevented Furnace from coming too close and the Prince escaped yet again. A course was set for Lochmaddy in North Uist, where they found another government warship and had to spend the night at sea. The enemy were everywhere. H.M. ships Greyhound, Baltimore, Terror and Raven were in the waters, shortly to be joined by Glasgow, Tryal and Happy Jennet. The next morning the fugitives beached their craft on a little island, perhaps Bearran, in Loch Uisgebhagh, Benbecula. The Prince laid down to rest in *'a poor grasskeeper's bothy or hut, which had so laigh a door that we digged below the door and put heather below the Prince's knees, he being tall, to let him go the easier into the poor hut.'*

The Prince sent for MacDonald of Clanranald, who brought Neil MacEachain with him to act as a guide. MacEachain was born in 1719 at Howbeg on South Uist and spent some time in the 1730s at the Scots College in Paris studying for the priesthood. He returned to the Long Island in 1738 after apparently giving up his religious studies and tradition has it that he was a schoolmaster for a while. In 1740 MacEachain, in the role of tutor, accompanied Clanranald's son, Young Clanranald, to France where they both became acquainted with Prince Charles. The two returned to Scotland some months before the rising began.

On 14 May MacEachain led Charles to a bothy in Glen Corradale on South Uist. This proved to be an excellent refuge, as the glen is isolated and difficult to reach by land. Charles and his companions spent three happy weeks in reasonable comfort in Corradale, hunting game, resting and being visited by supporters. The Prince was relatively safe, had sufficient to eat and brandy to drink. Both Neil MacEachain and Hugh MacDonald of Baleshare provide us with vivid snapshots of life at Corradale. MacEachain tells us that the Prince, *'took care to warm his stomach every morning with a hearty bumper of brandy, of which he always drank a vast deal; for he was seen to drink a whole bottle a day without being in the least concerned.'* Baleshare noted Charles' liking for brandy as well, *'We continued this drinking for 3 days and 3 nights. He still had the better of us, and even of Boystill* (Boisdale) *himself, notwithstanding his being as able a boullman, I dare say, as any in Scotland.'* Politics were often discussed and Baleshare leaves us with these illuminating comments regarding difficulties with the Prince's religion.

> *At last I starts the question if his highness wou'd take it amiss if I should tell him the greatest objections against him in Great Brittain. He said, Not. I told him that Popery and arbitrary government were the two chiefest. He said it was only bad constructions his enemys pat on't. "Do you 'no Mr M'Donald" he says, "what religion are all the princes in Europe of?" I told him I imagin'd they were of the same establish'd religion of the nation they liv'd in. He told me then they had litle or no religion at all.*

It is during the stay in Corradale that we hear of the restorative powers of 'treacle', as any palliative liquor seems to have been called at the time. Prince Charles was suffering from dysentery, which he attributed to drinking milk. The Prince *'took a loosenesse wch turned to a bloody flux'* and announced, *'if I had traicle, I'd be cured immediately.'* Remarkably, *'Sullivan remembered yt he had a little pot yt he carried about him when he was ill himself.'* The 'traicle' seems to have worked as we are told that *'in three days time the flux caissed.'* Clanranald visited Corradale again and the clothes he brought for Charles seem to have greatly impressed His Royal Highness. *'When the Prince got on his highland Cloaths he was quite another man. "Now," says he leping, "I only want the Itch to be a compleat highlander."'*

The interlude could not last forever and one day MacEachain brought the news that soldiers were combing the neighbouring islands.

Flight was called for again. The story of next couple of weeks is confused. The Prince and his party set sail and came ashore on the island of Wiay off Benbecula's south-east coast. A few days later Charles Edward and Felix O'Neil set out again and landed at Roisinis point. Donald MacLeod and O'Sullivan who stayed behind on Wiay decided that the Prince was in peril on Benbecula. They sailed across two days later to take him to a place of greater safety. It is possible they had chosen to return to Corradale, or perhaps it was bad weather drove them on to the coast of South Uist two or three miles north of Corradale, at Acarsaid Falaich (Hidden Harbour) near Uisinis point.

They were off again on the following day, this time for Lochboisdale. Royal Navy ships forced the fugitives to, *'a place called Cilistiela in South Uist.'* Cilistiela is thought to be the narrow channel, once printed as Kyle Stuley but today marked on the O.S. map as Caolas Stulaigh, separating the mainland of South Uist from the island of Stulaigh. The Prince hoped that MacDonald of Boisdale would again come to his rescue but unfortunately he had been arrested. The news was a serious blow. Evidence is scanty but it seems that the Prince was forced to set up camp on Calbhaigh (Calvay) island near the entrance to Lochboisdale. Neil MacEachain's narrative names the island as *'Stialay, a small island near the entry of Loch Boystile, within three long miles of Boystile's house.'* Ned Burke's account offers no name but provides some description. *'Afterwards coming ashore very much fatigued, we came to an old tower in the mouth of the island.'* MacEachain seems to have made a mistake in his recollection of the island's name perhaps confusing Stulaigh with Calbhaigh. There is a ruined castle on Calbhaigh and I think this must be the place. Despite Lady Boisdale's brave and generous efforts to provide the fugitives with food the Prince's situation became even more desperate. Two war ships blockaded the entrance to the loch and 500 soldiers were diligently searching not more than two miles away.

Landranger Maps

27 Nairn & Forres
33 Loch Alsh & Glen Shiel
26 Inverness & Strathglass
40 Mallaig & Glenfinnan
35 Kingussie
31 Barra & South Uist
34 Fort Augustus & Glen Albyn
22 Benbecula & South Uist

Faillie (27)	**NH712381**
'Nameless lochan' (40)	**NM892896**
Gorthleck House (26)	**NH547214**
Meoble (40)	**NM796877**
Invergarry (34)	**NH315005**
Roisinis (22)	**NF875536**
Strathan (33)	**NM979913**
Prince's Shore (31)	**NF786106**
Glen Corradale (22)	**NF834313**

I left the battlefield at Culloden by the B851 and joined the A9 at Balvonie. After a short walk along the main road I scrambled down an embankment to Daviot. Another mile or so brought me once again to the Ford of Faillie and the bridge over the River Nairn. Now it was back to the B851 for a long walk down Strath Nairn to the junction with the road to Gorthleck. Names have changed over the years and the Gorthleck House marked on modern maps is not the building the Prince visited. Fraser of Gorthleck's house is now called Gorthleck Mains and is a white painted farmhouse commanding magnificent views over Loch Mhor. The B862 continues through Whitebridge, past Loch Tarff and into Fort Augustus. Having already walked from Achnacarry and Loch Arkaig to Fort Augustus I decided not to repeat the experience in the opposite direction and hitch-hiked along the A82 into Spean Bridge. On the way I stopped for a few

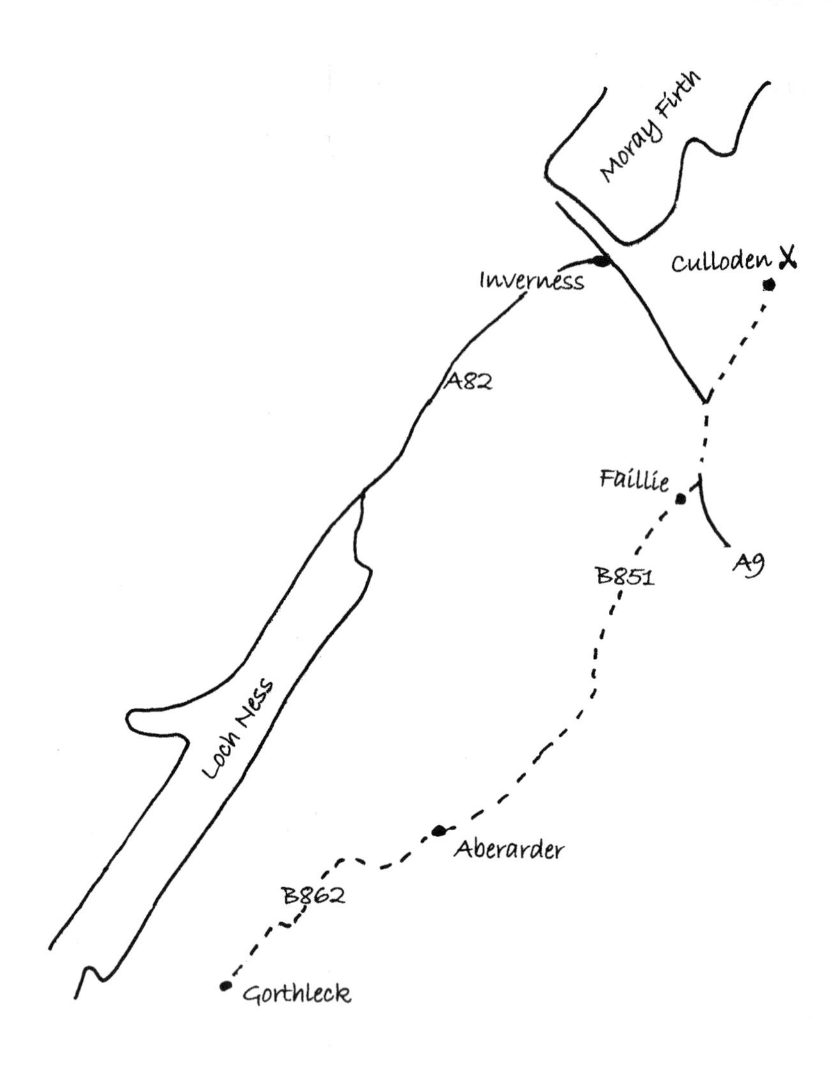

Culloden to Gorthleck (20 Miles)

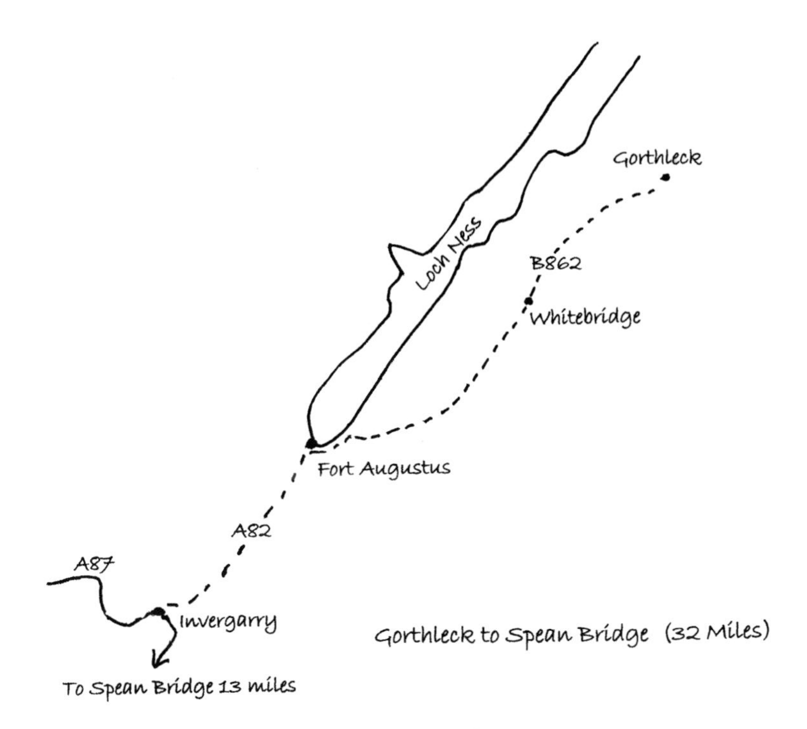
Gorthleck
Loch Ness
B862
Whitebridge
Fort Augustus
A82
A87
Invergarry
To Spean Bridge 13 miles
Gorthleck to Spean Bridge (32 Miles)

minutes to visit Invergarry Castle. The ruins stand in the grounds of the Glengarry Castle Hotel and are in a sorry state of repair. Notices on the fence surrounding the castle's sad little enclosure inform visitors of the fragile and dangerous state of the structure.

The next morning I prevailed upon Drew, my B&B host, to drive me to Clunes on the northern shore of Loch Lochy where the road known the 'Mile Dorcha' or 'Dark Mile' reaches out to the eastern end of Loch Arkaig. From here there are twelve more miles to the other end of the loch and a narrow road exists along the whole length of the northern shore. There are no established footpaths and Drew was kind enough to drive me to Strathan at the western end of the loch. A couple of miles from our destination we passed Muirlaggan, where the declaration was signed,.

From Strathan I struck out towards Meoble. There are a couple of sound, dry bothies along the way but this is isolated country and the walk must not be undertaken without due consideration of the weather, the distances involved and the shortage of places to sleep. The walk began well enough and after an hour and a half I arrived at the bothy in Glen Pean. From here the distinct footpath disappears but it was clear that I should follow the River Pean to Lochan Leum an t-Sagairt. There is no path along the shore of the lochan (picture p35) and I was forced to climb into the hills to the south and then return to the ever-narrowing burn. A few gnarled and stunted remnants of an ancient forest cling to life amongst the craggy cliffs that bear down and dominate the glen at its highest reaches. Eventually the stream vanished underground and I knew that I was approaching the top, but that there was still some wild and difficult terrain to negotiate. There are rocks as big as houses strewn about the place like the results of a giant game of dice. If the Bonnie Prince had known he was to have this journey to suffer he might well have stayed at home.

A tiny nameless lochan close to the source of the River Pean shows up on the map as a tiny circlet of sparkling blue nestling amongst woodland. The real thing is swampy, green, overgrown (picture p35) and closely guarded by gigantic rocks and twisted trees.

Which Way From Here?

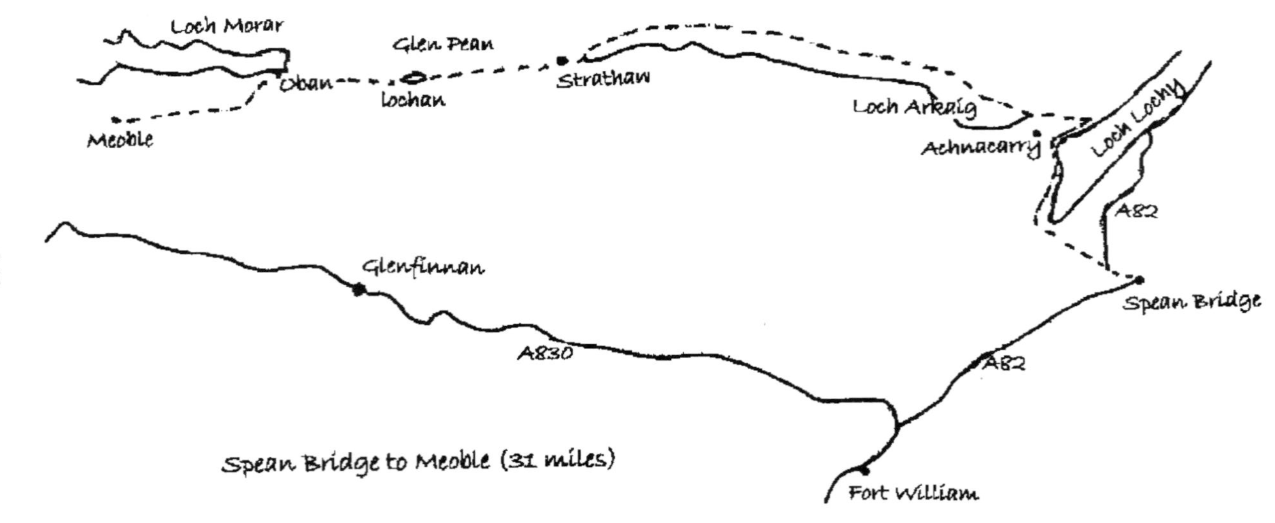

Spean Bridge to Meoble (31 miles)

The earth is sodden and the air is damp and silent. The place has a sinister and ghostly feeling. My imagination was working overtime and I could see the wicked witch of fairy stories waiting to jump out and scare me half to death in every tree and behind every rock. I had no wish to spend any more time here than was essential. My feeling of loneliness was compounded by the knowledge that I was in the centre of a wilderness and several hours walking in any direction from the nearest road or habitation. I discovered that it was possible to step along the edge of 'swampy green lochan', although I should think that at wetter times of the year this might be impossible. At the western end I climbed steeply, scrambling and scrabbling my way through rocks, higher and higher with no idea of how long the climb would last nor whether it would become so difficult I should be forced to descend and find another way. At last and with some sense of relief I found my way out to the left onto a less steep incline in open countryside. I could hear the welcome sound of a burn tumbling its way down the slope in the direction I needed to travel. My efforts were further rewarded with a heart-warming view of Loch Morar, a couple of miles away.

Loch Morar is a remarkable geological feature. Its western end is only a quarter of a mile from the sea, making the River Morar the shortest in the British Isles. The loch is the deepest in the kingdom. There are more than a thousand feet of water beneath the surface in places. Such depth is not matched off shore until the dip from the continental shelf is reached, some one hundred and seventy miles out to sea.

Oban bothy stands on the shore of Loch Morar in an outstanding location overlooking the glorious loch and surrounded by stunning mountains. The footpath leaves the shore and drifts south, ultimately running into Gleann Taodhail before turning west up to a tiny lochan at top of the pass. The way up is hard and steep and presented me with a number of disappointing false summits. From the top the Allt Slaite Coire flows gently through lumpy and boggy land for a couple of miles to Meoble. It is twelve or thirteen miles from the head of Loch Arkaig to Meoble and I had spent more than ten tough hours covering them. It was evening when I arrived and crucial that I found somewhere to sleep quickly. Meoble is a tiny place and its importance as a tourist destination can be gauged by the fact that it is, like Oban, inaccessible except on foot or by boat. There are a few well-furnished hunting lodges with inviting bedrooms but regrettably no one was in residence and despite ringing bells and blowing whistles I was unable to attract the attention of a living soul.

Clouds of the notorious Highland midges were driving me mad. I was growing increasingly weary and beginning to realise that I would probably have to sleep in the barn. I was not anticipating a comfortable night. Just before retiring to my bales of straw I noticed a caravan on the other side of the track. As a last resort I approached it with no expectation of anyone being in residence. No one was. Nevertheless I tried the door and to my surprise it opened. No alarm bells sounded and nobody came rushing out from the bedroom demanding that I leave at once. All was silent, so I went in and sat down. Oh, the relief of taking the weight off my feet for a few moments. I sat and no one came. I sat longer and took off my boots. I ate my remaining food and thought about trying to make the satellite T.V. work or making a cup of tea but did neither. At ten o'clock I unrolled my sleeping bag and lay down to watch the moon set behind a hill. As the last tiny crescent of moon disappeared there was a flash and a band of white light lit up the hillside. This was instantly replaced by a suffusion of light, which lasted some time as the moon sank lower. Still no one came. I fell asleep. In the morning I wrote a note thanking the owner and left a modest donation of five pounds for the night's rent. Shortly afterwards I left, but not before I had rustled around in the cupboards to find and eat a tin of tuna fish.

The route taken by the Prince from Meoble to Borrodale is not clear although two contemporary accounts describe the men emerging on the coast by Glen Beasdale. I was uncertain which route to take although I think the best way might be west from Meoble along the Abhainn Chlachach and Allt a' Bhlàir Dhairg and then south over Bealach a' Màma into Glen Beasdale. Drummond Norie, however, surmises that the party struck out south-west from Meoble past Lochan an Eas Bhàin and along the shore of Loch na Creige Duibhe. If so then the Prince must have finished the journey with a hard climb over the slopes of Druim Fiaclach into Glen Beasdale. My long and arduous journey the previous day had left me in need of some proper rest. I had no food to sustain me through the day so I chose to postpone my attempt and headed due south along a decent track to the western end of Loch Beoraid intending to finish up on the A830 Mallaig to Fort William road. Not long after crossing the River Meoble and using the eastern of two roughly parallel paths I began to climb steeply. The path, if such it can be called, entered a wild, woodland gully and I had to fight my way steeply uphill, cursing the pack I was carrying. Near the top there is a jumble of rocks, labelled on the map as 'Prince Charlie's Cave' although his Highness spent no time here on this part of his journey. He left that delight (if indeed he stayed here at all!) for his return trip from the Western Isles. At last, with great relief, I made it to the summit and followed the course of the Allt na Criche due south to the road and railway line at Arieniskill. With hindsight my recommendation to anyone attempting this walk is to stay away from the eastern path through the trees and use the western track that starts a mile or so closer to Meoble.

On my next visit I returned to the top of the hill near the royal cave. I couldn't face the struggle back to Meoble to begin the journey to Glen Beasdale and the miserable weather clinched it. I would walk west and leave the hills not in Glen Beasdale but in nearby Gleann Màma. On my previous visit Loch Beoraid had sparkled in the sunshine but now I could barely see it through the mist and drizzling rain. I turned left and slowly descended before beginning a long, slow drag over the pass between Cruach Thoraraidh and Creag Bhàn. I was certain that Loch na Creige Duibhe would come into view when I arrived at the top but as usual there were one or two false summits that crushed my optimism with the requirement for more effort. A final push produced a few moments of elation as I gazed down on the hazy outline of the loch far below.

That a footpath is marked on a Highland O.S. map is often

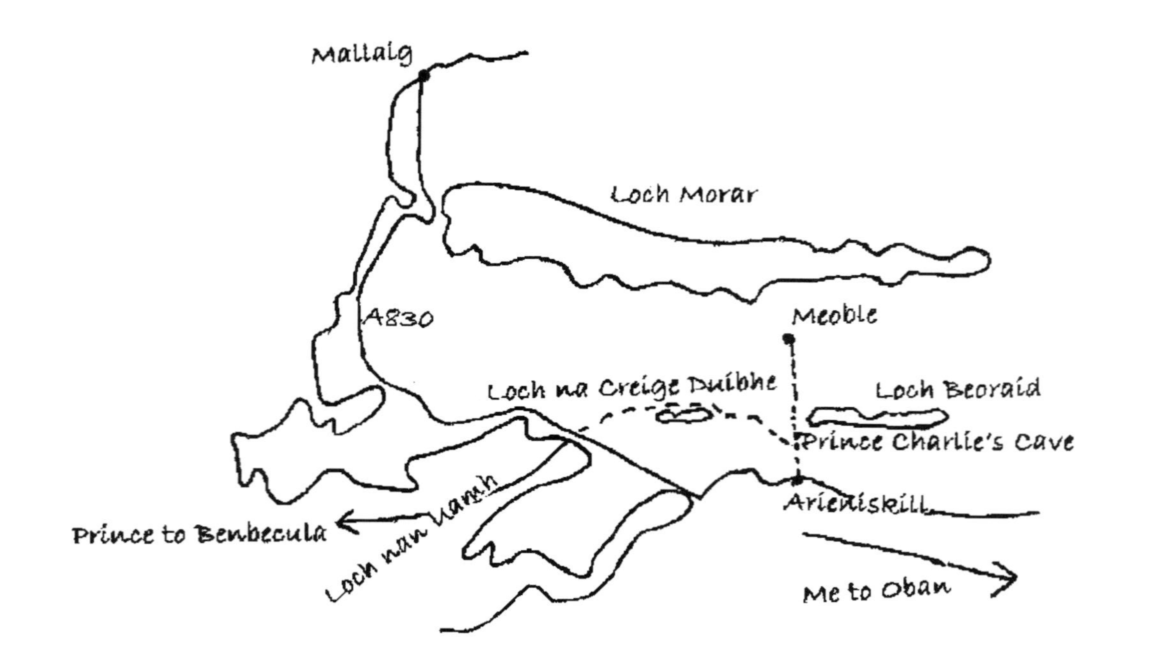

Meoble to Arieniskill and back to Loch nan Uamh (9 Miles)

simply an indication that others have been here before and if they have done it so can you. Such a path exists into Gleann Màma, along the northern shore of Loch na Creige Duibhe and its smaller neighbour, Loch Màma. At last I squelched my way onto the peninsula that does not quite separate the two lochs and at the western end of the second began to follow a stream that is not identified on my map but using the example of its two northern neighbours, Borrodale and Beasdale burns, I name the Màma burn. The map clearly identifies a path to the north of Màma burn but foolishly I was seduced by a wide track leading off from the southern edge of the loch. The track was easy to follow and I was not further tempted out of my way by the several paths that lead into the hills to the south. The trouble came when I was almost into the trees that cover both sides of the glen as it nears the coast. The burn ran deeper and deeper in its narrow gorge and my way forward became steep and difficult. The trees obscured the lie of the land and I knew that if I committed myself to this route and was unsuccessful then I should have to fight my way back up and cross the burn to the path marked on my map. My decision was easy. I must cross the burn at once and continue on the northern side. The implementation was more difficult. The burn, way below me, flowed fast and dangerous. To reach the far side I had to scramble down to the burn, pick my way over the water and haul myself and backpack up a steep heather covered gradient until I found the path. I did not enjoy the experience. I was no more than half a mile from the main road but a stumble or a twisted ankle could send me rolling down into the cold water rushing through the ravine where I might stay unnoticed for a very long time. Fortunately it didn't happen and I found the path where it was supposed to be. Even so I was heartily glad to reach safety and was sweating more than just a little when I did so. Once on the right track I made good progress, ironically recrossing the burn lower down, and arriving at last on the coast road at Loch nan Uamh.

Chartering a boat from Loch nan Uamh to Roisinis on Benbecula seemed unnecessarily extravagant and so I began my trip to the Hebrides from Oban on board the Caledonian MacBrayne ferry to Lochboisdale, South Uist. Promptly at 14:50 we steamed out of port through the Sound of Mull, across the Sea of the Hebrides, first to Castlebay on Barra and then on to Lochboisdale. I had booked bed and breakfast from the Tourist Information Office in Oban and stressed that as the ship docked at half past nine at night and I was on foot I would appreciate it if the accommodation were not too far from port. I was told not to worry and to watch out for a blue Nissan as I left the ship. Mr Ernie MacDonald would be there to pick me up. Sure enough he was and we sped away to a comfortable house where a night's rest was provided for a modest sum.

Charlie spent a lot of time dashing about the Hebrides both in boats and on land with no purpose other than to avoid the attention of his determined pursuers. I settled for visiting the significant Jacobite places on the islands in whatever order seemed convenient. I woke up on my first South Uist morning to a Hebridean breakfast, the like of which poor old Bonnie would never have seen during his time here. I was looking forward to the day, as it would fit in the missing first piece of the jigsaw. The Prince first set foot on British soil on the island of Eriskay and I felt a sense of achievement as I made my way to catch the ferry at Ludag pier. No doubt the service is subsidised as it provides a lifeline for the island but I was a little surprised to find myself the only passenger on the 0940 car ferry. I handed over my pound coin and fifteen minutes later the ship docked. The island is two and a half miles long and one and a half wide and the Coilleag a' Phrionnsa or Prince's Shore is a beautiful stretch of sandy beach not more than half a mile from the jetty. A pink convolvulus that grows on Eriskay is said to have grown from seeds brought from France in Charles' pocket. Quite why the Prince would have wanted to bring convolvulus seeds with him has not been adequately explained to me but it makes a good story. A cairn on the beach bears this message in English and Gaelic, '*This cairn was erected by the children of Eriskay school on July 23 1995 to commemorate the landing of Bonnie Prince Charlie here on July 23 1745.*'

I picked up a pebble as a souvenir and walked back along the beach thinking of the excitement and sense of expectation that the tiny band of adventurers must have felt at the beginning of their expedition to Britain. The day was fair and I lingered on the deserted strand meditating not just on Jacobite matters but using the solitude and the roll of the sea to examine my own life and times. Finding them less than perfect but pretty good compared with many others in our troubled world I arrived back in the village. The schoolchildren and teacher were outside and so I walked over to say hello and to thank them for building the cairn. The teacher had been a pupil at the school himself and we chatted about the imminent building of a causeway to South Uist and the advantages and drawbacks this might bring. The school will be affected with only the juniors remaining on the island, the seniors having to travel to school at Lionacleit on Benbecula. Only nineteen pupils attend Eriskay school at the time of writing so any reduction in numbers will seriously reduce the school's viability. The ending of 'island status' might also affect the speaking of Gaelic although the language is already under pressure from 'incomers' and television. Despite these reservations the academic staff of Eriskay school seemed to think that the causeway would bring more benefits than problems but I am pleased I was able to visit while this tiny island was still separated from its larger neighbour. Eriskay Catholic church is on the headland near the school and I opened its doors to enjoy a few moments of tranquillity. I lit a candle for the Prince and said a prayer for my family before coming out into the sunshine to take the ferry back over the water to South Uist.

Several months later I once more battled through the traffic on the M25, bound for a crowded Terminal 1 at Heathrow airport. The flight took me first to Glasgow and then on to Stornoway. The tourist office in town found me a suitable B&B and after settling in I spent a couple of hours trying to find Kildun House where Prince Charles stayed with Mrs Mackenzie. The house was on Arnish point a couple of miles south of Stornoway but the exact location seems to have been lost. There is a cairn at the end of the peninsula overlooking the North Minch. The plaque is topped by the Stuart rose and the inscription reads:

Eriskay Cairn

H.R.H. Prince Charles Edward with three attendants landed in Loch Seaforth 4 May 1746 and walking all night reached Arnish Loch at noon 5 May. In the evening he was received at Kildun House, Arnish by the Lady Kildun (Mackenzie). Early on 6 May he left Kildun in a boat and landed on Eilean Iubhaird, Loch Shell; remained there 6 to 10 May and sailed thence to South Uist and Skye.

Deoch-slàinte an Righ.

The Prince's faithful pilot was Donald MacLeod of Galtrigill, Skye.

Back in Stornoway I took a turn around the town centre to pick up the feel of the place. It was Saturday evening and the restaurants and bars were busy. The following morning everything changed. I was hit with the sort of culture shock only Stornoway on Sunday can provide. I knew the place would be quiet but I was not prepared for the total stoppage of almost all business and leisure activity. Stornoway is surely the only town in Britain where Sunday's newspapers are not available until Monday afternoon. The purchase of even the smallest items was impossible. Not a single shop was open. A modern sports centre was deserted. In the last year or so some travel restrictions have been relaxed but at the time of my visit it was not possible to travel to the island on the Sabbath. Aircraft did not fly and ferries did not sail.

The tourist brochures advise travellers to check that their proposed accommodation is open for business on Sundays. Many establishments do not allow guests to arrive or depart on that day. I heard an excellent story of a bed and breakfast landlady who accepted guests throughout the week but forbade the use of the television on Sunday. After returning from church she checked that her instructions had not been flouted by placing her hand on the back of the TV set to find out if it was warm!

The church has Stornoway Sundays in its grip. Presumably the people either like the way it is or at least are so used to it they find it perfectly normal. To the outside world, well to me anyway, it is somewhat bizarre. Churchgoing appears to be the only activity to find approval. Cars containing family groups streamed past me and they were all going to church. The men wore jackets and ties and occasionally sported trilbies. The ladies were all decked out in smart hats and Sunday best frocks. Little groups of people congregated outside churches after the service to swap gossip, invite each other for tea and perhaps even conduct a little clandestine business. It took me back decades. To have a day's rest from the business of earning a living is fine but whether it makes sense to forbid leisure pursuits as well as work is debateable. Stornoway's attitude to Sunday does nothing to encourage tourists to stay and makes it virtually impossible for them to spend any money.

I had no reason to remain in Stornoway until Monday morning but was unable to leave. There is no public transport and it is impossible to hire a car. My attempts to hitch-hike drew looks of disdain from the occupants of the few cars that passed and failed to stop. There was nothing for it but to walk back into town and try to amuse myself for the rest of the day. That proved to be difficult. Almost nothing was open. There were one or two hotels open for business, a tiny concession to the fact that people need food and drink even on Sunday. These places were mostly patronised by after church luncheon parties and in one hotel I felt sufficiently intimidated by the smartly dressed customers that I fled, feeling that my walking clothes, stout stick and request for a pint of heavy would not be appreciated. Another public house would happily serve me with a drink but only if I ate. I had already had a colossal breakfast and was not hungry. I declined and left. I walked up and down the almost deserted streets and was sufficiently bored to notice that the bank cash machines were working. It is possible to withdraw money in Stornoway on Sundays. I saw no one doing so. There is nothing to spend it on.

My last resort was the County Hotel. I marched in to the smart reception area and asked if the bar was open. The lady with the slightly wrinkled nose replied affirmatively. The 'public' bar was back out of the door and round the corner. I went in. It was packed. Almost all the clientele were young men. The place was bedlam and the point of being there seemed to be to consume as much beer and whisky as opening time would allow. Anyone looking for glass of chilled Chardonnay and a smoked salmon sandwich was definitely in the wrong place. Even so I stayed. There was nowhere else to go. In the evening things were a little better. The Indian restaurant stayed open seven days a week in sub-continental defiance of the prevailing attitude. The proprietors were from Bangladesh and unlikely to be members of the 'Wee Free' kirk. All the customers were visitors to the island.

Monday morning dawned and I hired a car. I drove south along the main road for fourteen miles to Baile Ailein. A mile or so further on I branched off left on the B8060 along the southern side of Loch Eireasort to the hamlet of Leumrabhagh at the end of the road. Clearly visible from the pier, but tantalisingly out of reach was Eilean Iubhaird. The paraphernalia of fish farming was all around and a chap pottering about with a small boat let me know that 'the boys were in and out all day' and would certainly take me to the island. I waited and sure enough a couple of dinghies with powerful outboards roared into the harbour. Fifteen minutes later one of them roared out again with a passenger and I was on my way. The dinghy pulled into a cleft in the rocks and I scrambled onto the shore after making quite sure that Neil, my pilot, knew that I wanted to be picked up again whenever he had cause to return to the harbour.

What of the *'low pityful hut'* where Prince Charles spent four days? Well, immediately above the rocks where I came ashore there are the remains of a bothy. Who knows when it was built? The island is protected on most of its coastline by serious cliffs and there is a good chance that the bothy used by Charlie was in the same place as the one there now. Iubhaird is small and is longer than it is wide. There is a hill at each end and a glen across the middle. I strode between the hills and in a few minutes was on the far side. I roamed around a little but soon realised that despite the bothy and the novelty of being the only person on the island there was no reason to stay very long. The dinghy arrived and jetted me back to the pier.

The Isle of Scalpay with its 350 inhabitants was my next

destination. I drove back to the main A859 road and continued south to Tarbert from where a single-track road stretches out to Scalpay. Access to the island used to be by ferry, but in 1997 a single-span, six million-pound bridge was built. There must have been doubts about the bridge diluting the island culture just as there are on Eriskay but at Mrs Rachel Cunningham's bed and breakfast business they were cock-a-hoop about it. They think a free road bridge is a huge improvement on the £11.35 car ferry.

Donald Campbell's house still stands, at least part of it does. The locals were in no doubt. I asked where Prince Charlie's House was and two people independently pointed me to a private residence that used to be the Presbyterian Manse. A cautious knock on the door brought the usual effusive island welcome. Donald MacSween invited me in for a chat and a cup of tea. A photograph of the house features in Drummond Norie's book, and the building looks remarkably similar to this day. In the nineteenth century photograph the house is depicted with an inscribed stone tablet over the front door. Regrettably the stone is no longer to be seen and even Mr Donald Morrison, who has lived opposite the old manse for a great number of years, cannot remember it being there. Fortunately he was able to recite the words of the Gaelic inscription and provided me with the English translation. *'On this foundation was the house in which Prince Charles passed some of his days as a fugitive in his own rightful kingdom.'* Exactly what happened to the stone tablet is not sure but I heard that when the building was a manse one of the Presbyterian ministers took a dislike to the inscription. The stories vary and the tablet was either covered over or possibly smashed out of the wall and destroyed. Norie dates the demolition of the old house to *'a little more than twenty years ago.'* This puts it in the 1870s and Mr Morrison placed the date of the construction of the house standing there today in the same decade.

I returned my hire-car to Stornoway and the following morning hopped on a bus to travel the fifty-six miles to Leverburgh in South Harris. As we journeyed the scene changed from an undulating landscape to a barren mountain panorama as Lewis gave way to

Harris. The village of Tarbert straddles the narrowest point on the island and guards the way into South Harris. This is an awesome corner of the Western Isles, an unyielding, rock-solid mountain wilderness, slashed through by burns and speckled with lochans. The main road squeezes its way through the middle of the landmass for three or four miles but at last admits defeat and heads west for the sea and the Sound of Taransay. In contrast with the rough and craggy east the west coast boasts beautiful sandy beaches and the Golden Road offers breath-taking views of the offshore islands. The ferry terminal is at Leverburgh or An-T-Ob as it is called in Gaelic. Lord Leverhulme (of Lever Brothers and Unilever fame) arrived in 1919 to set up the fishing company known as 'MacFisheries'. Leverhulme ran his business in South Harris with a view to the welfare of his employees as well as profit and in December 1922 the village was named after him. Sadly his lordship died in May 1925. Neither his executors nor the board of Unilever had much interest in the project and the work stopped. The pier and land were sold for a pittance but the village name remained.

Caledonian MacBrayne took me on the short but tortuous ferry crossing between Leverburgh and Otternish on North Uist. The MacDonald coach company turned up a minute or two later and my journey continued along the causeway that threads its semi-circular way along peninsulas and over tiny islands to Benbecula. I did not linger as I was keen to arrive on South Uist and visit one of Prince Charles' most secure and inaccessible hideaways, Glen Corradale. It is uncertain whether Prince Charles walked into Corradale or came by sea, perhaps he employed both methods of travel. The Lyon in Mourning has several accounts of the arrival in Corradale and only the account taken from the collective mouths of the Laird of Mackinnon, Malcolm MacLeod and Flora MacDonald states that they walked to the glen. Three others by Ned Burke, Alexander MacDonald and Felix O'Neil describe the Prince sailing to Benbecula but neglect to specify the method of travel into Corradale. Donald MacLeod's journal has a page missing and we are not privileged to read how he accounts for the Prince's travel to Corradale. Neil

MacEachain's account notes, *'About eleven aclock at night, they set out with Neil, who was their faithful guide, towards Corodale.'* W.B. Blaikie concludes that they walked but I wonder if this is correct? Firstly, the party had a boat so why not continue to use it? Secondly, the walk from Benbecula involved crossing the ford to South Uist. The passage could only be made at low tide and without doubt the crossing point was guarded twenty-four hours a day. Lastly all the accounts maintain Charles left Corradale for the island of Wiay by boat. It seems reasonable to argue that they may have arrived the same way.

I decided to approach Glen Corradale from the sea if I could persuade someone to take me. John Ure's book 'A Bird on the Wing' tells of the author being taken into Corradale and shown the remains of an ancient bothy by John Joseph MacDonald of Loch Aineort. I resolved to find him and see if he would repeat the journey for me. The telephone directory lists quite a number of MacDonalds but as Loch Aineort is not a big place J.J. was easy to track down. I phoned him and described what I wanted to do. The man had never heard of me, let alone met me, but he was immediately interested and helpful. 'When do you want to go?' he asked. 'Ideally tomorrow or the next day,' I replied, more in hope than expectation. John Joseph explained that as he currently had no boat on the water he would need to make a few telephone calls and get back to me that evening. The man was as good as his word and my mobile rang at 9.45pm. The boat was available, there would be four of us on the trip and John Joseph would take me to what he thought might be the remains of Prince Charlie's bothy. All I had to do was present myself at his house the following morning. Wild horses would not have kept me from the appointment but Loch Aineort is difficult to reach without a car. I rang Brian Walsh, the retired Lancastrian who I had met on a previous trip to South Uist and had been kind enough to show me around. He had had come to Uist thirty years before to complete a roofing contract and enjoyed island life so much he stayed on permanently. He too was happy to help. Thanks to island generosity and hospitality everything had fallen perfectly into place. I went to sleep praying that the weather would not let us down.

At precisely 10 o'clock on a fair but not brilliant morning with low cloud hanging over the tops of the hills we arrived at John Joseph's house. I was all for knocking on the door but Brian simply walked in, calling MacDonald's name. It seems that no one knocks on doors on the islands. I introduced myself to J.J. who began to weigh me up. He was friendly enough but I could tell he was figuring out whether I would be a suitable companion on the small fishing boat owned by one of his friends. I seemed to pass muster and we walked down to the large building where John Joseph used to store equipment during his days as an independent fish farmer. A Land Rover drew up. Inside were Murdo, whose boat it was, and Colin who proved to be the fastest filleter of fish I have ever seen. We gathered the fishing tackle together and loaded it and ourselves onto the dinghy that would take us to deeper water and the waiting motorboat. We clambered aboard and hauled the dinghy after us, roping it down on the cabin roof. The motor fired and we were away.

Glen Corradale is defended from the west, north and south by hefty mountains and from the east by magnificent cliffs dropping sheer into the sea. The only point of access is a miniature beach and once we were close the dinghy was heaved over the side for the final approach. John Joseph and I climbed in and paddled to the shore. We had to scale a short but steep incline into the glen proper and there it was stretched out before us with the mist-capped, magnificent mountains glowering over us as though they were irritated that we had penetrated the glen without struggling and sweating our way over the protective peaks.

The O.S. map marks the 'Uamh a Phrionnsa' (Prince's Cave) but as there is more than one account of Prince Charles sleeping in a house this is unlikely to be the Prince's refuge. John Joseph led me to the cave. It is on the northern side of the glen, (picture p36) not many yards from the shore and reasonably easy to locate. I imagine that the cavern was utilized as a shelter or as a storehouse occasionally but it would make a poor home for several men for three weeks. It definitely does not meet either Alexander MacDonald's description of his Highness taking refuge in *'his famous palace of Coridale (the house in the forest)'* or Neil MacEachain's account which observes, '*When they came near the house, Neil left him under a rock while he went in to see if there were no strangers there ~ he seemed extraordinary well pleased with the house, which he swore look't like a palace in comparison of the abominable hole they had lately left.'*

As we walked to the remains of the Prince's bothy John Joseph pointed to a hole in the ground and suggested that I crawl in. I wasn't keen but after donning oilskins I complied and wriggled my way into the aperture. I found myself in a man-made tunnel perhaps three feet wide and high enough for me to crawl on hands and knees. It was dark but the little light that penetrated from both ends illuminated stonewalls on either side with lintels laid over the top. After a few feet the tunnel roof became higher but despite John Joseph's opinion that the tunnel ought to be dry, it was not and my walking boots were unable to cope with the depth of water. I turned round and inched my way out again. Such tunnels are properly called souterrains. The script employed to mark them on the map is that used to denote ancient monuments, for it is believed that the Picts built souterrains several thousand years ago. It is thought that they were used as stores, hiding places and possibly for religious purposes but not for burial.

A little further up the glen we reached the main objective. The remains of the Prince's bothy are scarcely there at all. The shape of the building can barely be discerned and only the back wall, built into the hillside has more than two stones on top of each other. I would never have found it without John Joseph's help. Bracken overgrows the ruin and the foundations are difficult to spot at even the shortest distance. Had I been alone I should have walked straight past without a thought. We stood inside the ruin facing the back wall and J.J. indicated a large stone at ground level. I pulled it out of the wall to reveal the dark entrance to another souterrain. The bothy had been built over the entrance of this advantageous Neolithic feature although it is unlikely that Prince Charles used the tunnel as a hiding place as Corradale is geographically secure and the bothy well placed to spot advancing intruders. John Joseph thought I might like to creep into this souterrain as well. The opening was too small for my shoulders but I squeezed in as far as I could and shone a torch into the darkness. The tunnel widened into an underground cave perhaps four feet high. A few yards from the entrance, the roof had collapsed although enough light filtered through from the exit to show me that the structure was littered with dead animals in an advanced state of decay. I contented myself with taking a photograph and, fascinating though the souterrain was, declined to explore further.

My mission was completed and John Joseph pointed out the 'V' of Bealach Crosgard as the way I should walk back to the road at Loch Aineort. It is only four miles or so but tough going. It was mid-day but the clouds were still obscuring the tops and I was unsure if the weather would improve or worsen. I had left my walking stick in the dinghy and as we returned to collect it I expressed my doubts and explained that I had not been in these mountains before. As Prince Charles left Corradale by boat I needed no persuading at all when it was suggested that I might forgo the walk and spend the rest of the day on a fishing trip.

The experience was splendid. The weather improved until there was not a cloud in the sky. Staying close to the shore we tried our luck with rods and lines. The sea was packed with pollock (picture p36) and even a complete novice like me pulled a dozen out of the water after a little tuition from Colin. Murdo gunned the engine every now and then and we moved off to another position while the splendid cliffs of the coastline slipped past. Murdo looked after the boat, John Joseph and I fished and Colin showed his prowess with a sharp knife. Each fish was pulled from the box and Colin had it gutted, filleted and skinned in next to no time. When the boat was not under power the calm sea produced only a small swell and Colin's fingers were in no danger. At the end of the day, as we returned to harbour, the boat bucked as it breasted the waves but Colin was not deterred. If anything his knife flew faster. He clearly intended to have the job done by the time we docked. The entrails and carcasses sailed over the stern and screaming gannets and fulmars plummeted into the sea to fight over the discarded scraps. As we arrived back in Loch Aineort Colin's fingers were miraculously intact and the large bucket at his feet was full of washed and neatly skinned pollock fillets.

My task the following day was to find a way onto Calbhaigh in the entrance to Loch Boisdale. I needed to hitch another ride on a fishing boat so I wandered about on the pier, examined the piles of lobster pots and other fishing paraphernalia and generally watched the world slowly go by. The sun was shining and I was in no hurry. After a while a large truck arrived in port and the driver and his mate both in trademark yellow oilskins and Wellington boots jumped out. This looked promising. I approached them and explained my requirements. They were pleased to be able to help as people usually are in these friendly islands. They enlightened me that their boat drew too much water to land on Calbhaigh but that when close to the fish farm I could transfer to a rubber dinghy and complete the journey. 'Can you drive?' one of the men asked. I confirmed that I could. 'OK, take the truck to the end of the pier and we'll go and get the boat.' With that they disappeared, leaving me in charge of an essential part of their livelihood. I carefully selected the correct gear and gingerly reversed. Emboldened by this success I more confidently manoeuvred the vehicle several hundred yards to the place they had indicated, thankfully applied the handbrake and switched off the engine. I left the keys in the ignition of course; that's what everyone does here. The fishing boat chugged round to the pier, I climbed down the vertical ladder on the side of the jetty and we sailed out of Lochboisdale, past the island of Gasaigh towards Calbhaigh. Everything went according to plan and before long I stepped ashore on my second uninhabited island of the week. Calbhaigh is even smaller than Eilean Iubhaird but it is graced with a ruined ancient castle and a modern lighthouse. The castle is in a sorry state but its presence makes it reasonably sure that this was the island on which Prince Charles took refuge after being chased up and down the coast from Glen Corradale. Fortunately the weather was still fine and I amused myself by scanning the horizon with my binoculars and watching the farmers in their dinghies bobbing in and out between the fish cages. In time one broke off from its task and cruised towards my island. Fifteen minutes later I was back in Lochboisdale, well pleased with my day trip to Calbhaigh.

ELEVEN

OVER THE SEA TO SKYE

Speed bonnie boat like a bird on the wing,
'Onward' the sailors cry;
Carry the lad that's born to be king
Over the sea to Skye.
Skye Boat Song, Sir Harold Boulton

The presence of warships at the entrance to Loch Boisdale persuaded Charles that remaining on Calbhaigh any longer would be foolish. Further escape was required and the fugitives made a quick run by boat to the head of the loch. Charles knew that the party with which he was travelling was too big for anyone's safety. On 20 June he paid off his boatmen with a shilling a day and parted company from Donald MacLeod and Colonel O'Sullivan. MacLeod was captured on Benbecula on 5 July and was brought before General John Campbell of Mamore on board the Furnace. After admitting his association with the Young Pretender the General asked MacLeod if he knew of the reward offered for the Prince and commenting that the money, *'no less a sum than thirty thousand pounds sterling, which would have made you and all your children after you happy for ever.'* Donald's reply is illustrative of the Highland importance of offering hospitality to others and the loyalty on which the Prince was often able to rely. *'What then? Thirty thousand pounds! Though I had gotten't I could not have enjoyed it eight and forty hours. Conscience would have gotten up upon me. That money could not have kept it down. And tho' I could have gotten all England and Scotland for my pains I would not allowed a hair of his body to be touch'd if I could help it.'*

MacLeod was eventually taken to London and was not released until 10 July 1747. He returned to Skye and died on 8

September 1749. Charles' manservant Ned Burke parted company with the Prince at this time and went to North Uist, where he almost starved. He was never captured and eventually returned to his former occupation of carrying one end of a sedan chair in Edinburgh. He died in the capital on November 13 1751. At nightfall on 20 June, the Prince, Neil MacEachain and Felix O'Neil crossed South Uist, heading for Milton, a house owned by Angus MacDonald. Angus had a sister named Flora who kept house for him and looked after the cattle from a shieling at Ormiclate. Prince Charles had come to Milton in response to a message from Flora's stepfather, Hugh MacDonald of Armadale on Skye, indicating that it might be possible to send him to that island disguised as Flora's maid. Armadale could provide government passes through any military cordons they might come across and suggested that, improbable as it might seem, Charles could expect help from the wife of MacDonald of Sleat, Lady Margaret.

Flora agreed to the plan and promised to meet the Prince again in a cottage at Roisinis. She then left for Clanranald's house at Nunton on Benbecula to make preparations. The Prince and his two companions made off towards Glen Corradale. They rested for most of 21 June on the slopes of Hecla, a hill three miles from the glen. The Prince became anxious. No message had arrived from Flora so MacEachain was sent to Nunton to find out what was happening. The channel separating South Uist from Benbecula can be forded at low tide, but the water was deep when Neil arrived. While deliberating what to do he was pounced upon by sentries who arrested him. The same fate had befallen Flora the day before. Neither of them had the permit needed to cross between the islands. Fortunately Hugh MacDonald was the captain in charge of the militia and he arranged for the two of them to be released. Miss MacDonald continued her journey to Nunton unimpeded and MacEachain returned to Prince Charles.

It was difficult to transport Charles to Roisinis. Travelling by land was too dangerous as the fords were constantly guarded. Fortunately MacEachain recognised friends fishing in Loch Sgiopoirt (Skiport) and they agreed to ferry the party as far as the island of

Wiay. The island was deserted, and so a decision was taken to make landfall on Benbecula and walk the rest of the way to Roisinis. They arrived at midnight and MacEachain entered the shieling expecting to meet Flora but she was not there. To make matters worse a government militia was camped a few hundred yards away. The men spent the night in the bothy but left at first light as soldiers visited each morning to fetch milk. The Prince and his friends were reduced to hiding under rocks on the shoreline in pouring rain. In the evening their discomfort was lifted a little by the arrival of food and wine from Lady Clanranald but there was no alternative that night but to remain on the beach. A better place to hide was clearly required and so MacEachain took the Prince to a bothy on Ruabhal, a hill between Roisinis and Nunton. The following day the welcome news arrived that the boat for Skye was at last ready. The bearers of the information were Flora's cousins. They were also officers in a regiment hunting for the Prince but clan loyalty and Highland hospitality took precedence over allegiance to the crown.

Neil MacEachain left the Prince in the care of the MacDonald cousins and walked over to Lady Clanranald's house at Nunton to check the preparations for the Prince's escape. MacEachain found Flora, her brother Angus and his wife together with Lady Clan and her seven year old daughter ready to sail around the north of Benbecula to Roisinis. With them they had a blue and white flowered dress for Charles to wear. *'The gown was of caligo, a light coloured quilted petticoat, a mantle of dun camlet made after the Irish fashion with a cap to cover his royal highness whole head and face, with a suitable head-dress, shoes, stockings etc.'* Flora and Lady Clan arrived at the Rosinis bothy and were greeted by the Prince. They were all eating a meal when news came that General Campbell had landed near Nunton with 1,500 men. Charles and his companions had to escape again, this time by rowing across Loch Uisgebhagh. It was time to leave Benbecula and try to reach Skye. Armadale had provided only one government pass for a manservant and so it was necessary that either O'Neil or MacEachain left the Prince's company. MacEachain spoke Gaelic and so accompanied the Prince and Flora. MacDonald had also written a letter to his wife introducing Flora's make-believe servant.

My dear Marion

I have sent your daughter from this country lest she be in any way frightened by the troops lying here. She has got one Betty Burke, an Irish girl, who, as she tells me, is a good spinster. If her spinning pleases, you can keep her until she spins all your lint; or if you have any wool to spin, you may employ her. I have sent Neil MacEachain along with your daughter and Betty Burke to take care of them.
I am your dutiful husband,

Hugh MacDonald, 22 June 1746.

The Prince put on his disguise and wanted to carry a pistol under his petticoats. Miss MacDonald would not hear of it and protested that should he be searched the pistol would straight away give him away. Prince Charles replied, *'Indeed, Miss, if we shall happen to meet with any that will go narrowly to work in searching as what you mean they will certainly discover me at any rate.'* Flora must have had a very persuasive personality for the Prince gave up his pistol and carried only a wooden cudgel.

On returning home Lady Clanranald was interrogated by General Campbell and Captain Ferguson and she was arrested with her husband some days later. Felix O'Neil tried to make his own escape and, as luck would have it, a few days after he parted company with the Prince a French ship, Le Hardi Mendiant, approached Benbecula. Colonel O'Sullivan had made his way from Loch Boisdale to Benbecula and was fortunate to be taken on board the ship. O'Neil, sensing an opportunity to facilitate the Prince's escape, went after His Royal Highness after first arranging to join the ship in four days time at Lochmaddy. Charles had already left for Skye and so, try as he might, O'Neil could not find him. On reaching Lochmaddy O'Neil discovered no sign of Le Hardi Mendiant and after skulking in the area for several days in the hope the ship might turn up was captured and taken aboard HMS Furnace. He was imprisoned in Edinburgh Castle from where he was released on parole in 1747. Flora MacDonald had her own opinion as to the reason for the non-appearance of the French ship recounting to Bishop Forbes in The Lyon in Mourning that, *'The timorous O'Sullivan, having a fair wind, and not having the courage to stay till O'Neil's return, being resolved to take care of Number One, obliged the captain to set sail directly, lest he should be taken and should lose his precious life.'* Perhaps there is something in that argument but it is more likely that the attention of the Royal Navy prevented the appearance of the vessel in North Uist. The French ship evaded capture and sailed to Norway, from where O'Sullivan made his way to France.

At 8p.m. on 28 June, MacEachain, Flora and the Prince embarked for Skye and at dawn on 29 June were off Waternish Point where they hoped to make landfall. The point was occupied by enemy troops and so they rowed another twelve miles across Loch Snizort to the Trotternish peninsula, where they landed at a place, now called 'Prince Charlie's Point', close to Monkstadt, a house owned by Sir Alexander MacDonald of Sleat.

Sir Alexander MacDonald's wife, Lady Margaret, was an ardent Jacobite but had no wish to make life difficult for her husband who was providentially away serving the government in Fort Augustus. The news of the Prince's arrival had put her into a state of agitation if not sheer panic. Her state of mind was not improved by the knowledge that Lieutenant MacLeod of the Skye militia was at that moment dining upstairs. The Prince could not stay in the area long and Lady MacDonald began to think of what should be done. Lady Margaret had recently communicated with the Prince via Captain Donald Roy MacDonald of Baleshare and it was from him that she hoped for advice. She talked first with her husband's factor, Alexander MacDonald of Kingsburgh and as she did so Donald Roy arrived to be greeted by Lady Margaret's exclamation, *'Oh, Donald Roy, we are ruined forever!'* The conversations produced the suggestion that the Prince should be smuggled to the neighbouring island of Raasay and then back to the mainland where he could hope for more help.

The Prince persuaded himself from time to time that the Laird of MacLeod was sympathetic to his cause and had to be talked out of approaching him on more than one occasion. He would have been completely convinced that the opposite was true should he have been able to read a letter written by MacLeod to MacDonald of Kinsburgh. Written during the time *'of the young Pretender's skulking in the Long Island,'* the letter advises Kingsburgh to capture Charles and take the reward of thirty thousand pounds. *'I am persuaded he will pay you a visit in expectation of your protection. It will then be in your power (I hope you will use it) to aggrandize your family beyond many in Scotland. I need not enlarge on this.'* As MacLeod cannot have been certain that Prince Charles would visit Kingsburgh, possibly he wrote in the same vein to others in his efforts to ingratiate himself with the government.

Charles must have made an incongruous sight as he walked towards Portree. It was Sunday and they met many churchgoers, some of who commented on the size of Betty Burke and the way she hitched up her skirts every time there was a burn to cross. The party reached Kingsburgh where Mrs MacDonald was preparing for bed. Not knowing the identity of the visitors she said that although they were welcome to stay, she could not see them that evening. In a while her daughter came to her saying, *'Oh mother, my father has brought in a very odd, muckle, ill-shaken-up wife as I ever saw!'* Kingsburgh persuaded his wife to provide food for the visitors and at last admitted to her that their guest was Prince Charles.

> *'Why, my dear it is the Prince. You have the honour to have him in your house.' 'The Prince', cried she. 'O Lord, we are a' ruin'd and undone for ever! We will a' be hang'd now!' 'Hout, goodwife,' says the honest stout soul, 'we will die but ance; and if we are hanged for this, I am sure we die in a good cause.' Pray make no delay; go, get some supper. Fetch*

what is readiest. You have eggs, butter and cheese in the house, get them as quickly as possible.' 'Eggs, butter and cheese!' says Mrs MacDonald, 'what a supper is that for a Prince?' 'O goodwife,' says he, 'little do you know how this good Prince has been living for some time past. These, I can assure you will be a feast to him.' ~ After he had made a plentiful supper, he called for a dram; and when the bottle was brought, he said he would fill the glass for himself; 'for,' said he, 'I have learn'd in my skulking to take a hearty dram.' He filled up a bumper and drank it off to the happiness and prosperity of his landlord and landlady.

That the relationship between the Prince and Lord George Murray was strained seems to have filtered through to Skye and a report of a conversation between Charles and Kingsburgh is illuminating. *'Kingsburgh said that he asked particularly at the Prince about Lord George Murray, whether or not he could lay treachery or any such thing to his charge. The Prince answered that he would never allow anything of treachery or villainy to be laid to the charge of Lord George Murray. But he could not help owning that he had much to bear of him from his temper.'*

Charles rested at Kingsburgh House all the next day and resumed his journey in the evening. He left the house in female disguise but quickly shed it in favour of Highland dress. Kingsburgh remained at home but provided Prince Charles and Neil MacEachain with a guide to help them on their way. Flora preceded the three of them on horseback using a different route. Approximately a week after Charles had left Kingsburgh the house was visited and searched by Captain Ferguson's men.

When Ferguson asked Kingsburgh where Miss MacDonald and the person along with her in woman's cloaths lay all night in his house, he answered, 'I know in what room Miss MacDonald herself lay, but where servants are laid when in my house, I know nothing of that matter, I never enquire anything about it. My wife is the properest person to inform you about that.' Then he had the impertinence to ask Mrs MacDonald, whether or not she had laid the young Pretender and Miss MacDonald in one bed? To which she answered, 'Sir, whom you mean by the young Pretender I shall not pretend to guess; but I can assure you it is not the fashion in the Isle of Skye to lay the mistress and the maid in the same bed together.' Then Ferguson desired to see the different rooms where their late lodgers had slept; and after seeing them he said, it was pretty remarkable that the room in which the maid had slept seem'd to look better than the one where the mistress had been laid.

Kingsburgh was arrested and eventually ended up a prisoner in Edinburgh Castle. He was released on July 4 1747 and returned to the management of his lands on Skye. He died on February 13 1772 at the age of eighty-three. His epitaph reads, '*Let all the world say what they can. He liv'd and died an honest man.'*

Flora and Donald Roy MacDonald were waiting for the Prince when he arrived at MacNab's Inn in Portree. Malcolm MacLeod of Brea and two of his cousins had a boat waiting nearby for the journey to Raasay so Charles took his leave of Flora and asked if he could repay *'a crown of borrowed money.'* She replied that it was only a half crown and the Prince duly handed over the coin. As they parted Prince Charles was optimistic enough to comment, *'For all that has happened I hope, Madam, we shall meet in St. James' yet.'* Neil MacEachain also parted with Charles in Portree and in the early hours of July 1 the Prince once more set out across the sea. The party found Raasay had been pillaged as retribution after Culloden. Cattle were slaughtered and houses burned, leaving the island unable to offer even the smallest hospitality. Prince Charles returned to Skye the next day, desperate for help.

The small band of men landed back on Skye at Nicolson's rock, north of Portree harbour. After some discussion Charles announced his intention to travel the thirty miles into the Mackinnon country of Strathaird and asked Malcolm MacLeod to accompany him. MacLeod agreed and suggested the Prince pretend to be his servant and to call himself Lewie Caw. The two walked along Glen Varragill and then close to the head of Loch Sligachan on the night of 3 July. Although there seems to be no direct evidence of the route, W.B. Blaikie in his 'Itinerary of Prince Charles' comments that the local belief is that the presence of troops in the area forced them to the shore of Loch Ainort and south through Strath Mor to Loch Slapin on their way to Elgol.

Malcolm MacLeod and the Prince seem to have struck up a friendship during their journey that was close enough for Malcolm to teach Charles the ways of a servant should they meet others. The Prince learned how to walk several paces behind his 'master' and to carry the baggage when necessary. They talked about disguising the Prince and he exchanged his waistcoat of *'scarlet tartan with a gold twist button'* for the less ostentatious one worn by MacLeod. Charles also proposed *'blacking his face with some one thing or another'* but decided against it and instead *'pulling off the periwig and putting it into his pocket took out a dirty white napkin and desired the Captain to tye that about his head, and to bring it down upon his eyes and nose.'* After a discussion comparing clothes suitable for the climate in Italy to those required for the Highlands Charles comments, *'I have had this philibeg* (kilt) *on now for some days, and I find I do as well with it as any the best breeches I ever put on. I hope in God, MacLeod, to walk the streets of London with it yet.'* Health was another topic of conversation and,

> *The Captain, happening to see the Prince uneasy and fidging, took him to the back of a know, and opening his breast, saw him troubled with lice for want of clean linen, and by reason of the coarse odd way he behoved to live in, both as to sustenance and sleep. He said, he believed, he took fourscore off him. ~ The Prince, even when warm and sweating, used to drink a great deal of water in his wandering from place to place, and the Captain was always sure to*

desire him to take a dram above the water to qualifie it. The Captain intreated him not to drink water when he was sweating lest he should thereby injure his health. 'No, no', said the Prince, 'that will never hurt me in the least. If you happen to drink any cold thing when you are warm, only remember, MacLeod, to piss after drinking, and it will do you no harm at all. This advice I had from a friend abroad.' The Captain said the Prince was always sure to observe this direction.

The two men made their way to John Mackinnon's house in Elgol where they were made welcome as Mackinnon was married to MacLeod's sister. On the way to Elgol the Prince,

Happened to fall into a bogue almost to the top of the thighs and MacLeod behoved to pull him out by the armpits and thereby was bogued himself. The Captain desired the servant lass, who could talk nothing but Erse, to bring some water for his feet, which she did; and being much fatigued he desired her to wash his feet and legs. When she was washing them he said 'You see that poor sick man there, I hope you'll wash his feet too. It will be a great charity, for he has as much need as I have.' 'No such thing,' said she, 'although I wash the master's feet, I am not obliged to wash the servant's. What! He's but a low countrywoman's son. I will not wash his feet indeed.' However, with much intreaty Malcolm prevailed upon the maid to stoop so low as to wash poor Lewie's feet. While she was washing them she happened to use him right roughly, and the Prince said to Malcolm, 'Oh MacLeod, if you would desire the girl not to go so far up.'

When Prince Charles announced a new plan to return to the mainland the elderly clan chief Mackinnon of Mackinnon took it upon himself to see that the journey was successful. The Prince was reluctant to lose the services of Malcolm MacLeod but it was the clan chief, accompanied by John Mackinnon and four boatmen, who made the hazardous voyage across the Sound of Sleat. In the early hours of 5 July they made landfall at Mallaig but could find neither shelter, nor anyone to help them and were in constant danger of being discovered.

Landranger Maps
18 Sound of Harris & St Kilda
32 South Skye & Cuillin Hills
23 North Skye
22 Benbecula & South Uist

Monkstadt (23)	**NG378675**
Kingsburgh (23)	**NG395553**
Flora's Grave (23)	**NG400719**
Luib (32)	**NG565279**
Milton (22)	**NF741269**

A visit to Flora Macdonald's birthplace was essential, so I set off for Milton, north of Lochboisdale. Nothing now remains of the house except a few stones. The cairn's inscription states:

> *Clan Donald raised this cairn of remembrance to their kinswoman Flora MacDonald, daughter of Ranald, son of Angus of Milton, South Uist. She was born in 1722 near this place and spent her early life in the house that stood on this foundation. When pursuit was drawing near to the Prince in the Long Island she greatly aided him by her heroism and endurance to gain shelter in the Isle of Skye.*

Flora was born into a family of some influence, her father being tacksman in the service of his clan chief MacDonald of Clanranald. Tacks were leases of land, granted by the Chief to those clansmen thought suitable. Flora's father held two tacks, one at Baile Mhanaich on Benbecula and the other, Milton on South Uist. Flora's mother

Marion was the daughter of the Reverend Angus MacDonald, a Presbyterian minister. Flora's father died when she was only a year old and Marion married Hugh MacDonald of Armadale in Skye. In 1746 Armadale was a captain in the government militia on Benbecula but was, in common with many others in a similar position, a Jacobite sympathiser.

Folklore makes much of the fact that despite the £30,000 reward for the Prince's capture, he was never betrayed. Highlander loyalty to the Stuart cause combined with a tradition of hospitality is supposed to have kept Charles safe. Eighteenth century island life was hard even for the relatively well off. Much of the land was unproductive and slowly tilled with hand ploughs. Harvests were late and often poor, producing an inadequate diet for almost everyone. *'Their food oatcakes, butter or cheese and often the coagulated blood of their cattle spread on their bannocks.'* Such economic conditions make it inconceivable that no one gave the redcoat army information in the hopes of acquiring the reward. The price on the Young Pretender's head was enormous, more than two million pounds at today's values. There must have been informers, otherwise the Prince would not have come so close to capture so frequently. It is also possible that some of those who went out on a limb for Charles were ignorant of the reward money or, more likely, did not trust the government to pay up. Perhaps even the saintly Flora had no idea of the money she could make by turning in the heir to the Stuart throne. In the event Prince Charles was not captured and so the money was never paid.

Brian, the retired roofer, took me to Milton and offered to show me the Clanranald house at Nunton as well. Nunton has been extended and altered several times over the years but is at least partly original and it is clear from the number of outbuildings that the estate was impressive at one time.

My final tasks on the Outer Hebrides were to walk to the top of Ruabhal where Charles was hidden for a while and then to search for the bothy at Rosinis where he met Flora and Lady Clanranald. Benbecula is mostly flat and it was an easy walk from the main road at Stansa na Fèille out to Ruabhal, the highest point on the island. I could see no signs of the Prince's visit so I added a stone to the cairn at the top and walked back down. The track gives way to a footpath and that fades away into the heather as Rosinis is approached. In the distance I could see a house on sand dunes and made that my destination. The derelict house is of relatively modern style and was built to replace the blackhouse that stands in ruins nearby. The buildings stand on a sheltered inlet of the sea in an ideal spot from which to launch a boat and may well be the place where Prince Charlie was first introduced to Betty Burke.

It was time for me to sail over the sea to Skye. Maggie Mackinnon of the BBC's Gaelic service drove me to Lochmaddy and CalMac provided the ferry. Altogether an easier way of leaving the Uists than was available to Prince Charlie. Ships leave every day for the two-hour voyage to Uig. As I stepped off the boat the heavens opened and I was soaked to the skin. I took shelter in the Ferry Inn, where I dried out for a while, sampled a couple of pints of 70/- ale and chatted to a couple of poor souls who were camping. A little local knowledge provided me with some accommodation and the next day, in much better weather, I walked up the hill to Monkstadt. The house (picture p37) is in ruins but the steadings are undergoing restoration work. There are also a few occupied cottages, some of which may have been in existence in 1746.

My next destination was Dunvegan Castle, the hereditary seat of Clan MacLeod. One of the rooms contains artefacts relating to the Forty-Five. There is a portrait, painted by Allan Ramsay, of Norman MacLeod, the 22nd chief. A waistcoat worn by Prince Charles Edward made from white silk with straw-coloured grass seed motif stitching hangs on a wall. It was donated to the MacLeods by one of Flora MacDonald's daughters. A painting of Duncan Forbes of Culloden occupies pride of place over the mantelpiece. Donald MacLeod of Galtrigill's spectacles are displayed in a glass cabinet as is a transparent pendant containing a lock of Prince Charlie's hair allegedly cut from his head by Flora MacDonald during the visit to Kingsburgh.

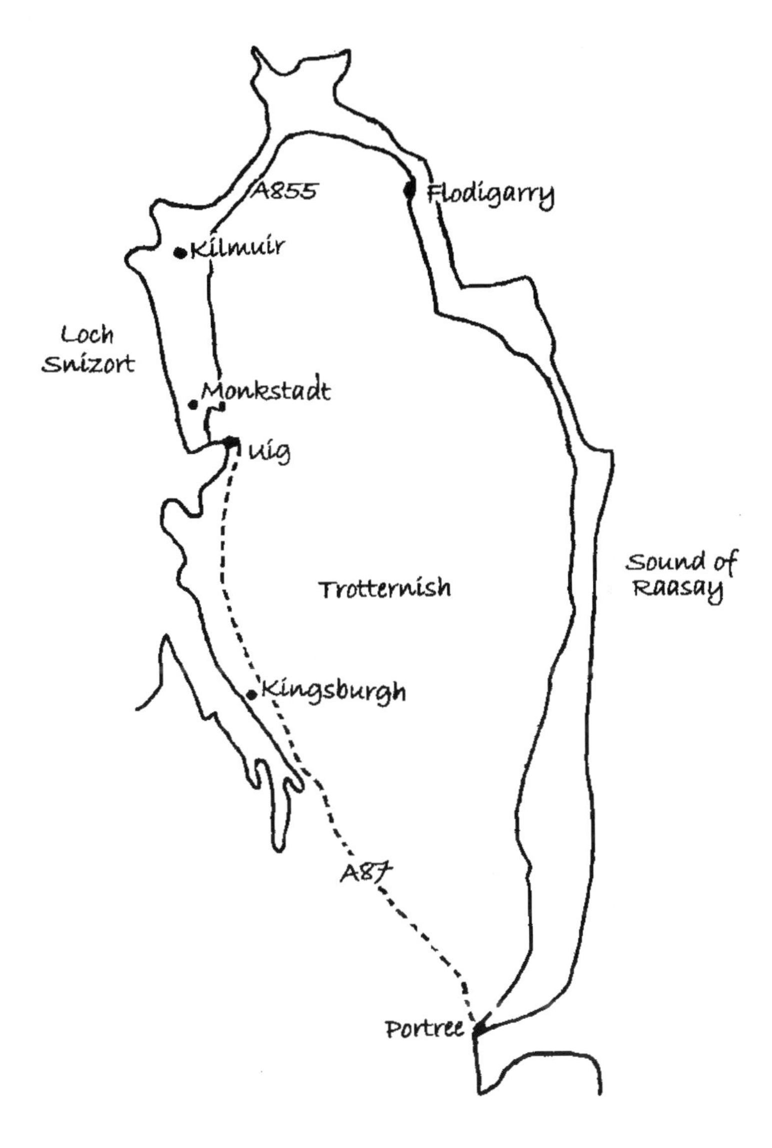

Uig to Portree (13 Miles)

I left Dunvegan and headed south, first to Kingsburgh and then to Portree. Kingsburgh House is in a perfect position on the edge of Loch Snizort but is sadly derelict. The same family has owned it for decades and now only a small cottage attached to the main building is occupied. MacNab's inn in Portree has changed out of all recognition since the Prince was there and is now called the Royal Hotel. If any of the original building still stands then it has been well camouflaged over the years.

After parting company Flora and the Prince were never to see each other again. Their association had lasted twelve days. On her way home she was arrested and taken on board HMS Furnace. The captain was John Ferguson who had a deserved reputation for using torture to extract information from those unfortunate enough to fall into his hands. Providentially, Major-General John Campbell was also on board and he saw to it that she was reasonably treated. Flora was transferred to the floating prison, HMS Bridgewater and later placed under house arrest with William Dick, a government messenger at arms in London. This was a frequent occurrence for prisoners who presented little risk and could pay for their keep. Friends raised £1500 to pay the sums demanded and perhaps leave some over for when she was released. On 4 July 1747, Flora was freed under the terms of the Act of Indemnity and returned to Scotland where she married Kingsburgh's son, Allan MacDonald, at Armadale on 6 Nov 1750. The Scots Magazine reported the marriage. '*Nov. 6, 1750. At Armadale, in Sleat, Allan MacDonald, eldest son of Alexander MacDonald of Kingsburgh, married to Miss Flora MacDonald, daughter of Ronald MacDonald of Milton, deceas'd. This is the young Lady who aided the escape of the young Chevalier.*'

Shortly after they married, Flora and Allan lived at Flodigarry (picture p38) in north-east Skye. Their cottage is now part of the Flodigarry Hotel. Five of their seven children were born at Flodigarry but when Allan's father began to suffer from ill health the couple moved to Kingsburgh. Unfortunately for the family, life in the Highlands and Islands was rapidly changing. The role and influence of the tacksman was diminishing and the rent he was required to pay forever increasing. In the end bad winters and economic woes including the collapse in the price of black cattle forced many Highlanders to emigrate to America and Canada. Flora's stepfather, Hugh, left for North Carolina in 1773, followed the next year by Allan and Flora.

Ironically Allan fought for the British in the American War of Independence. Perhaps he supported the loyalists rather than the rebels as he remembered what could happen as a consequence of defying the Hanoverian monarchy. In the event he found himself on the losing side once again and was captured after the Battle of Moore's Creek Bridge. Those who bitterly opposed British rule harassed loyalists like Mrs MacDonald and the time when Flora was deprived of her husband took on an air of fear and uncertainty. Allan spent eighteen months as a prisoner and was released on parole in August 1777. He travelled to New York where he was exchanged for an American prisoner and freed. His new regiment sent Allan to Nova Scotia. Flora joined him later but she was lonely and unhappy, concluding that the transatlantic adventure had not been a success. Eventually MacDonald agreed that his wife should return to Skye where she arrived in June 1780. Allan followed in 1785 and the couple lived together until Flora's death at the age of sixty-eight on March 4 1790. Allan died two years later at Kingsburgh, on 20 September 1792.

Flora MacDonald is buried at Kilmuir on Trotternish and an imposing monument (picture p37) stands above her grave. It was erected in 1880 to replace an earlier one that was constructed in 1871 but blew down in a gale two years later. The cross is inscribed with the words:

> *Flora MacDonald. Preserver of Prince Charles Edward Stuart. Her name will be mentioned in history and if courage and fidelity be virtues, mentioned with honour. Born at Milton, South Uist 1722. Died at Kingsburgh, Skye 1790.*

Six days a week the ferries sail from Sconser, on Skye, to the Isle of Raasay but on Sundays the seas are quiet. I arrived in Sconser on Saturday afternoon. An immediate visit to the island meant either returning on the last ferry of the day at 9pm or spending two nights there. I chose the former and so only had a very few hours in which to explore. About one hundred and fifty people live on Raasay and Inverarish is the main centre of population. Many of the houses are set in woodland interspersed with huge rhododendron bushes and if you can ignore the abandoned cars it is a pretty place to live. The only shop was similar to rural establishments I remember from my childhood, all dark wood and mysterious drawers with not a bar code recognition machine in sight. The hotel has seen better days but it provided me with a decent pint of beer and a reasonable meal. The most affluent and efficient looking enterprise I saw was an Outdoor Centre based in imposing Raasay House. The place was bubbling with young people who were obviously enjoying the experiences the Centre offers. I walked north, out of the woods and uphill to the Youth Hostel from where there are panoramic views of the island and of Skye. On my way back to the jetty I noticed Raasay's playing field. A prominent official notice banned the use of both field and play equipment on Sundays. That attitude explains the absence of ferries on the Sabbath.

A bus from Portree took me to the Sligachan Hotel at the head of the loch from which the hotel takes its name. The footpath along Glen Sligachan extends all the way to Elgol but as Prince Charles is reputed to have headed over the hills to Loch Ainort I had to do the same. I chose a path accompanying the Allt na Measarroch to its source and in two hours I reached flat ground at the top of the pass. The respite was short lived. The Allt Coire nam Bruadaran flows steeply down the other side and my knees were complaining bitterly by the time I emerged on the A87 not far from Luib at the head of Loch Ainort. From Luib I walked through Strath Mor for about four miles. The path is not difficult although boggy in places. It passes to the west of Lochain Stratha Mhóir and at the lochan's southern end crosses the burn to continue east of Loch na Sguabaidh.

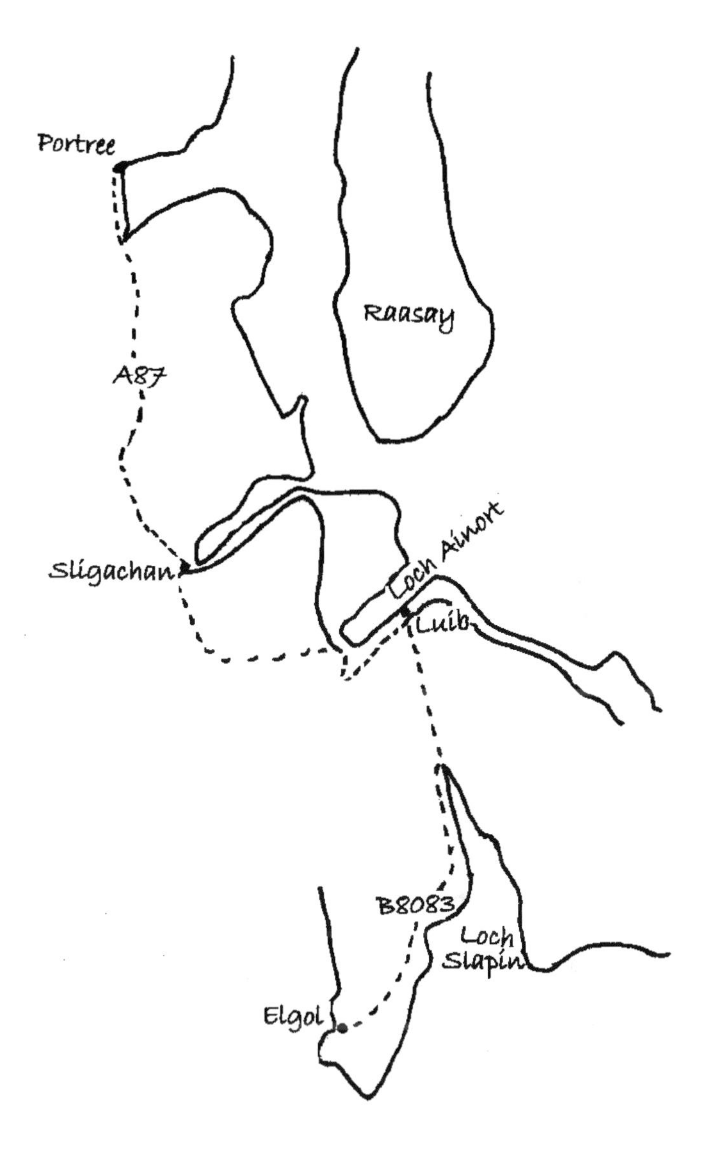

Portree to Elgol (22 Miles)

I failed to see the crossing point and continued along the western side of the burn through rough ground with no footpath at all. I could probably have struggled out onto the road eventually but fortunately saw a group of walkers on the far bank. I consulted the map, noticed my mistake and plucked up enough courage to wade across the cold water to finish this part of my journey on the excellent path I found there.

From the head of Loch Slapin the road hugs the coast for a couple of miles before turning inland and ending in a steep drop to the coast on the western side of the Strathaird peninsular at Elgol. The village has a school by the sea and a Post Office that was due to close permanently a few days after my visit. Elgol is still Mackinnon country and I stayed at Ach a Chleat with Anne and Shay Mackinnon. As I retired that evening I contemplated the good fortune that had led me to spend the night in Elgol in a Mackinnon household. I had an excellent dinner inside me and that had been finished off with the offer of a dram of Prince Charlie's own liqueur, the famous Skye Drambuie. The next morning the weather was brilliant. I wanted to see the bay in which there is yet another 'Prince Charlie's Cave' and so strode out along the spectacular cliffs south of Elgol. There is no evidence that Charles stayed in this particular cave although His Royal Highness must have waited somewhere as the boat approached to take him to Mallaig. W.B. Blaikie makes the astute comment that, *'All caves where he was known to have travelled have a way of developing myths.'*

There was no boat was waiting in Elgol to take me to the mainland. My journey to Mallaig would be less direct but more comfortable than that endured by Prince Charlie. I had to make my way first to Broadford and then south into Sleat where I should board the Armadale ferry. Another of the Mackinnon clan helped me in this venture. Only the Post Bus provides public transport from Elgol and that was not due for hours. I was walking and indifferently hitch-hiking when a battered old Volkswagen, driven by an elderly gentleman, drew up and offered me a lift. I leapt in with some gratitude and we set off at a sedate pace along the narrow road. The driver,

Mr Adam Mackinnon assessed me for a few minutes and then stopped the car and asked if I could drive. I said I could and we swapped seats. My host explained that his hip gave him constant trouble. Driving while rolling, lighting and smoking a cigarette was becoming difficult as he grew older! During the journey I took lessons on clearing a way through cattle on the road without startling them and learned that the closing of the Post Office in Elgol was a great disappointment to my new friend. He would have to go to Broadford once a week to collect his pension and settle up with the 'Top Shop' that provided his needs courtesy of the Post Bus. When he was a young man there were several retail suppliers within walking distance and although he admitted to an improvement in the roads Mr Mackinnon could not see how the state of things today could be regarded as progress. I agreed of course.

Before boarding one of the frequent ferries to Mallaig I visited Armadale Castle and Gardens. The Clan Donald Lands Trust is the custodian of Armadale Castle and the 20,000 acres of the Armadale Estate. There are beautifully landscaped gardens (picture p38) and a restaurant but the building that interested me most was the new Museum, Library and Study Centre opened in 2002. The Centre specialises in genealogical research and assists academic studies and has an extraordinary collection of more than 6,000 books and documents facilitating research into most areas of Scottish history and culture.

TWELVE

GLENMORISTON MEN

'They knew well the reward declar'd to give for apprehending or destroying H.R.H., but all the bribes in the world cou'd not make them betray that trust.'
MacDonell of Lochgarry's Narrative ~ Itinerary of Prince Charles

After spending three nights in the open near Mallaig, Old Mackinnon and one of the boatmen went off to try and find a cave that might offer them some shelter. While they were gone Prince Charles and John Mackinnon were rowed along the shores of Loch Nevis. They hoped to cross the loch to the Knoydart side where Old Clanranald was staying in a house that belonged to MacDonald of Scottas who was killed at Culloden. The boat was spotted and chased by a government militia but the oarsmen managed to put into shore and hide Prince Charles at the top of a hill. Eventually the fugitives managed to cross the loch undetected and land the Prince on a tiny island thought to have been Eilean na Glaschoille. John Mackinnon rowed on to meet Clanranald. *'Well then, what muckle devil has brought him to this country again?'* was the unenthusiastic response to the news that Charles was close by. Clanranald had helped in the past but now was understandably frightened of doing more. There was no choice but to row back to Mallaig and walk several miles south to Cross in the hope that MacDonald of Morar would help them. The infamous Captain Ferguson had burned down Morar's residence and he was living in a bothy. He welcomed his guests with food and being frightened to let them remain in the house led them to a cave for the night. The cold light of morning concentrated Morar's mind on the consequences of being arrested for assisting Charles and he offered no further co-operation. In desperation the Prince resolved, not for the first time, to ask help from Angus MacDonald of Borrodale. John Mackinnon agreed to accompany

Prince Charles but left his elderly clan chief at Morar.

Ferguson had been busy. The house at Borrodale had been added to the list of those burned to the ground. Despite his difficulties Angus agreed to assist saying, *'I shall lodge him so secure that all the forces in Britain shall not find him out.'* John Mackinnon left the Prince at Borrodale and returned to Morar. Tradition would have us believe that as Mackinnon departed, Charles gave him the recipe for Drambuie in gratitude for his help. The following morning Old Mackinnon was arrested but John managed to escape and returned home. He was taken prisoner almost as soon as he arrived in Elgol. The two of them were transported to London where they remained in custody until July 1747.

For the next two weeks Prince Charlie was continually on the run and his movements were without pattern. The terrain was difficult and the travelling hard. It appears that Charles stayed hidden in a cave or bothy in the woods at Borrodale for three days. He sent a message to Alexander MacDonald of Glenaladale before moving again to *'McLeod's Cove, upon a high procipes* (precipice) *in the woods of Borradil,'* four miles to the east. On July 15 Glenaladale joined the group and the next day they all moved to a refuge near Meoble in Morar that had been prepared by Angus MacEachine, Borrodale's son-in-law. Nowhere was safe for long, yet movement was a risky business too. General John Campbell had several ships anchored in Loch Nevis and Captain Caroline Scott was hunting the Prince in Arisaig. Inland, a redcoat cordon stretched from Loch Eil to Loch Hourn to cut off escape to the north and east. Nonetheless, remaining where he was meant certain capture and so, leaving behind Borrodale and MacEachine, the Prince set out again along *'a road so wild and rugged, as to be almost impervious even in daylight.'* Glenaladale, his brother John and Borrodale's son, another John MacDonald, now accompanied the Prince,

It seems that the party made their way to the east, south of Loch Beoraid, *'and by twelve o'clock they came to the top of a hill in the outmost bounds of Arisaig called Scoorvuy'* (O.S. Sgurr a' Mhuidhe) from where Glenaladale's brother was dispatched to

Glenfinnan for news. A rendezvous between them was arranged at *'about ten o'clock at night on the top of a hill, above Locharkaig in Lochiel's country, called Scoorwick Corrichan'* (O.S. Sgurr nan Coireachan). The Prince's party continued its slog eastwards *'and by two o'clock came to the top of a neighbouring hill called Fruighvein'* (O.S. Fraoch-bheinn). Glenaladale noticed clansmen moving their cattle and learned from them that 600 enemy soldiers were at the head of Loch Arkaig making escape in that direction impossible. A messenger was sent to recall Glenaladale's brother and another to find Donald Cameron of Glenpean. If Glenpean could be found, his local knowledge would provide a chance of finding a safe way through the cordon to the north.

The man sent to recall Glenaladale's brother returned unsuccessfully from his mission and brought the bad news that a hundred men of the Argyll Militia were at the bottom of Fraoch-bheinn. There was nothing for it but to move north without waiting for Glenpean to arrive but happily they chanced upon him later as they tramped through *'Corrour'* (O.S. Coire Odhar) at about eleven o'clock that night. Glenpean supplied information regarding the position of enemy soldiers and guided the group *'through roads almost impassable even in daylight, and travelling all night they came at four o'clock in the morning to the top of a hill in the Brae of Locharkaig, called Mamnyneallum.'* They rested here all day, within half a mile of an enemy camp, secure in the knowledge that the hill had already been searched. Glenaladale's brother, having not found the Prince at the top of Sgurr nan Coireachan as arranged, rejoined the group here.

The location of Mamnyneallum is not entirely clear. W.B. Blaikie believes that Mamnyneallum is *'a mistranscription for Mamnyn Callum'* and *'is without doubt a phonetic spelling of the Mam (elevated moorland) or shoulder of the Sgor Choileam of the Ordnance map. It is a pass down the slope of that high peaked hill, with a hollow running longitudinally through it capable of screening a party who might desire to proceed without being observed.'* Unfortunately the name 'Sgor Choileam' seems to be no longer in modern use although the mountain is so named on the map used by Drummond Norie in his 'Life and Adventures of Prince Charles Edward Stuart'. The modern 'Sgurr Thuilm' is geographically in the right place and phonetically similar. It also has a shoulder to the west separated from the main peak by a concealing deep hollow.

The route from 'Mamnyneallum' northwards is equally difficult to define. The contemporary account says no more than that Prince Charles *'continued in the top of the said hill all that day, and about nine o'clock at night set out with his retinue to the northward, and by one o'clock in the morning came to a place called Corrinangaul* (O.S. Coire nan Gall) *on the confines betwixt that part of Glengarry's country called Knoydart, and that part of Lochiel's country called Locharkaig.'* It is seven miles as the crow flies between Mamnyneallum and Coire nan Gall at the western end of Loch Quoich and at least twelve by any probable walking route. This forced march through a mountainous landscape in gathering darkness was, we are told, accomplished in four hours although this is difficult to believe.

Glenpean hoped that they might meet up with some of Lochiel's clan in Coire nan Gall and so obtain some food *'as they had entirely run out of provisions, excepting a very small quantity of oatmeal, and as small a remainder of butter.'* Unfortunately the corrie was deserted and the men were compelled to struggle on for another mile to the slopes of Druim Còsaidh where they all rested for an hour. The requirement for sustenance was becoming desperate and so Glenpean and Glenaldale's brother were dispatched to find food. The two exhausted foragers returned at three in the afternoon but brought only two small cheeses and the unwelcome news that about a hundred redcoats were marching up the other side of the hill. *'Notwithstanding this alarm (the search for his royal highness being general and very narrow all around), they stayed in the same place till about eight o'clock at night.'*

At last the fugitives moved across Gleann Còsaidh, narrowly avoiding a government camp. *'We passed so near that little camp as to see the soldiers passing betwixt us and the fires, and to hear the sound of their talk.'* In spite of the huge danger, the night of 20 July ended with the Prince almost triumphantly slipping through the redcoat cordon. According to Glenaladale, *'There was but one line of troops in our front, but were planted in little camps pitched in a line from the head of Loch Uirn to the head of Loch Eil, being 27 in all, so that once we crossed the one line of these we had none more near us to cross.'* Prince Charles Edward Stuart was still free and never again quite so close to capture.

The journey continued towards Glenshiel and Glenpean now pronounced himself out of the territory he knew well and returned home. Donald MacDonald, a Glengarry man known to Glenaladale, joined them and took over as guide. The Prince had heard that a French ship was searching for him at Poolewe on the west coast and he intended to go there but this plan was discarded when a message arrived indicating that the ship had abandoned its mission and left. Threatened again by troop movements they moved north into Glen Shiel and then east, by night, towards Glenmoriston. They found themselves on a hillside above Strathcluanie and *'chusing a fast place, took some rest till towards three o'clock afternoon.'* The night was spent in *'an open cave where he could neither lean nor sleep,'* possibly somewhere near the top of Sgurr nan Conbhairean.

The next day, July 24, yet another John MacDonald came into the Prince's life when he brought them milk. This MacDonald was a member of a band of dispossessed Jacobites that subsisted by raiding government forces. They are frequently referred to as 'The Seven Men of Glenmoriston' although for some of the time there were eight. The others were Alexander MacDonald, the brothers Alexander, Donald and Hugh Chisholm, Gregor MacGregor and the man usually acknowledged as the leader, Patrick Grant. The eighth man was Hugh MacMillan, *'who came one day accidentally upon us a little before we left Chissolm's country; and knowing us all, we kept him with us and proved very faithfull.'* Prince Charles was taken to their cave *'in the Brae of Glenmoriston in a place called Coiraghoth'* where, *'his royal highness was lulled asleep with the sweet murmurs of the finest purling stream that could be, running by his bedside, within the grotto, in which romantic habitation his royal highness pass'd three days.'* Troops, as always, were closing in on Charles' position necessitating a *'move into a place within two miles of them called Coirmheadhain, where they took up their habitation in a grotto no less romantic than the former'* where they stayed for a further four days.

Hearing that Captain Campbell and his militia were no more than four miles away Charles moved again, northwards to the Fasnakyle forest between Glen Affric and Glen Cannich. MacDonald of Glenaladale has it that *'they set out and climbed a hill on the northmost side of Glencanna,'* and Patrick Grant names the hill as *'Peinachyrine'* (a phonetic version of Beinn a' Chairein) and points out that this was the most northerly point of the Prince's wanderings. Charles' hopes of rescue were dashed when he heard that a French ship had docked at Poolewe but departed soon afterwards. However, *'a couple of gentlemen who had come on board of her had actually landed and were making the best of their way for Lochiel's country in search of the Prince.'* Charles moved east towards Strathglass and arrived at Fasnakyle on 9 August. The Prince now decided that he must journey southwards towards Achnacarry and Loch Arkaig in hopes of meeting Lochiel as well as hearing news from the two Frenchmen.

On August 13 a messenger was sent to summon Cameron of Clunes and the following day, as Glengarry was reported to be free of the enemy, Charles travelled first along the River Loyne and then south to ford the River Garry. Once safely across the party spent the night on the side of a hill in the rain and next morning came to the northern shore of Loch Arkaig at Achnasaul. A secure cave was found in the woods of Torre Chrone at the eastern end of Loch Arkaig. MacDonell of Lochgarry and Cameron of Clunes joined the group and on 16 August accompanied the Prince to another part of the same wood. From one of these hiding places a messenger was sent to try and find Lochiel who was known to be 'skulking' in

Badenoch with another firm friend, Cluny Macpherson. Lochgarry was of the opinion that further resistance was possible and that an army of at least two thousand men could easily be assembled. His Royal Highness agreed and so Lochgarry, Dr Archie and Cameron of Clunes departed for Badenoch to ask Lochiel and Cluny for their opinions and ideas.

Once again the security of the Prince made another move essential and on 21 August a new hiding place was found in the woods at Torr a' Mhuilt about a mile from Lochiel's ruined house at Achnacarry. Soldiers under the command of Lieutenant-Colonel Edward Cornwallis had burnt the house to the ground on 28 May. During the three days that were spent here Prince Charles, adopting the identity of a Captain Drummond, met the French officers at last. Unfortunately they had no useful information and subsequently left. The activities over the next few days are somewhat obscure but it seems likely that a force from Louden's regiment threatened the Prince, resulting in him fleeing by way of Gleann Cia-aig to the top of Meall an Tagraidh for a couple of days.

On 27 August Lochgarry and Dr Archie returned from Lochiel and Cluny with discouraging news of their thoughts on a further uprising. *'They answered, in their opinion, as the kingdom was so full of the enemy, it wou'd be of much worse consequence to rise in arms than doe otherwise.'* If Prince Charles had any lingering fantasies of once again marching at the head of a fearsome army of Highlanders they were surely dashed now. Having no alternative Charles travelled to Lochiel's secure hideaway and hoped for news of a ship that could take him to France.

Landranger Maps

40 Mallaig & Glenfinnan
25 Glen Carron & Glen Affric
33 Loch Alsh & Glen Shiel
26 Inverness & Strathglass
34 Fort Augustus & Glen Albyn
41 Ben Nevis, Fort William

Arieniskill (40)	**NM788831**
Kinloch Hourn (33)	**NG951071**
Charlie's Cave (40)	**NM796850**
Ceannacroc Bridge (34)	**NH226105**
Sgurr a' Mhuidhe (40)	**NM854825**
Glenmoriston Cave (34)	**NH139156**
Fraoch-bheinn (40)	**NM896837**
Tomich (26)	**NH310275**
Sgurr Thuilm (40)	**NM940880**
Liatrie (25)	**NH249326**
Corryhully (40)	**NM913845**
Fedden (34)	**NN210941**
Coire nan Gall (33)	**NM927977**
Achnacarry (41)	**NN176878**
Sourlies (40)	**NM869950**

From Mallaig I took a trip aboard the motor vessel 'Western Isles' to Inverie on Knoydart (picture p39) where I hoped to find the house that once belonged to MacDonald of Scottas. Knoydart is almost as remote today as it was in 1746 and the ferry is an essential link to the rest of the world for the one hundred souls who live there. There are a few miles of road but they fail to connect this exhilarating wilderness to other parts of the country and so, except for a few dedicated walkers, all visitors and supplies arrive by sea.

It was a glorious day as we sailed over Loch Nevis and docked right in front of the 'Old Forge Public House', surely the most remote pub on mainland Britain. Scottas is a mile or so to the west of the pier and I was pleased to find a striking house overlooking the sea that I thought worthy of investigation. It was the right place. The present owner has done a superb job of renovation and maintenance and told me that the house was on the site of that existing in 1746 but had effectively been completely rebuilt. There is a scroll-shaped date stone under the eaves at each end of the house and although I could read neither with the naked eye, binoculars revealed the number 17 carved in relief on the left-hand stone. The number on the right-hand side was impossible to make out from the ground, as it was both eroded and obscured by tree branches. I borrowed a ladder and climbed to the eaves to discover that the house was built in 1775. The tiny and unremarkable Eilean na Glaschoille is another mile down the road opposite Glaschoille house. I took a couple of photographs and walked back to 'The Old Forge' where I drank an excellent pint of the Skye brewery's 'Young Pretender' hand-pumped beer while waiting for the ferry to return.

W. B. Blaikie comments that MacDonald of Morar's bothy no longer stands but positions it at *'Cross ~ a long mile south of the bridge over the Morar river.'* There is a cross set on a hill near the railway station in Morar and the views from the top are extraordinary. Through the shimmering heat haze I could see the silhouettes of the islands of Eigg and Rum and the jagged points of the Cuillins on Skye. Behind me, deep and mysterious, Loch Morar spilled across the landscape. However, this is not the place to which Blaikie refers and the exact location of Cross is not certain. There is a Glenancross Farm a couple of mile south-west of Morar and I was informed that this used to be named simply Cross Farm. For my money this is as good a bet as any for the site of Morar's house.

The whereabouts of the cave in Morar has also been lost. Ordnance Survey is not shy about any number of 'Prince Charlie's Caves' in the Highlands but it offers no location in Morar. Blaikie notes that *'the cave is a mile from the site of the house, near the mouth of the river, in the face of a cliff some twenty-five feet high.'* The estuary of the River Morar occupies a charming sandy bay and there are several caves on the southern shore. I tried to reach them and imagine that at low tide it is a simple matter. At high tide it is perhaps impossible. I couldn't manage it and so conclude that this is not a likely place for Charlie's cave. Drummond Norie tells that local tradition sites the cave at Scamadale, on the southern shore of Loch Morar about a mile from its western end. It's not likely but who am I to argue?

Arisaig House, now a hotel, stands on the site of Angus MacDonald's house at Borrodale. The O.S. map marks a 'Prince

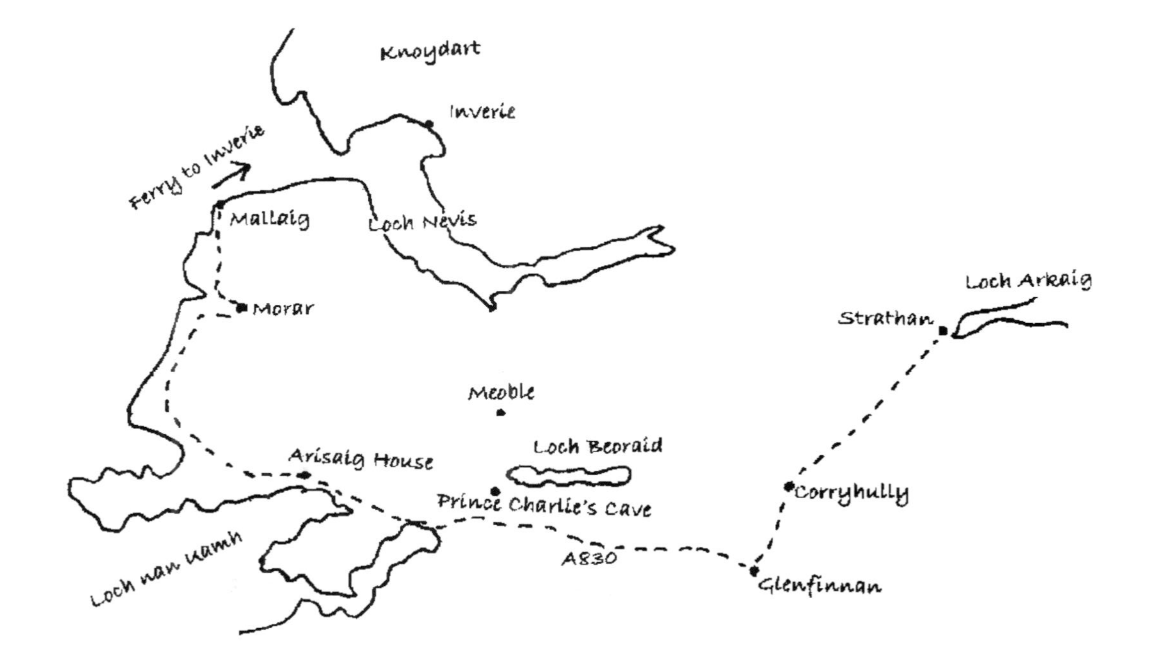

Mallaig to Glenfinnan and Strathan (35 Miles)

Charlie's Cave' immediately to the south and those who are prepared to search diligently may find it. Of the Prince's next hiding place 'MacLeod's Cove', mentioned in John MacDonald's narrative, there seems to be no trace.

I travelled from Morar through Arisaig to Arieniskill on the A830 at the western end of Loch Eilt. I had been here before and had already climbed my way past 'Prince Charlie's Cave' from Meoble when following the Prince's flight from Culloden. As recounted I did not much enjoy the experience. The cave is in trees, high on a hill overlooking the River Meoble and Loch. There is no certainty that this is 'MacEachine's refuge' but it is as likely as any other location in the area.

I made up my mind not walk to the cave again, justifying my decision with the thoughts that the Prince is reputed to have marched to the south of Loch Beoraid and the marked path today is north of the loch. As it seems likely that some of his men used Sgurr a' Mhuidhe and then Fraoch-bheinn as vantage points they may have tramped well to the south, quite near the modern road perhaps! For those determined to walk every step I suggest using the footpath to Kinlochbeoraid where, although the map indicates no bridge over the Allt a' Choire it ought to be possible to cross somewhere. Once over the burn then it looks relatively simple to walk along Gleann Donn if the forested area is not too difficult. Up on the top at the watershed the Allt a' Chaol-ghlinne provides a guide for the walk to Corryhully north of Glenfinnan.

I used the road and at Glenfinnan turned left into the glen for the pleasant and undemanding walk up to Corryhully. I stopped at the bothy for a while and was amazed to find it supplied with electricity. Such luxury is rare if not entirely unprecedented. The road ends at Corryhully but the walk along Gleann a' Chaorainn to Strathan at the western end of Loch Arkaig is straightforward. Sgurr Thuilm, where I think 'Mamnyneallum' is to be found, rises 3,000 feet above the glen. A cairn marks the watershed and mid-point of the walk to Strathan. From here the path runs downhill and the trickles of water merge to form the Allt a' Chaorainn that ultimately contributes to the

River Pean. A rickety bridge over the burn leads to another over the Pean and from here the map indicates that the path dives into the forest to emerge at Strathan. I found a couple of high stiles over the fence into the woods but try as I might I could not find a path through them. In the end I gave up and as the forest does not extend to the bank of the river I walked along the fence line into Strathan. This last part of the walk was the hardest. The ground is flat, low-lying and extremely boggy. A bootful of water was unavoidable.

The route from 'Mamnyneallum' to Allt Coire nan Gall at the western end of Loch Quoich is difficult to discern from contemporary accounts. In a footnote Drummond Norie relates that local tradition maintains that the Prince descended into Glen Pean from 'Mamnyneallum' and then followed the course of the Dearg Allt and the Allt a' Chinn Bhric. Somewhere near Kinbreack in Glen Kingie Prince Charles turned to the west and crossed the slopes of Sgurr Beag and Druim Buidhe into Coire nan Gall. Norie mentions that this information came to him too late for him to include it on his map, apparently forgetting that as the Dearg Allt flows into the River Dessarry right at the head of Loch Arkaig where hundreds of the enemy were encamped, the fugitives had abandoned this line of escape. To avoid the soldiers the route from Mamnyneallum must have been due north across Glen Pean and into Glen Dessarry, two or three miles west of the head of Loch Arkaig. A possible route might then have been to continue due north, passing between Garbh Chioch Bheag and (confusingly) another mountain named Sgurr nan Coireachan and finally into Coire nan Gall.

I chose to find my way from Strathan up Glen Dessarry following the path that extends past Lochan Mhàim to Sourlies at the head of Loch Nevis. My intention was to turn north about a mile before the lochan and climb around the shoulder of Garbh Chioch Mhor, along the Allt Bealach na h Eangair and finally into Coire nan Gall. I must have been mad! Not only could I not pronounce the names I could not possibly conquer those places in a single day and still have time to find a way out to Kinloch Hourn. Unless I was prepared to spend a night on the hills I should have to radically rethink my tentative plans.

I called in to Upper Glendessarry where Jim from Wallasey was in residence. He concentrated my mind and suggested that I should stride through to Sourlies bothy and walk out to Kinloch Hourn via Barrisdale the next day. This itinerary is at considerable odds with the Jacobites' journey of course but then the Prince had a guide, he was desperate and he was half my age! I continued my slog up the glen until Lochan Mhàim came into view. By now I had decided that Sourlies ought to be my destination but was lured to the north by footprints and an apparently uncomplicated path. This was a big mistake. I climbed and climbed until a narrow scree slope between the two highest mountains in the region came mistily into view. There were still miles and miles to go to Kinloch Hourn, the weather was not good and I pictured the crossing of the pass leaving me stranded several hours from shelter. I knew I was beaten and reluctantly began to descend. Instead of retracing my steps I headed west and followed the course of Allt Coire na Ciche for a while until to my despair I found myself looking down a precipitous incline at the bottom of which I could see the Finiskaig River as it flowed towards Sourlies on Loch Nevis. I needed to be at the bottom of that slope and was not looking forward to getting there. Slowly and carefully I picked my way through the scree and at last made it down to the river. The detour had cost me at least a couple of hours and I did not arrive at Sourlies (picture p40) until three o'clock.

As I knew that my day was to be difficult I had completed a form stating my route for the day before I left my B&B that morning. My host was aware that should I not phone him by say ten at night he should inform the police who would consider sending out the mountain rescue people to look for me. I was nowhere near where I had said I would be and a very long way from a phone box. Fortunately it was mid-summer and as I still had at least six hours of daylight left I thought I'd have a go at walking north to Barrisdale and possibly even Kinloch Hourn. I began by walking up the course of the River Carnach. All went well for a couple of hours but at about 5.30p.m. the path disappeared into woodland in the bottom of the river's steep-

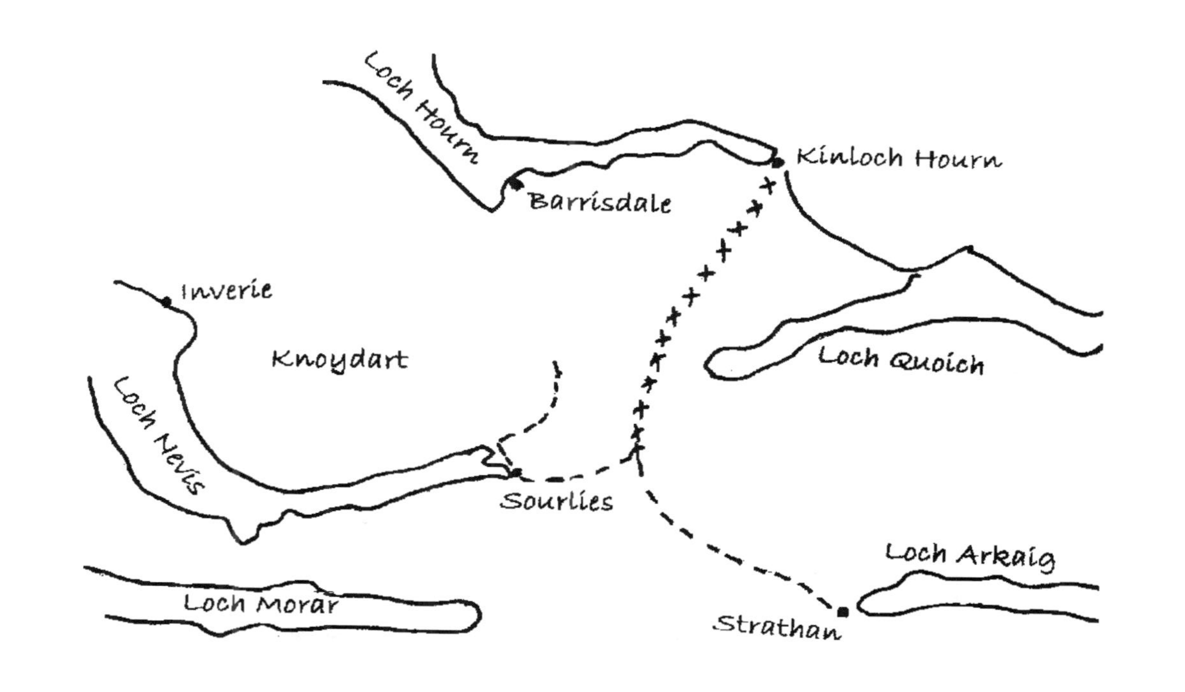

Strathan to Sourlies (12 miles)
Prince's route (xxx) to Coire Sgoireadail (Kinloch Hourn)

sided gorge. These tiny wooded areas in the Highlands are often difficult to negotiate, as the trees only exist because the land on which they grow is almost inaccessible by people or deer. Although I knew it was theoretically possible for me to force a way along the river and climb up to join the path that runs east-west from Loch Quoich to Loch Hourn I once again started to worry about spending a night on the hills and turned back. At least Sourlies bothy would provide me with a roof over my head.

Seven o'clock saw me back at Sourlies and I was now almost certain that I would be unable to telephone to say I was safe and so resigned myself to the consequences. There was one long shot left. I had spotted an elegant lodge, Camusrory, on the shore of Loch Nevis. If anyone was in residence perhaps they might have a satellite phone or radio transmitter. It's a couple of miles from Sourlies to Camusrory and I had already been walking for over ten hours but nevertheless I set off with no great hope of success. I passed the estate buildings and headed for the main house. It was unoccupied as I had more than half expected. I trudged away disappointed. My last throw of the dice was to be the other house in the small complex of buildings. My hopes were raised as I passed a water-powered electricity generating plant that was gently humming away. I knocked on the door of the house and was amazingly rewarded by the sound of a barking dog followed by human speech. The door opened and I knew that things could only get better. Two estate workers lived there permanently and they had means of communication with the outside world. The mountain rescue helicopters would not be scrambled for me after all! We chatted for a while and, after ascertaining that I was about to spend the night at Sourlies, Victor suggested that I might like to spend three hours or so walking over the hills to Inverie in Knoydart. When I expressed my reluctance to do that as I was already exhausted the two men proposed that they could possibly launch their dinghy and powerboat me down Loch Nevis to Inverie. Inverie has bed and breakfast, Inverie has telephones, Inverie has a pub! It was irresistible. A fee was negotiated: the Land Rover provided transport to the pier at Torr Cruinn and the boat was launched. Forty minutes later I was standing in the dining room of the Pier House in Knoydart thanking my lucky stars that a room was available and that my exciting day had ended so well.

The following morning I woke with the knowledge that I had not yet achieved my ambition of following the Prince's direct route to the north. I had also attempted to get through to Barrisdale and been unsuccessful there as well. With a full day in front of me perhaps I could try again but reluctantly decided that I should have to leave that expedition for another occasion. I bade farewell to Knoydart and embarked on the 'Western Isles' bound for Mallaig.

So that the dedicated may attempt the direct journey if they wish I offer both Drummond Norie's itinerary and my own thoughts on the Prince's journey. Norie is led by local tradition to conclude that the route took the men from Coire nan Gall around Meall an Spardain, along Gleann Còsaidh to Loch an Lagain Aintheich. Turning north-east the travellers rounded Sgurr à Chlaidheimh and descended to Coireshubh near Kinloch Hourn. This sounds possible although I cannot see why the fugitives needed to twist and turn quite so much. My suggestion is that the Prince crossed Gleann Còsaidh somewhere near the present day shore of the Loch Quoich reservoir and climbed up to Coire Beithe before dropping down to the glen through which the present day road to Kinloch Hourn runs.

Soon after leaving Gleann Còsaidh Prince Charles had an accident that could easily have cost him his life. The Prince stumbled and *'would certainly have fallen one hundred fathoms perpendicular over the rock had he not catched hold of a tree on the very top of the rock with one of his legs.'* Cameron of Glenpean came to the rescue and the journey continued without further incident. At last the men came *'betwixt two and three in the morning to a place on the Glenealg side of the head of Lochuirn called Corriscorridill,'* (O.S. Coire Sgoireadail) where they paused for the day.

The Prince spent time in a *'fast place'* in *'Corriscorridill'* and the Coire Sgoireadail rises high out of Kinloch Hourn to Bealach Duibh Leac before descending along the Allt Mhàlagain to the A87 main road in Glen Shiel, south of Achnagart Farm. The route up Coire Sgoireadail looks very hard especially near the top where the ground rises to about 2,700ft and is very steep on both sides of the summit. I chose a different way and was helped in my decision by Donald Cameron of Kinloch Hourn. Donald Cameron of Glenpean had guided Charles Edward into the area and so it seemed fitting for me to take Cameron advice on a suitable route into Glen Shiel. Donald's advice was to follow the line of electricity pylons north-west from his house for a couple of miles and then branch off right to cross the burn named Allt a' Choire Reidh towards Allt Coire Mhàlagain. In recommending this route Donald was in good company as W.B. Blaikie writes, *'The natural, indeed the only practicable pass from Loch Hourn to Glenshiel is by Coire Mhalagain, and the path is in use to this day.'* The path was steep but easy to follow all the way to the burn where it disappeared. Here, it seems, most walkers turn round and go back the way they came. Not me: I crossed the flow of water and with Mulloch Gorm on my left, followed the stream up into the hills, accompanied for most of the way by dazzling views over Loch Hourn. The watershed is at the tiny lochan on Bealach Coire Mhàlagain.

The great thing about the top of this pass (picture p39) is that there is no endless series of false peaks to tease tired walkers; the crest that can be seen from the bottom of the hill is indeed the summit. Away down in the distance on the other side I could see the road snaking through the glen. It appeared to be much closer than it was, as my feet had no hesitation in confirming hours later. Another burn, confusingly also called Allt Coire Mhàlagain, rises from the summit and flows into Allt Mhàlagain and the River Shiel. There was no path to follow on this descent. The terrain began benignly enough, but gradually grew worryingly steeper. The gorge in which the burn flows became narrow and sheer-sided and I thought it prudent to remain as high on the hills as possible. I was happy when the struggle was over and my knees could take a well-earned rest from constantly applying the brakes as gravity and my backpack tried to roll me downhill. My welcome on the road was a stream of cars quite

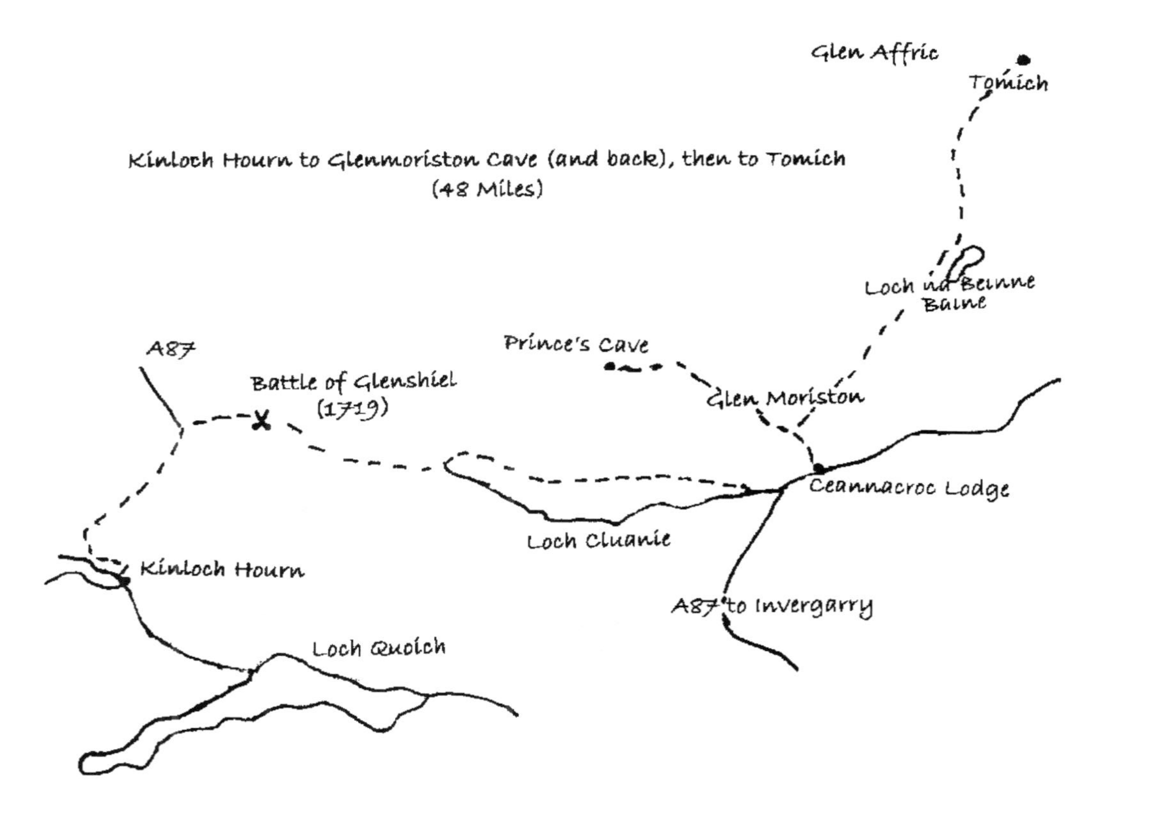
Kinloch Hourn to Glenmoriston Cave (and back), then to Tomich
(48 Miles)
Glen Affric
Tomich
Loch na Beinne Baine
Prince's Cave
Glen Moriston
A87
Battle of Glenshiel
(1719)
Ceannacroc Lodge
Loch Cluanie
Kinloch Hourn
A87 to Invergarry
Loch Quoich

disinterested in the tiredness of my legs and no bus was due for a couple of hours. Ah well, at least the sun was shining and I was well pleased with my achievement for the day.

The range of hills known as The Five Sisters rears up with formidable steepness from the riverbank to the north of Glen Shiel. One of the mountains is named Sgurr nan Spainteach, (the Peak of the Spaniards) after the Spanish troops who fought on the Jacobite side at the battle of Glenshiel during the rising of 1719.

The Glenmoriston Men allegedly took the Prince to two caves. The contemporary accounts rely on phonetic renditions of place names, which makes identification of either cave questionable. Glenaladale describes the first cave as being in 'Coiraghoth', which is reasonably interpreted to be Coire Dho. He goes on to mention a second cave in 'Coirmheadhain', which is undoubtedly Coire Mheadoin. Patrick Grant's account confirms the existence of two caves. It locates the second one at 'Coirskreaoch' and describes it as *'no less romantic ~ than the former.'* John of Borrodale mentions only one cave, that being at 'Corrichido' and offering the description that it *'is one large stone in the strath of this corry near these huts you see; under that stone fourty men can accomodate themselves, and the best water in the highland runen throu it.'*

Blaikie believes that two caves exist but that the whereabouts of the one the Prince hid in first has been lost. I am not so sure. If we are to believe Glenaladale, then the first cave is to the east of the second. If the Prince came over the hills from the west then he would have had to pass the isolated location of the cave in Coire Mheadhoin to reach the one in the less remote Coire Dho. Today there appears to be only local knowledge of the cave in Coire Mheadhoin and that fits the description given by Borrodale quite well. We have 'Corrichido' and 'Coiraghoth' described as locations of the first cave and 'Coirskreaoch' as the location of the second. Could these be all referring to the same place? The Allt Coire Mheadhoin flows into the River Doe and it is difficult to be certain where one ends and the other begins. Is it not possible that there was only one cave, high up the glen, near the source of a burn that eventually becomes the River Doe? The contemporary accounts were taken down some time after the events. The Prince was constantly on the run and frequently changing hiding places. Many of these might have been described as 'caves' for want of a better description. As the years passed I imagine one uncomfortable night out on the hills swiftly merged with others in the memories of those who were there.

The route to the Glenmoriston Men's cave is uncertain and even the redoubtable W. B. Blaikie offers nothing definite, simply mentioning a hillside above Strathclunie and then going on to say, *'they turned northward, climbing to the top of a high hill between Glenmoriston and Strathglass. (Sgurr-nan-Conbhairean, probably).'* If the Prince approached the cave from the south, west or even north he must have had a trying time of it. The cave is hemmed in on three sides by fearsome cliffs protecting difficult, high and steep mountains. There would have been no room for error and reaching the cave in darkness would have been close to impossible.

Drummond Norie walked to the Glenmoriston cave in 1899. He took Blaikie as close to his word as he could and comments, *'to reach this wild spot I had to spend the night at Claunie Inn, drive to Lundie, climb Carn á Ghluasaid, over 2000 feet, Sgurr nan Conbhairean, 3632 feet, and descend the precipitous Corrie Mheadhain to the cave.'* Norie goes on to *'recommend the excursion to those of my readers who are fond of a good day's climbing.'*

Well good for Mr Norie. I don't doubt his word but that journey seems only suitable for a mountain goat and, not having half the British army at my heels, I settled for a less arduous route. I travelled by road, east along Loch Claunie to the Ceannacroc Bridge near the confluence of the rivers Doe and Moriston. A track through the valley of the Doe leads four miles into the Ceannacroc Forest to a couple of bridges near the confluence of the Allt Coire Mheadhoin and the Allt Coire Sgreumh that together make up the Doe. The route follows the course of the Allt Coire Mheadhoin to another bridge from where there is neither track nor footpath but I continued to follow the burn west through sodden moorland into the corrie containing 'Prince Charlie's Cave'. The corrie is enormous and finding the cave was difficult. I looked everywhere, searching out the most unlikely clefts in the rock face to no avail. Time was running out for I had to return over the same route. In the end I even began to doubt that I was in the correct corrie and with a heavy heart and even heavier legs I gave up.

It was not until the following spring that I had a chance to try again and this time I took some local advice. It turned out that I had been searching for the cave according to my preconceived and unfortunately incorrect ideas. I had expected to find the cave in the face of the corrie and presumed I should find its mouth facing me as I walked to the end of the glen. Wrong! The cave (picture p40) is simply a large space conveniently formed by the rolling together of several huge boulders as they split off from the cliff face thousands of years ago. Had I read Blaikie's 'Itinerary' in detail before I began my search the task would have been easier. Before my second visit I learned that the hiding place is *'a cavern formed by the great masses of rock at the bottom of a talus* (scree) *from the hill above ~ in fact a cavity in a cairn of stones.'*

A plaque *'In Memory of the Seven Men of Glenmoriston'* has been placed at the entrance of the cave informing the visitor that the object of the hard day's walking has at last been discovered. The inscription names the men, with the exception of MacMillan, and describes them as *'hosts and protectors of Prince Charles Edward Stuart in this cave between 28 July and 1 August 1746 and were not tempted by the rewards offered to betray him to his enemies.'* It continues, *'A great sum of money or reward did not cause them to betray me. The memory of these devoted men will go down to generations yet unborn.'* On the left of the clump of boulders is a cleft that also offers access to the dark interior and the *'finest purling stream'* of MacDonald's narrative trickles out to the right. The man must have had an ironic sense of humour for although the cave would certainly provide shelter from wind, rain and prying redcoat eyes, it is difficult to see how Prince Charles could be *'as comfortably lodged as if he had been in a royal palace.'*

Blaikie's 'Itinerary' suggests the route north from the Glenmoriston Men's hideout is *'over the shoulder of Tigh Mor into the pass of Alt na Ciche, which debouches into Glen Affrick at Ardnamulloch at the head of Loch Affrick, and thence down Glen Affrick to the fast places of Fasnakyle.'* The journey to Gleann na Ciche involves some difficult terrain and there are several possible routes that run north to Glen Affric to the east of the one Blaikie suggests. They provide easier walking and as there is no evidence to the contrary I see no reason why Prince Charles should not have taken one of them.

One way involves the track I had previously used through Glen Doe. About three miles north-west from Ceannacroc Lodge a footpath pushes north and then north-east into the Guisachan Forest. Unfortunately the path begins on the wrong side of the river and if there ever was a bridge it is not there now. The river was high and impossible to ford and I so decided against this route. A few miles east is the 'pylon road' leading north from Dundreggan but that is probably way off track for the Prince's journey north. After consultation with my B&B host I chose a route to the west of a large stand of trees, due north of Ceannacroc Lodge. After struggling for a mile over waterlogged ground I reached the unmade road built to link the various dams that are part of a hydroelectric scheme in this district.

Walking was easy at first. I travelled east and then north-east to a dam at the end of the road. The map shows a trail heading north through woodland on the other side of the burn. In reality the path is scarcely discernible but I made good progress. I intended to follow the course of the Allt na Muic to the watershed and join the marked path over Bealach Feith na Gamhna into Glen Affric but I failed to concentrate adequately on my direction. The driving wind and rain pushed me steadily eastwards until I came to within half a mile of Loch Beinne Baine and realised that I must either backtrack or figure out a new route. The terrain was flat but boggy and criss-crossed with deep gullies through the peat. My feet were soaked and the cloud was too low for comfort. The likelihood of being enveloped in mist fills even the most experienced walkers with apprehension. It is easy to become disorientated when landmarks are invisible and the chances of falling or twisting an ankle are much greater in poor weather.

I knew that the pylon road was just east of the loch and that if the weather got worse my compass would bring me to it without too much difficulty. I resolved to head north from my position a little west of the loch and soon found myself following the course of the Allt Cas a Chuirn north towards Garve Bridge. At the point where the burn enters the forest the gorge through which it flows became steep and difficult and so I headed off left, along the forest fence. A couple of miles later I joined the pylon road at the junction with the track to Hilton Lodge. There was even a welcome signpost confirming my position. My choices were to walk north to Hilton Lodge or follow the other arm of the signpost to the village of Tomich. The prospect of accommodation meant that Tomich won hands down and I strolled along the forest road for several miles into the village.

There are few buses between Tomich and the rest of the world and so I was lucky to arrive in the village at four o'clock just as the bus from Inverness arrived to drop off the last of its cargo of school children. I could not resist jumping on and at first simply intended to travel the few miles to Cannich where I thought there would be a greater choice of places to stay. I was wet, tired and had endured enough for one day. The lure of the big city was too great and I found myself buying a ticket all the way to Inverness. Presumably the service is heavily subsidised as I had the bus all to myself for the whole journey. The weather brightened up as we drove along the shore of Loch Ness and I was much more cheerful and a good deal drier when I disembarked in the centre of town.

My next visit was in much better weather a couple of months later. My first challenge was to visit the most northerly place the Prince reached during the '45 described as being to the north of Glen Cannich and, recounted by Patrick Grant as *'Peinachyrine'*. My difficulty was that modern maps show Beinn a' Chairein to be south, not north, of the glen. However many names have changed over the years and maps of the period provide evidence that the hill due north of Liatrie Farm in Glen Cannich was known in 1745 as Binachren. This hill is now named Meallan Odhar but I feel reasonably sure that this is where Prince Charles climbed as he impatiently waited for messengers returning with news of shipping at Poolewe.

The minor road that heads to Loch Mullardoch from Cannich provided the approach to Meallan Odhar. At Liatrie I struck off north along the course of the Liatrie burn. There is no path and progress was slow. The thigh deep covering of bracken and heather hampered my efforts and I was forever worried about my inability to see where I was putting my feet. Once into the trees the conditions improved but it was not until I was north of the copse that I reached clearer ground. At the top I was rewarded by a magnificent view into Glen Stathfarrar with Loch Monar glinting in the sunlight over to my left.

A few minutes later I began the easier task of the return journey. I emerged on the road satisfied with my achievement but with wet feet and trousers and the unwelcome attention of a cloud of midges. I returned to Tomich to pick up the road leading to Hilton Lodge and the pylon road back into Glenmoriston. The track is well defined and runs due south through the Guisachan Forest, east of Loch na Beinne Baine to the A887 road at Dundreggan. Once back in Glenmoriston I had to find a way around Loch Gary to the western end of Loch Lochy near Achnacarry. I hitch-hiked along the A887 and as we travelled I persuaded my driver to stop for a few moments at the cairn dedicated to Roderick Mackenzie.

> *At this spot in 1746 died Roderick Mackenzie an officer in the army of Prince Charles Edward Stuart. Of the same size and of similar resemblance to his Royal Prince when surrounded and overpowered by the troops of the Duke of Cumberland gallantly died in attempting to save his fugitive leader from further pursuit.*

The story is not well documented but apparently at his moment of

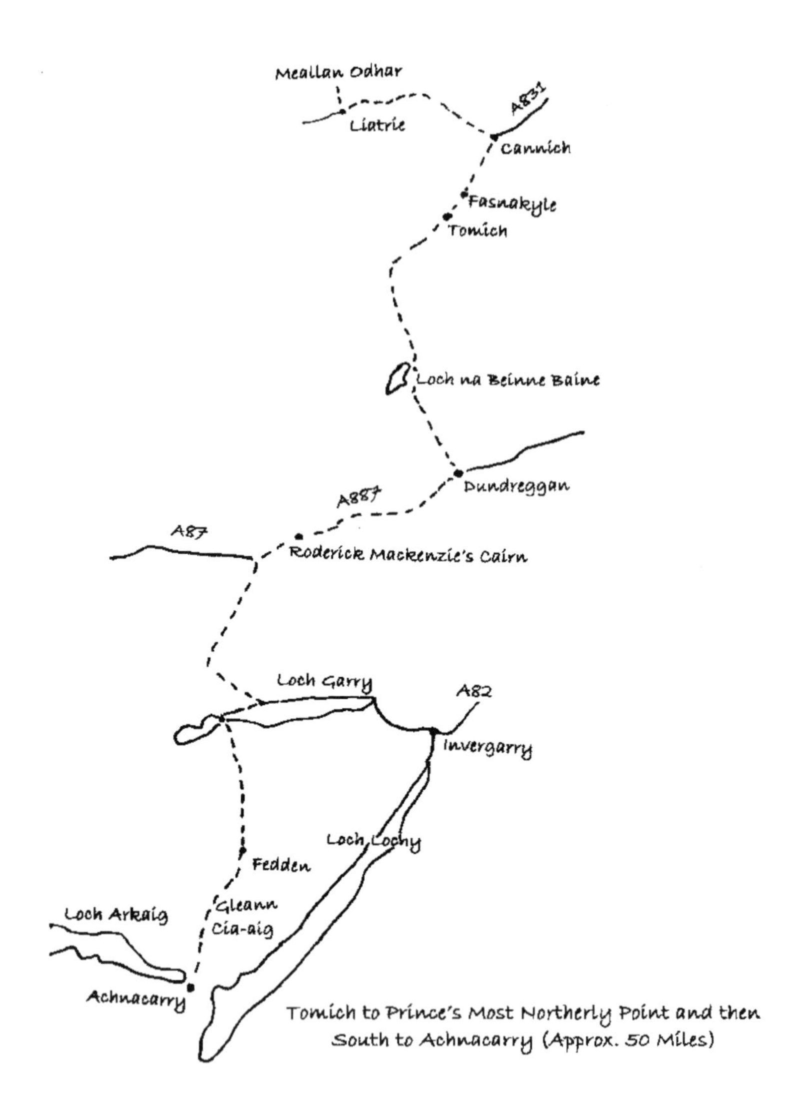

Tomich to Prince's Most Northerly Point and then South to Achnacarry (Approx. 50 Miles)

death Mackenzie claimed to be the Prince. The soldiers believed him, cut off his head and took it to Fort Augustus for identification.

The A87 took me south to the Tomdoun road and this leads to the western end of Loch Gary but rather than crossing the River Gary as the Prince did, I made use of the modern bridge over the loch. I intended to walk directly to the woods at the southern end of Gleann Cia-aig where Prince Charles hid in *'a very fast place'* after moving east from Achnasaul. I stood on the bridge and contemplated my good fortune to be there on this loveliest of days. The water was mirror flat and the surrounding hills were clearly reflected in all their picture postcard beauty. A good track thrusts south and then east past Greenfield and then south again through the Glengarry forest. In places the trail is waymarked by the Scottish Rights of Way Society and is quite easy to follow. The path comes to an old iron fence and as any discernible track more or less disappears the fence became my companion and guide for the next few miles. The path is flanked by steep mountains and burns flow down from both sides making progress along the glen a wet and boggy business. At last I caught a glimpse of a building in the distance. This was Fedden, a sorry, dilapidated shieling at the foot of Meall an Tagraidh. The ruin consists of four low walls and a chimneystack that looks in imminent danger of collapse. The place is marked on the O.S. map and was confirmation that I was in the right place. From Fedden a clear path reaches south along Gleann Cia-aig and I emerged on the 'Mile Dorcha' close to Achnacarry.

THIRTEEN

CLUNY'S CAGE

'The Cage was no larger than to contain six or seven persons, four of which number were frequently employed in playing at cards, one idle looking on, one becking, and another firing bread and cooking.'
Donald Macpherson's account ~ Lyon in Mourning

Charles' journey into Badenoch and then to Cluny's Cage in Ben Alder is poorly documented. Lochgarry's account is the only one available and this gives little information. The narrative reports that the journey began on 28 August when Prince Charles, accompanied by Dr Archie, Lochgarry and others, rounded the southern end of Loch Lochy and walked the fifteen miles along Glen Gloy to the River Tarff, *'to pass within two short miles of Fort Augustus.'* From here it is probable that the men travelled south along Glen Tarff and over the Corrieyairack exactly one year to the day after previously crossing the pass. Fearing that sentries patrolled the bridge at Garvamore, the little band of men might have turned off the military road and headed towards Loch Laggan.

Tradition has it that the Prince was conducted down the Allt Coire Adair to Ranald MacDonell's house at Aberarder. Robert Forbes met MacDonell and his brother Alexander in 1760 but their account of events makes no mention of a visit to the house. Alexander simply states that he was honoured to supply the Prince with *'a brown short coat, a shirt and a pair of shoes.'* It seems unlikely that Prince Charles visited Aberarder. The Creag Meagaidh range of hills to the north-west is steep and difficult and as the house is the only one in the area it was probably under observation by the redcoats.

From the southern end of Loch Laggan Charles marched across the Ardverikie Forest towards Loch Pattack. This long and arduous journey ended when *'the Prince lay the first night at Corrineuir at the foot of Benalder after his coming to Badenoch from which he was conducted next day to Mellanmuir in Benalder, a shieling of very narrow compass.'* Exactly where Corrineuir and Mellanmuir are to be found is not entirely clear but it was in the Mellanmuir shieling that Charles was at last reunited with Lochiel. The Prince *'was gay, hearty and in better spirits than it was possible to think he could be, considering the many disasters, misfortunes, disappointments, fatigues and difficulties he had undergone.'*

Perhaps Charles' good mood could be attributed, at least in part, to the preparations made at Mellanmuir, *'where there was more eatables and drinkables provided for his entertainment than he expected. There was plenty of mutton newly killed, and an anker of whiskie of twenty Scotch pints, with some good beef sassers made the year before, and plenty of butter and cheese, and besides, a large well cured bacon ham.'* On 1 September Cluny Macpherson, who had earlier left for Achnacarry to look for the Prince, returned to the Mellanmuir shieling. The Prince kissed him *'as if he had been an equal'* and said, *'I'm sorry Cluny, you and your regiment were not at Culloden. I did not hear till of very late that you was so near to have come up that day.'*

The next day Charles Edward was recommended to move on to a more secure place two miles further into the wilderness of Ben Alder, *'to a little sheill called Uiskchilra where the hut or bothie was superlatively bad and smockie.'* Charles stayed here for three nights before travelling on to the primitive, two-story hiding place constructed from boulders and timber and known as Cluny's Cage.

> *The habitation called the Cage in the face of that mountain was within a small thick bush of wood. There were first some rows of trees laid down in order to level a floor for the habitation, and as the place was steep this rais'd the lower side to equall height with the other; and these trees, in the way of jests or planks, were entirely well levelled with earth*

and gravel. There were betwixt the trees, growing naturally on their own roots, some stakes fixed in the earth, which with the trees were interwoven with ropes made of heath and birch twigs all to the top of the Cage, it being of a round or rather oval shape, and the whole thatched and covered with foge. The whole fabrick hung as it were by a large tree, which reclined from the one end all along the roof to the other, and which gave it the name of the Cage.

The Cage was securely hidden in a thicket of trees. It was reasonably comfortable and Cluny reasoned that if no ship could be found to take Charles to France then it would be possible to spend the winter there. Others using the Cage as a last refuge were Lochiel, his servant Allan Cameron, Dr Cameron, Lochgarry, Macpherson of Breakachie, and a few of Cluny's servants. Fortunately for Prince Charles the French government was still making an effort to rescue him. Previous attempts had met with failure not least because Prince Charles was always well hidden. In June the Comte de Maurepas wrote, *'It seems certain that the Stuart Prince is in one or other of the small islands of the north of Scotland. But he is so well concealed from his enemies and from those who would help him, that both seek him with the same lack of success.'*

In mid August the thirty-four-gun L'Heureux and Le Prince de Conti with her thirty guns were despatched for Scotland and sailed into Lochboisdale on 4 September. They discovered the Prince was not there and so crossed the Minch to the mainland under the guidance of Captain MacDonald of Clanranald's regiment. They flew British colours to avoided detection and made contact with Cameron of Clunes. The news of the ships' arrival was told to John Macpherson who set out to bring the message to the Prince at the Cage. Macpherson was lucky enough to come across Cluny and Dr Cameron who were on a mission to Loch Arkaig, probably in connection with the gold buried there. Cluny provided a man to guide Macpherson to the Cage and Prince Charles learned of his good fortune in the early hours of 13 September. On the same day the escape party set out for the coast and spent the first night at the Uiskchilra bothy where John Roy Stewart joined them.

The next day the men skirted the southern end of Loch Laggan and crossed the River Spean at Moy. They had to be sure of avoiding the enemy and so trekked north to *'Uisknifichit'* (probably Uisge nam Fichead) and then turned west across the River Roy into Glen Gloy. At the southern end of Loch Lochy the river had to be crossed but the water was very high. A leaky old tub was found and with some difficulty the men made it to the other side. On 16 September they reached Lochiel's burned out house at Achnacarry and in the evening set out for the western end of Loch Arkaig. Two days later they reached Borrodale where the Prince, Lochiel, Dr Cameron, John Roy Stewart, Lochgarry and more than a hundred others boarded the ships. In the early hours of 20 September 1746 the vessels sailed for France. The Jacobite rising of 1745 was over.

Landranger Maps

34 Fort Augustus & Glen Albyn
42 Glen Garry & Loch Rannoch
35 Kingussie

Laggan (35)	**NN615945**
Melgarve (34)	**NN463959**
Luib-chonnal (34)	**NN394936**
Roughburn (34)	**NN375813**
Ben Alder (42)	**NN496718**
Uiskchilra? (42)	**NN523762**
Prince Charlie's Cave (42)	**NN499684**
Leitir na Lic Cluny's Cage? (42)	**NN511692**

I decided upon a compromise in making the journey from Achnacarry to Ben Alder. The Prince's exact route is in some doubt and as I had already walked along Loch Lochy from Achnacarry to Fort Augustus and then over the Corrieyairack pass when following the Prince's trek south I excused myself from doing it again. I made my way to

Laggan Bridge and the southern end of Wade's road over the Corrieyairack. The road is accessible by car for about eleven miles and I am grateful to David whose arm I twisted for a lift the moment he stepped outside the village shop. He needed little persuading and generously drove me to Melgarve from where a track follows the River Spey to Shesgnan. Here the path disappeared although I could just discern and follow the tracks of all-terrain vehicles to the source of the river, tiny Loch Spey. A couple of miles more brought me to Luib-chonnal and then White Falls (picture p41) at the head of the River Roy. The path widens to become a track suitable for rugged motor vehicles and then develops into a road that follows the river and emerges in Glen Spean at Roybridge. My travels did not take me quite as far as the road and I needed to cross the river and head south. The bridge is a mile west of Leckroy and once across I backtracked along the other bank to Annat where I picked up the path leading through the Braeroy Forest to the Burn of Agie. I marched south along the burn past Dog Falls before following one of its tributaries, the Allt Sguadaig, to the point where an unnamed rivulet joins from the south. The Allt a' Chaorainn rises in the hills close to a shelter-shaped cairn and I followed its flow due south until it spilled itself into the River Spean reservoir on the A86 at Roughburn.

Before following the Prince into the wilds of Ben Alder I made a quick detour to see the places where two notable Jacobites lived. MacDonald of Keppoch and MacDonald (or MacDonell) of Tiendrish both lived in this area. Keppoch's house was burned down after Culloden and the estate forfeited. Today the place is back in MacDonald hands and the present house dates from 1763. The government troops were not as thorough as they might have been and fortunately failed to burn the building now employed for agricultural purposes but used as barracks for Jacobite troops during the rebellion. Tirindrish, as it is now spelled, is on the outskirts of Spean Bridge, less than a mile east of the village. This house suffered the same fate as Keppoch's but the present owners believe that the thickness of the walls at the back of the house indicate that these at least are probably original.

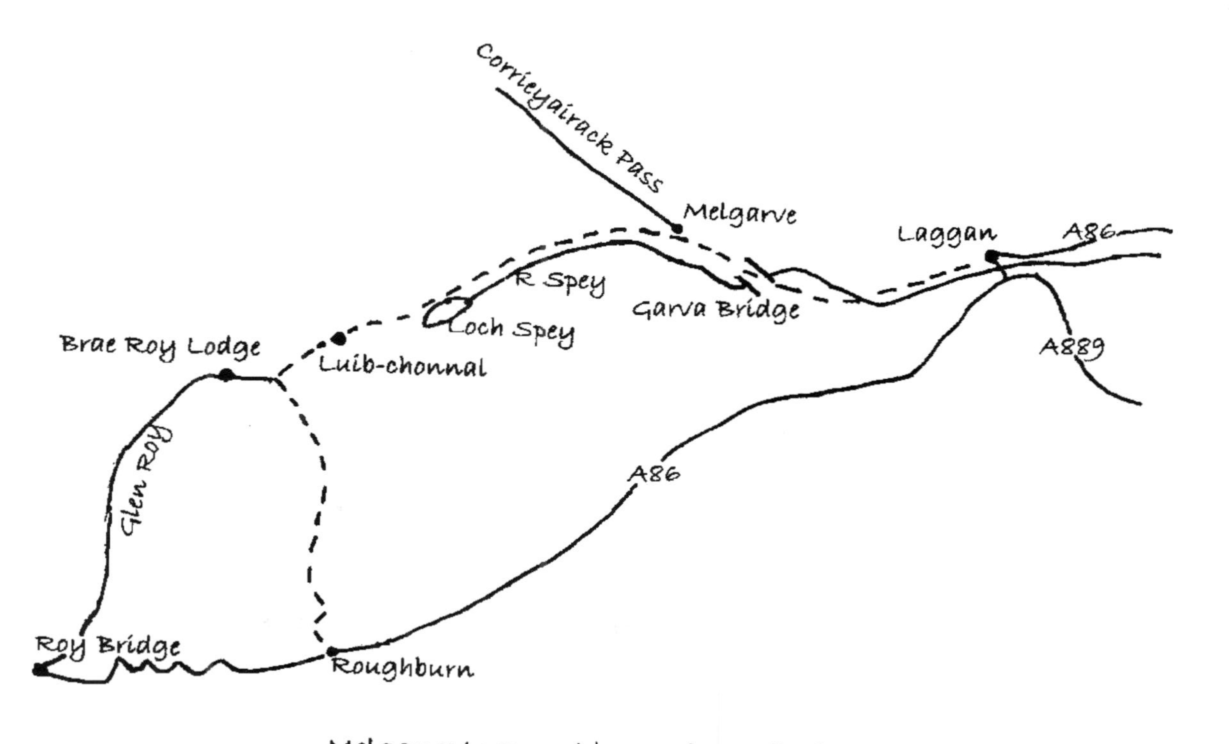
Corrieyairack Pass
Melgarve
Laggan
A86
R Spey
Garva Bridge
Loch Spey
A889
Brae Roy Lodge
Luib-chonnal
Glen Roy
A86
Roy Bridge
Roughburn
Melgarve to Roughburn (16 Miles)

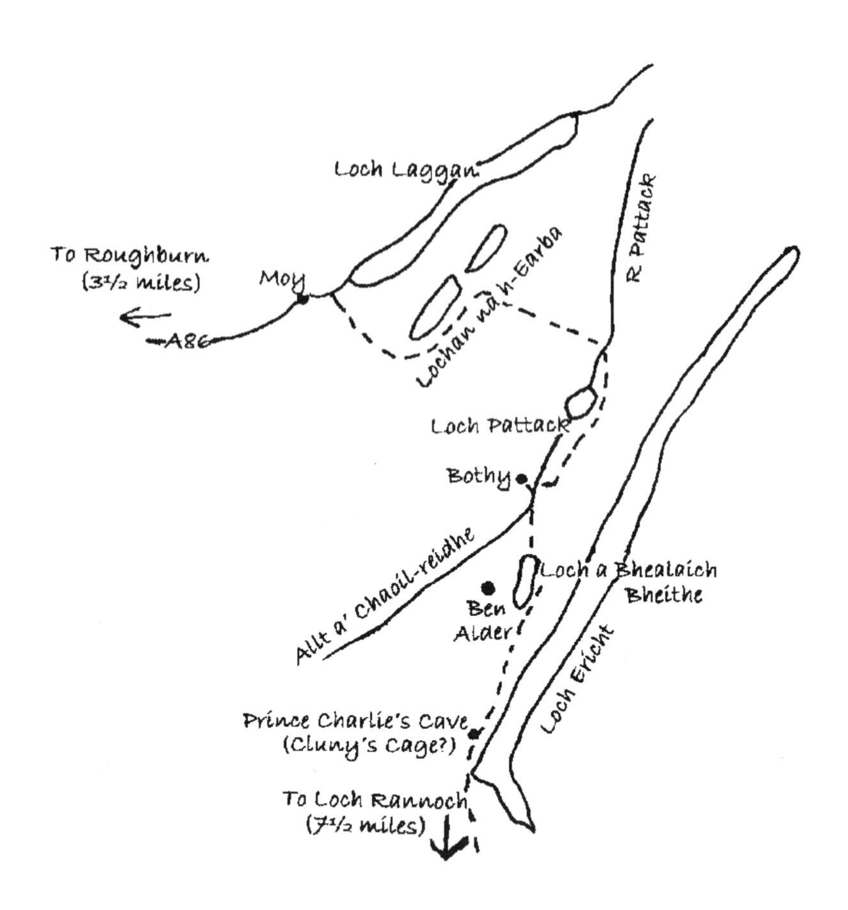

Loch Laggan to Loch Ericht (18½ Miles)

The bridge over the River Spean between the reservoir and Loch Laggan leads to a track along the southern shore of the first of twin lochans known as Lochan na h-Earba. At a point midway between the two the Allt a' Mhaigh provides a useful guide uphill across the Ardverikie Forest to the pass between Meall Bhuidhe and Geal Charn. It was an easy walk, steadily gaining height but with no discernible path to follow. At the top the way forward was unmistakable. In front and to the right Loch Pattack glittered in the sunlight. I headed down the slope and joined the Allt Dubh as it tumbled its way into the River Pattack. At the river I turned to the south and began the gentle mile and a half to the loch. About halfway there I came across the ruins of a bothy on the left of the track. There was hardly any of it left; just a depression in the ground with the back wall cut into the slope of the hillside and enough remaining stones to indicate that walls were there at one time. The building was twelve strides long but only three wide. Could this have been the *'shieling of very narrow compass'* mentioned by Cluny's brother Donald in 'The Lyon in Mourning'? The bothy is described as being in *'Mellanmuir in Ben Alder'* and according to Blaikie 'Mellanmuir' is probably Meallan Odhar marked on the modern Landranger map just west of Loch Pattack. We shall almost certainly never know for sure and there are probably several ruined shielings in the area. The one I found has as much claim to be the genuine article as any other.

From Loch Pattack I followed the path alongside the Allt a' Chaoil-reidhe deeper into Ben Alder. Both Blaikie and Norie point out that this burn could be called Uisge Chaoil-reidhe and the *'Uiskchilra'* of Macpherson's account is likely to be a phonetic spelling of the name. I found no sign of an ancient shelter but a modern bothy stands close to the burn and as I stretched out in my sleeping bag that night I persuaded myself that I was resting in the place used by Prince Charlie all those years ago. I wondered if the ancestors of the midges that consumed me for dinner had eaten him alive as well.

The next morning the day dawned bright upon the Ben and I set off early, following the burn further into the wilderness. After about a mile the path veered away from the stream and climbed until it and I reached beautiful and isolated Loch a' Bhealaich Bheithe. I was feeling fit and happy. The sun had driven away the appalling midges and the pressures of modern life seemed unimportantly distant. I tramped along the eastern shore of the mile long loch, with Ben Alder and Beinn Bheòil towering above me. I was sorry to leave the sparkling loch and a little reluctantly commenced the climb over Bealach Breabag. I reached the top to be rewarded with a spectacular view of Loch Ericht stretching away in front of me with Ben Alder Cottage nestling on its shore. The bothy was a welcome sight, as I knew it would provide rest and shelter for a while. As I descended I kept my eyes open for a possible site of Cluny's Cage. After some mistaken wanderings through the detestable deep tufted grass and heather on the steep hill I spotted the conglomeration of large rocks (picture p41) marked on the O.S. map as Prince Charlie's Cave. The Lyon in Mourning describes the Cage as being *'a very romantic comical habitation made out for him by Cluny, at two miles farther distance into Benalder.'* As this location is about five miles from the Allt a' Chaoil-reidhe and the possible site of the Uiskchilra bothy there is doubt as to its authenticity.

Another account of the Cage, written in French, was found in the Cluny charter-chest. This document was produced in about 1756 and describes the Cage as *'overlooking a beautifull lake of twelve miles long'* and *'in a thicket of hollywood.'* There is no holly in Ben Alder today and it seems likely that the writer mistook rowan for holly as both have similar red berries. Today only a solitary rowan grows from the rocks at Prince Charlie's Cave and there is no significant number of trees anywhere in the immediate area. Although the precise location of the Cage will probably remain a mystery a contemporary source describes it as being *'situate in the face of a very rough high rockie mountain called Letternilichk which is still a part of Benalder.'* There is a rocky outcrop marked Leitir na Lic on the nineteenth century map used by Drummond Norie and this could be the *'Letternilichk'* mentioned. It is not named on my modern map but overlooks Loch Ericht about a mile north-west of

Ben Alder Cottage.

When Prince Charles left the Cage for the last time it was to make his way to the coast and his final escape to France. His path took him back to Loch Laggan, to Achnacarry and out west to Borrodale. I did not want to retrace my steps over ground previously covered and so my long journey of adventure and discovery ended in the wilds of Ben Alder. I walked south feeling satisfied with my achievement yet a little sad that after six summers of effort, study and exploration it was all over. The path finally brought me to the road at Loch Rannoch and I hitched a lift to my final night's accommodation in Pitlochry.

FOURTEEN

WILL YE NO COME BACK AGAIN?

'Bonnie Chairlie's noo awa', Safely ower the friendly main; Mony a heart will break in twa', Should he ne'er come back again.'
Caroline Oliphant (Lady Nairne)

Lord George Murray remained in hiding in the Highlands and eventually escaped to Holland on 16 December. He wanted to meet Prince Charles again and even visited Rome to ask the 'King over the Water' to intercede with Charles on his behalf. James did his best and wrote to his son encouraging a meeting between the two men. However, Charles could not forgive Lord George for what he saw as acts of betrayal and especially the bitter letter written after Culloden. Prince Charles wrote back in less than friendly terms. The letter ends, '*En fin besides for what he deserves I humbly represent your Majesty, it would be of ye most Dangerous Consequences iff such a Divill was not secured immediatly in sum Castle where he might be at his ease, but without being able to escape, or have ye Liberty of Pen or paper.*' Lord George visited Paris hoping they might meet but Charles refused and asked the French government to have Murray arrested. Lord George returned to Holland where he died at Medemblik on 11 October 1760.

Of the 'Seven Men of Moidart', Sir John MacDonald was captured at Culloden. He claimed French citizenship and was eventually exchanged for English prisoners. Sir Thomas Sheridan had been sent to Rome to keep King James up to date with events and died of a fit in 1746. Francis Strickland is reputed to have died *'of a dropsy'* in Carlisle. Aeneas MacDonald missed Culloden having been sent to Barra to collect a consignment of Spanish money. He was captured, eventually released and later died in the French Revolution. George Kelly had been sent to France with news of the Jacobite victory at Prestonpans. He joined the Prince in exile in Paris and died in 1762. William, Duke of Atholl drifted south from Culloden and was captured near Loch Lomond. He was incarcerated in the Tower of London and would probably have been executed with the Lords Balmerino and Kilmarnock on 18 August if he had not died in captivity on 9 July 1746. John William O'Sullivan escaped to France on Le Hardi Mendiant and married Louise Fitzgerald, a woman of some means, in 1749. He died in the early 1760s.

Neil MacEachain, who parted from the Prince on Skye, was never captured and eventually escaped to France. He took the name MacDonald, joined the French army and married a French woman. His son distinguished himself as Napoleon's Marshall MacDonald and was rewarded with the title of Duke of Tarentum. MacEachain died in Sancerre in 1788. John Roy Stewart died in Boulogne in the summer of 1747. A cairn near his birthplace at the Knock of Kincardine on Speyside commemorates his part in the Forty-Five.

Lochiel escaped to France with the Prince and died in the military hospital at Bergues, near Dunkirk, on 26 October 1748. Murray of Broughton was imprisoned in the Tower of London but escaped execution by turning King's evidence. He was pardoned and granted a pension of £200 per annum in 1748. He lived until 1777. Many Jacobites found it difficult to forgive Sir Alexander MacDonald of Sleat for not supporting Prince Charles. MacDonald died at the age of thirty-five on November 28 1746. An unknown poet wrote:

If Heav'n is pleas'd when sinners cease to sin;
If Hell is pleas'd when sinners enter in;
If Earth is pleas'd, freed of a truckling knave;
Then all are pleas'd — MacDonald's in his grave.

Simon Fraser, Lord Lovat was a Jacobite at heart despite his ability to declare loyalty to both sides at the same time. The British army came hunting for him at the end of the rising and he was captured on a remote island at the western end of Loch Morar. Lord Lovat was transported first to Fort William and then to London where he was convicted of treason, not least because of the skin-saving testimony of Murray of Broughton. Simon Fraser was beheaded on 9 April 1747. Defiant to the last he offered the executioner ten guineas to do his work well.

Ewan Macpherson of Cluny remained in Scotland at the end of the rising. He had been entrusted with the guardianship of the buried Loch Arkaig treasure. Using his 'Cage' as a secure base, Cluny skulked in the Highlands and successfully evaded capture for nine years. Prince Charles at last authorized his friend and faithful servant to come to France and to bring with him whatever remained of the treasure. Cluny Macpherson died in Dunkirk on 30 January 1764.

Prince Charles spent the rest of his life in exile. He never quite gave up hope of a Stuart restoration and even in his darkest hours was always convinced of his right to the throne. The Treaty of Aix-la Chapelle ended the War of Austrian Succession in 1748 and brought peace between France and Britain. The treaty demanded that Prince Charles must be removed from French soil and we have a wonderful insight into Prince Charles' character in his reaction to this edict. On 16 July he issued a public proclamation in flowery and verbose language.

> *We regard and always will regard, as null, void, and of no effect, everything that may be statuted or stipulated which may tend to the acknowledgement of any other person whatsoever as sovereign of the kingdom of Great Britain besides the person of the most high and most excellent prince, James the Third, our most honoured lord and father, and, in default of him, the person of the nearest heir, agreeably to the fundamental laws of Great Britain.*

In short he disregarded the treaty and despite being approached in the most polite way by emissaries from Louis XV refused to leave France. The British continued to pressurise the French king and preparations were made to seize the Pretender and remove him from France by force if necessary. The plans for the detention were leaked well in advance but still Charles ignored the threat. On 10 December as the Prince was about to enter the opera house the arrest was made. They *'bound him with silk cord, of which the duke* (de Biron) *had provided ten ells on purpose, and hurried him into a hired coach, which was immediately driven off, attended by a strong guard.'* The Prince was first taken to Vincennes and then after giving his word that he would not return to French territory taken to the papal city of Avignon. Even this would not satisfy the British who were determined to drive Charles back to Rome. Under the threat of a naval bombardment of the port of Civitavecchia the Pope instructed Charles to leave Avignon at once.

In 1750 Charles made the journey to London in an attempt to engender support for another rebellion He ordered 26,000 muskets and 10,000 swords and, in an attempt to ingratiate himself with the Protestant population, renounced Catholicism and joined the Church of England. The Prince possibly stayed in Essex Street, off the Strand, where there is a plaque noting the visit. Support was not forthcoming and, braving the wrath of King Louis, Charles returned to Paris in bitter disappointment.

A further attempt to return to Britain in triumph occurred in 1752 with the unlikely promise of help from Sweden. This plan, 'The Elibank Plot', involved a body of Swedish troops landing in Scotland at the same time as other Jacobite supporters were to depose George II in London. During the planning of this ambitious scheme the Prince was betrayed by Alistair MacDonald, Young Glengarry, who was one of the conspirators. Glengarry who was a spy known by the code name 'Pickle' provided the government with details of the plan. Dr Archie Cameron was betrayed and arrested for his involvement in the plot. He was taken to Edinburgh Castle and then the Tower of London. He was hanged without trial at Tyburn 7 June 1753, the last man to die for the Jacobite cause.

Shortly after this depressing episode Clementine Walkinshaw re-entered Charles' life. The Prince sent orders that she should join him although it is probable that there had been no contact between the couple since 1746. It is just possible, but not likely, that the couple met during Charles' visit to England in 1750 and furthered their relationship on that occasion. Under the circumstances it might be considered strange that Clementine immediately complied with the Prince's request and left home for Paris. Not many eighteenth century women would have responded favourably to a summons to travel far from home into a foreign country to join a man who had been neither seen nor apparently heard from for six years, even if that man was a Royal Prince. Do we assume that Clementine was deeply in love with Charles and so rushed to his side when so commanded? If not then perhaps she regarded the whole business as an adventure that might bring her fame and fortune. Is it possible that she saw herself as a potential queen of England? We shall never really know. Another possibility is that Clementine thought herself married to Prince Charles and maybe, just maybe, she had given birth to their child. There are those who have tried to demonstrate that Charles and Clementine were legally married according to Scottish law. This irregular form of legal marriage required no involvement of the church and depended upon such things as mutual consent, sexual intercourse and cohabitation as man and wife. Unfortunately the rules validated marriage only if the conditions were fulfilled in Scotland and the few weeks when Charles and Clementine were together in Bannockburn are unlikely to have been enough to satisfy a court of law. Whatever the situation in the past Charles and Clementine became lovers and their daughter Charlotte was born in Liège on 27 October 1753. They seem to have been happy for a time but still had to live under assumed names, at one time styling themselves Dr and Mrs Thompson while living in Basle during 1755 and 1756.

Why didn't Prince Charles marry Clementine with all the pomp of a Royal wedding? He certainly needed to produce a legal heir. Clementine was a single woman, able to give birth and in love with her Prince. Perhaps part of the answer is that as she was not of Royal blood he thought she was not good enough for him. If the Prince's previous relationships are anything to go by then it is certain that Charles and Clementine would have numerous difficulties to reconcile. Before he took up with Clementine Charles had embarked on two serious affairs. That both rapidly descended into acrimony perhaps suggest that he thought no woman good enough for him. One liaison was with Louise de Montbazon who had been suggested as a possible wife as far back as the late 1730s. By the time Prince Charles found time to notice her in 1747 she was married. The two had a torrid affair and Louise became pregnant. Louise's husband accepted the child, Charles Godefroi, as his own but as frequently happened in those days the baby died before he was six months old. The association between Charles and Louise ended with tears and recrimination in April 1748 and the Prince immediately embarked upon a liaison with Anne-Marie, Princesse de Talmont, another married woman. At forty-seven she was twenty-one years older than Charles. The love affair was disastrous and ended in May 1751.

Prince Charles' inability to mount another invasion of Britain was telling on him and he increasingly sought solace in alcohol. His relationship with Clementine deteriorated to the extent that in July 1760 she left him and found refuge in a Parisian convent. She took Charlotte with her and, although Charles expressed no sorrow at the departure of Clementine, he made strenuous but unsuccessful attempts to have the little girl brought back to him.

Charles said goodbye to his father when he left Rome in 1744 and despite pleading letters from James over many years they were never to meet again. After the failure of the Forty-Five both the 'King over the Water' and his second son, Henry, had given up any realistic hopes of regaining the throne. Charles felt personally betrayed and was further disappointed when his brother became a Roman Catholic cardinal and so diminished the chances of a Stuart heir in direct line to the throne. By 1764 King James was seriously ill and Prince Henry wrote to Charles seeking reconciliation. Although Charles had not seen his father for almost twenty-two years, he replied curtly that he wished to see neither of them. By the end of 1765 James was close to death. Charles relented and travelled to Rome but the journey was in vain. James died before his son's arrival on the night of 1 January 1766. He was buried in St Peter's, honoured by a sermon from the Pope. Charles III as he now styled himself was not recognised as the rightful king of Great Britain by the Roman Catholic Church. Perhaps if the Prince had swallowed his pride and sought an early reunion with his father, Pope Clement XIII might have looked upon his claim to the throne more favourably.

By 1771 the Pretender was being encouraged to marry before it was too late to produce a legitimate heir to the Stuart fortunes, such as they might be. France, ever wishing to be a thorn in the side of Britain, supported the idea and Louise, eldest daughter of the penniless Princess of Stolberg, agreed to the match. The couple married on Good Friday, 17 April 1772. Louise was only nineteen years old. For a short time all went well. Charles Edward drank less and the couple attended numerous social functions in Rome. By the end of the year when there was no sign of an heir being born Charles became depressed and reverted to the bottle. Not surprisingly the marriage began to go the way of his previous relationships. In 1774 the couple moved to Florence and three years later bought the Palazzo San Clemente. Charles was still sufficiently self-important to have the British coat of arms painted above a door in the vestibule and not content with that pretentious fantasy he persisted in his self-delusion by commissioning a weathervane for the roof, styled 'C. R. III'.

Louise was young, beautiful and rapidly becoming disenchanted with marriage to this drunken, older man. A fateful meeting occurred between Louise and Count Vittorio Alfieri, a twenty-seven year old poet. They fell in love but it seems to have taken Charles a long time to realise the nature of their relationship. At last, on 30 November 1780 Charles accused his wife of adultery, attacked and perhaps tried to strangle her. Louise had endured all she could and followed Clementine Walkinshaw's example in seeking sanctuary with the nuns in a nearby convent. Once safely inside nothing would persuade her to change her mind and in the winter of 1783 the couple were granted a legal separation. Louise and Alfieri lived together until his death in 1803. Louise died in 1824.

In March 1783 Charles believed himself to be dying and wanted desperately to exclude Louise from his will. He had not seen Clementine Walkinshaw or Charlotte for twenty-four years but acknowledged Charlotte as his daughter and made her his heir. Charles wrote to Clementine asking if it would be possible for Charlotte to live with him. Neither Clementine nor her daughter objected and Charles and Charlotte moved into the Palazzo San Clemente. Their relationship became good enough to produce some reconciliation and the exchange of several friendly letters. Charlotte was concerned for her mother's well-being and persuaded her father to make adequate financial provision for Clementine. Charles seems to have been pleased with his daughter and spent a few happy years in Florence. Unfortunately Charles' health was becoming a serious cause for concern and in 1785 father and daughter left Florence and travelled to Pisa to take the waters. They did not return to the Palazzo San Clemente but took up residence in the Palazzo Muti in Rome.

As the French Revolution got under way Charlotte became ill with cancer but despite her poor health she made efforts to persuade her mother to leave France and move to Switzerland for safety's sake. After she died on 17 November 1789 Charlotte's will provided for Clementine but the difficulties for aristocrats in Paris at the time eventually stopped the pension being paid. Clementine fled to Switzerland and died in poverty in Fribourg at the end of 1802.

In time, Charles' health became worse and on the evening of 30 January 1788 he suffered a stroke and died. His death was recorded as the 31st so as not to coincide with the date of the execution of Charles I. The Pope forbade his burial in St Peter's and so the body was at first interred in the cathedral of Frascati, where his brother Henry was Bishop. When Henry died in 1807 he was buried alongside his father in St Peter's and the Pope agreed that Charles' coffin should go there too. In 1819 the future King George IV of Great Britain commissioned a white marble monument by Antonio Canova to stand over the grave.

JACOBO III
JACOBI II MAGNAE BRIT REGIS FILIO
KAROLO EDVARDO
ET HENRICO DECANO PATRVM CARDINALIUM
JACOBI III FILIIS
REGIAE STIRPIS STVARDIAE POSTREMIS

To James III, son of King James II of Great Britain, Charles Edward, and Henry, Dean of the Cardinal Fathers, sons of James III, the last of the royal house of Stuart

The monument is a splendid memorial to the last of the Stuarts but it is dwarfed amongst the grandeur of St. Peter's and tourists and the faithful alike pass by without a second glance. Perhaps in the quiet of the evening when the crowds have departed Bonnie Prince Charlie is at peace and Pretends no longer.

BIBLIOGRAPHY

Ang, Tom & Pollard, Michael, *Walking the Scottish Highlands, General Wade's Military Roads* (André Deutsch, 1984)

Aronson, T. *Kings over the Water* (Cassell, 1979)

Bailey, Geoff B. *Falkirk or Paradise* (John Donald, 1996)

Barron, Evan MacLeod, *Prince Charlie's Pilot* (Carruthers & Sons, 1913)

Berry, C. Leo, *The Young Pretender's Mistress* (Charles Skilton, 1977)

Blaikie, W. B., *Itinerary of Prince Charles Edward Stuart* (Scot. Hist. Soc. 1897)

Blaikie, W.B., *Origins of the '45* (Scot. Hist. Soc. 1897)

Brown, Iain Gordon & Cheape, Hugh, *Witness to Rebellion* (Tuckwell Press, 1996)

Chambers, Robert, *History of the Rebellion of 1745-6* (7th edition, W. & R. Chambers Ltd, London & Edinburgh, 1869)

Craig, Maggie, *Damn' Rebel Bitches*. (Mainstream Publishing, 1997)

Daiches, David, *Charles Edward Stuart. The Life and Times of Bonnie Prince Charlie* (Thames and Hudson, 1975)

Douglas, Hugh, *Flora MacDonald. The Most Loyal Rebel* (Alan Sutton)

Douglas, Hugh, *The Private Passions of Bonnie Prince Charlie* (Sutton, 1998)

Elcho, David Lord, ed. Hon. Evan Charteris, *A Short Account of the Affairs of Scotland*, (David Douglas, 1907)

Erickson, Carolly, *Bonnie Prince Charlie* (Robson Books)

Fergusson, James, *Argyll in the Forty-Five* (Faber and Faber, 1951)

Dunn, Michael, *Walking Ancient Trackways* (David and Charles, 1986)

Duke, Winifred, *The Rash Adventurer* (Robert Hale Ltd, 1952)

Duke, Winifred, *Prince Charles Edward and the '45* (Robert Hale, 1938)

Forbes, Rev. Robert, *The Lyon in Mourning*. Three vols, ed. Henry Paton (Scot. Hist. Soc. 1859)

Forster, Margaret, *The Rash Adventurer* (Secker and Warburg, 1975)

Gibson, John S., *Ships of the '45* (Hutchinson & Co.1967)

Hobson, W. *The History and Topography of Ashbourne* (1839)

Home, John, *History of the Rebellion in 1745* (Cadell, Jun. and Davies, London, 1802)

Jarvis, Rupert C., *Collected Papers on the Jacobite Risings. Vol II* (Manchester University Press, 1972)

Johnstone, Chevalier de, *A Memoir of the Forty-Five* (The Folio Society 1958. First published, 1820)

Kybett, Susan Maclean, *Bonnie Prince Charlie* (Unwin Hyman, 1988)

Lang, Andrew, *Prince Charles Edward* (Goupil & Co., Manzi, Joyant & Co., 1900)

Linklater, Eric, *The Prince in the Heather* (Hodder and Stoughton, 1965)

Maclean, Alasdair, *A MacDonald for the Prince* (Acair Ltd 1982)

Maclean, Fitzroy, *Bonnie Prince Charlie* (Weidenfeld and Nicholson, 1988)

McLynn, Frank, *Charles Edward Stuart. A Tragedy in many Acts* (Routledge)

McLynn, Frank, *The Jacobite Army in England* (John Donald, 1983)

McLaren, Moray, *Bonnie Prince Charlie* (Hart-Davis, 1972)

McLaren, Moray, *Lord Lovat of the '45* (Jarrolds, London, 1957)

MacLeod, John, *Highlanders, A History of the Gaels* (Hodder and Stoughton, 1996)

MacLeod, Ruairidh, *Flora MacDonald* (Shepheard-Walwyn, 1995)

McLynn, Frank, *The Jacobites* (Routledge and Kegan Paul, 1985)

Lenman, Bruce, *The Jacobite Clans of the Great Glen 1650-1784* (Methuen)

Nicolson, Alexander, *History of Skye* (MacLaren and Sons, 1930)
Norie, W. Drummond, *The Life and Adventures of Prince Charles Edward Stuart* (Caxton, 1903)
Pennant, Thomas, *A Tour in Scotland, 1769* (Birlinn Ltd, 2000)
Pennant, Thomas, *A Tour in Scotland and Voyage to the Hebrides, 1772* (Birlinn Ltd, 1998)
Pittock, Murray G.H. *The Myth of the Jacobite Clans* (Edinburgh University Press, 1995)
Prebble, John, *Culloden* (Secker & Warburg, 1961)
Preston, Diana, *The Road to Culloden Moor* (Constable, 1995)
Selby, John, *Over the Sea to Skye* (The History Book Club, 1973)
Speck, W.A., *The Butcher. The Duke of Cumberland and the Suppression of the '45* (Welsh Academic Press)
Tayler, A. & H., *1745 and After* (Nelson and Sons, 1938)
Tayler, H., *Jacobite Epilogue* (Nelson and Sons, 1941)
Terry, Charles Sanford (Editor), *The Forty-Five. A Narrative of the Last Jacobite Rising by Several Contemporary Hands* (Cambridge University Press, 1922)
Tomasson, Katherine, *The Jacobite General* (William Blackwood, 1958)
Tomasson, K. & Buist, F., *Battles of the '45* (B.T. Batsford, 1962)
Ure, John, *Bird on a Wing* (Constable, 1992)
Whitworth, Rex, *William Augustus Duke of Cumberland* (Leo Cooper)
Youngson, A.J. *The Prince and the Pretender* (Croom Helm, 1985)

Walking With Charlie

Steve Lord

We hope you enjoyed reading "Walking With Charlie" and will find the book useful when you visit the Highlands of Scotland